SAN DIEGO TRIVIA

To George

Have fun reading
about San Diego!

Evelyn Kooperman

SAN DIEGO TRIVIA

by Evelyn L. Kooperman

Silver Gate Publications
San Diego, California

Cover by Mark-Elliott Lugo

Library of Congress Cataloging
Card Number 88-061524

ISBN 0-929629-01-9

Laserset by Able Printing Company, Santee, California
Printed in the United States of America
by Delta Lithograph Company, Valencia, California

10 9 8 7 6 5 4 3 2 1

To order:
Silver Gate Publications
7159 Navajo Road, Suite 296
San Diego, CA 92119

PREFACE

This book is for everyone who enjoys being in San Diego. The project began in July 1986 when KFMB Radio contacted the San Diego Public Library where I work, asking if the librarians would submit 75 San Diego trivia questions that would be aired over the radio. I have always been interested in San Diego history, so I went to work and came up with 172 short questions; each one led to another, and the research was so addicting that I couldn't stop. I turned up so many interesting tidbits about San Diego that I thought that others would enjoy sharing the fun. I continued the research for another two years, adding over 600 more questions and expanding those I already had, and finally had enough for a book. The entries are still brief, so I hope that each of you who picks up this book will want to seek out more information on the subjects that are of particular interest to you.

Though this book is not an in-depth research work, extreme care has been taken to insure accuracy. History books did not always agree, so I consulted the original or definitive sources whenever possible and practical. Also, current events keep changing, so unless otherwise specified, all dated questions are accurate as of January 1, 1988.

Enjoy!

ACKNOWLEDGMENTS

Special thanks are due-

To the tireless workers at the San Diego Public Library California and Newspaper Rooms: Mary Allely, Eileen Boyle, Marilyn Filderman, Edna Gonzales, Lance Haim, Mary Castro, Linda Davis, Paul Isner, Janet Johansson, Joann Johnson, Jim McLinden, Marie Terry Mulloy, and Marie Templeton.

To my friend Mary Alys Skulavik, my father Rex Roy, and my husband Larry Kooperman for driving all over San Diego County with me.

To my friends who took the time to read my manuscript and offer valuable suggestions: Donna Bauer, Linda Griffin, Larry Kooperman, Diana Logue, Mary Alys Skulavik, and Vere Wolf.

To Rhoda Kruse, my friend and local history expert, for her competent assistance in reviewing my text for historical accuracy. (Any errors, however, are my own.)

To all those who contributed ideas and advice: "Downtown" Sam Minsker, Ralph de Sola, Margaret Kazmer, Charles Wyborney, Chuck Valverde, Judy Swink, and Mark-Elliott Lugo.

To Tom and Pat Lindsay of Able Printing Company and Maria Johnson of Delta Lithograph Company for their valuable assistance in the printing of this book.

To Mark-Elliott Lugo for his beautiful cover.

To the many helpful librarians at all the public, college, university, museum, and historical society libraries in San Diego County.

To Dayna Monroe of KFMB Radio for the original idea.

Grateful acknowledgment is made to the following persons or institutions that responded to my phone calls, visits, and letters of inquiry: Chuck Ables; Joyce Abrams; Rudolf Aguilar, Marston's; Dominic J. Alessio, Mr. A's Restaurant; Cynthia Allen; Richard W. Amero; Ralph Armstrong; Karen Arter; Beve Ashley, Dudley's Bakery; W. C.Babcock, Pioneer Pharmacy; Thomas H. Baumann; Frank Belock Jr., San Diego Engineering and Development Dept.; The Big Kitchen; Don Borgen; Max Bradshaw; Dr. Ray Brandes; Gordon Browne; Tom Burfield, Carnation Company; Clair W. Burgener; John Cash, San Diego High School Alumni Association; Ron Cervantes, San Diego Fire Department; Florence Christman; Chula Vista Chamber of Commerce; William E. Clarke, San Diego County Office of Education; Anthony Coker; 1st Lt. J. E. Coonradt, U.S. Marine Corps; Sgt. Harold L. Cox, San Diego Police Department; June Crosby; Crystal Pier Motor Hotel; Chris Cullen, TraveLodge; Dick Dalton, Rohr Industries Inc.; Jeanne Danis, Coronado Playhouse; Theodore Davie, San Diego Trust and Savings; Dr. Michael Dean; Del Mar Racetrack; Virginia L. De Marais; Karen Dirks; Aubrey Dunne; Paul Ecke Jr.; Dr. Benjamin Elkin; Sue Ellis, Horton Plaza; William L. Evans, Bahia Hotel; Donna J. Farrell, Marketplace at the Grove; Sandy Fitzpatrick; Joe Forand, Theatre Organ Society of San Diego; Dale Frost, Port of San Diego; Lois Furr, Coleman College; Stan Fye; Jim Galloway, Galloway's Pharmacy; Ron Gardner; Gaslamp Quarter Association; Murney Gerlach, San Diego State University; Herbert G. Goldman; Jackie Hall, Sea World; Thomas Hamecher; Paul R. Handlery, Handlery Hotels; Tom Hanscom, San Diego Wild Animal Park; Ben Harroll; Michael Patrick Hearn, International Wizard of Oz Club, Inc.; Stacy Heckman, Waterfront Promotions; E. M. Herrell, Oceanside Community Development Department, Engineering Division; Mike Highfill, San Diego Sockers; Sam Hinton; J. E. Hopkins, Naval Submarine Base; Mary Hranka, Mission San Diego; Edith Hughes, National City Chamber of Commerce; Helen Hussey, San Diego High School Alumni Association; Frederick Jee, Anza-Borrego Desert State Park; Joseph E. Jessop; Jim Joiner, San Diego Zoo; Bob Johnston; Julian Chamber of Commerce; Julian Drug Store; KFMB-TV; E. R. Kearns, Woolworth Company; Nick Kerasiotis,

World Boxing Association; Frank Kern, Hall of Champions; Larry Killmar, San Diego Wild Animal Park; Don Kinnel; Barry P. Knudson, Walker Scott Co.; Carmen Lacey, San Diego Museum of Art; Frankie Laine; Daniel LeBlanc, Sea World; Raymond Lemke; Liz Linderman, San Diego Repertory Theatre; Durwin Long, Foodmaker, Inc.; Ed Lubic; Brian Luscomb, Great American; Judy McCarty; Roberta McClellan, Starlight Opera; Tim McGrath, Cleveland National Forest; Jonathan McMurtry; Frank Maitski, San Diego Utilities Dept., Water Production; Bud Maloney; Hamilton Marston; Judy Sanders Mazzarella; Catherine Miller, San DiegoSportfishing Council; K. D. Mitchell, Naval Air Station, North Island; Juliette Mondot, Save Our Neon Society; Archie Moore; Neil Morgan; Katherine Nash; Lowell North; Stephen Oakford, Hotel del Coronado; Oceanside Chamber of Commerce; Debora O'Connor, Marriott Hotels; Office of the Mayor; Manny Oliva, San Diego Firefighters; Joan Oppenheimer; Felipe Ortiz, Town and Country Hotel; Palomar Observatory; Jacqueline Parker, Scripps Institution of Oceanography; Robert Pastore; Curtis L. Perkins, San Pasqual Academy; Gordon Pettit, Marston's; Robert Plimpton, San Diego Civic Organist; Larry Pluth, County Planning & Land Use Dept., Street Names Section; Jeff Poe (and others), U. S. Post Office; Joanne M. Powell, San Diego Hardware Company; Nancy E. Price, California Ballet Co.; Dr. Philip R. Pryde; Dorothy V. Rock, ZLAC Rowing Club; Frances B. Ryan; Colin H. Saari, Dept. of the Navy, Recruit & Training Command; Robert St.Clair, Fort Rosecrans National Cemetery; San Diego Chamber of Commerce; San Diego Chargers; San Diego Convention and Visitors Bureau, Dept. 700; San Diego Department of Maps and Records; San Diego Gas & Electric Company; San Diego Medical Health Center; San Diego Symphony; Julie Scaramella, Centro Cultural de la Raza; Susan F. Schafer, San Diego Zoo; Elton Schiller, San Diego Padres; Diane Scholfield; George A. Scott, Walker Scott Co.; Carole Seaton, San Diego Zoo; Doug Shakespeare, Valley Center Chamber of Commerce; Wilbur Shigehara, National Weather Service; Wendell Shoberg; Laurie Singer; Richard C. Smith, Otis Elevator Co.; David Starcevick, Arthur Hotel; Robert Stevenson; Andy Strasberg, San Diego Padres; A. Ted Talano, Hotel San

Diego; Gunnery Sgt. Teeling, MCRD; Helen Vazquez, San Diego High School Alumni Association; Armand Viora; Gloria Walton; Don Ward; Gary Ware, Carnation Co.; John Warren family; Julie West, Home Federal; Whitey Wietelmann, San Diego Padres; Commander R. E. Wildermuth, Naval Air Station, North Island; Doug Willoughby, Rosicrucian Fellowship; Senator Pete Wilson; Thomas M. Wilson, Vista Irrigation District; Donna Witherspoon, US Grant Hotel; Bob Wright, *San Diego Union*.

Quotations are reprinted with permission from the *San Diego Union*.

TABLE OF CONTENTS

HISTORY I

EXPLORERS, INDIANS, PADRES

1. Juan Rodríguez Cabrillo, the discoverer of San Diego, sailed for what country?

2. What were the names of Cabrillo's two ships?

3. For what navigable body of water was Cabrillo searching as he made his way up the California coast?

4. What name did Cabrillo give to San Diego Bay?

5. What explorer gave San Diego its present name?

1. Spain. He was a Spanish or Portuguese soldier and navigator who sailed from Navidad, New Spain (Mexico) June 27, 1542, under the patronage of Charles V of Spain and Antonio de Mendoza, viceroy of New Spain. Cabrillo and his crew were the first white men to sail into San Diego Bay, on September 28, 1542.

2. *San Salvador* and *La Victoria*. The *San Salvador*, his flagship, was probably a galleon about 100 feet long, and the *La Victoria* was probably a smaller carrack. In addition, there may have been one or more smaller accompanying vessels with his party.

3. The Strait of Anián (called the Northwest Passage by the English). This was a legendary waterway connecting the Atlantic and Pacific oceans, which was supposed to provide a short cut to China and the Spice Islands.

4. San Miguel. He named it after St. Michael the Archangel, whose feast day was September 29, the day after he discovered the bay. Cabrillo and his men sailed into the bay and probably anchored and stepped ashore at Ballast Point.

5. Sebastián Vizcaíno. He sailed into the bay in 1602, and although he had been instructed not to make any changes in place names, renamed it for San Diego de Alcalá (St. Didacus). San Diego was a fifteenth-century Spanish saint on whose feast day (November 12) Vizcaíno and his men set up chapel and said Mass on Ballast Point, and was also the name of Vizcaíno's flagship, giving him two reasons for his choice of a name.

6. In the late 1760s, Spain sent expeditions of soldiers and padres into Alta (Upper) California largely because what country was threatening to encroach upon her territory from the north?

7. In what year was the first Alta California mission founded?

8. How old was Father Serra when he arrived in San Diego?

9. To what religious order did Father Serra and his fellow padres belong?

10. Who was the military leader of the 1769 land expeditions from Baja California to San Diego?

11. Where in San Diego was Alta California's first mission located?

12. Who was the first Christian martyr in California?

6   Russia. The Russian fur trappers had been working their way from Siberia across to Alaska and down toward Spanish California.

7.   1769. It was founded in San Diego by Father Junípero Serra. On July 16, 1769, he raised a crude cross and said his first Mass here. This date is regarded as the birthday of San Diego.

8.   Fifty-five.   Though troubled with an infected leg, he had traveled close to 900 miles by foot and muleback after leaving Loreto, Baja California on March 28, 1769. (There is some disagreement about his age, but most biographers agree that he was born November 24, 1713, which would make him 55 upon his arrival here on July 1, 1769.)

9.   Franciscan   (founded by St. Francis of Assisi). The first missions in Baja California had been established by the Jesuits in 1697. That order was expelled in 1767-68, and the Dominicans and Franciscans were brought in to replace them. The Dominicans eventually succeeded the Franciscans in Baja California, while the Franciscans continued to establish missions in Alta California.

10. Captain Gaspar de Portolá, governor of Baja California.

11. Presidio Hill. It was founded there July 16, 1769, by Father Serra. Soon construction on an adobe chapel was begun. In 1774 the mission was moved to its present location in Mission Valley to be near a better water supply and farming land, and to separate the Indians from the soldiers at the presidio.

12. Father Luis Jayme (Jaume). In 1775 he was killed at Mission San Diego by Indians. He was the only Franciscan in California to meet martyrdom at the hands of the Indians.

13. What name did the Spaniards give to the Indians that they met here?

14. What was the staple food of the native San Diego Indians?

15. In 1774, what Spaniard led the first overland expedition from Sonora, Mexico, through the back country of San Diego and up the California coast?

16. What navigator sailed the first non-Spanish ship into San Diego Bay?

17. What mission was called the "King of the Missions"?

13. The Diegueños. The Indians called themselves the Kumeyaay, but they were named Diegueño (originally San Diegueño) by the Spaniards because they were under the jurisdiction of Mission San Diego. Likewise the Luiseños to the north were named for Mission San Luis Rey.

14. The acorn. These were gathered in the hills; then they were ground on stones, and the poisonous tannin was leached out in loosely woven baskets. Other common foods were wild plants, animals such as rabbits and deer, nuts, seeds, roots, fruit, and for those along the coast, fish and shellfish. Agriculture was not practiced.

15. Captain Juan Bautista de Anza. He was accompanied by Father Francisco Garcés and a small party of soldiers. The following year he led 240 soldiers and settlers over the same route to what is now San Francisco. The Anza-Borrego Desert through which he traveled is named for him.

16. Captain George Vancouver. In 1793 this British sea captain stopped here in the sloop-of-war *Discovery* while on a voyage to explore and survey the northwest coast of America.

17. Mission San Luis Rey. It was founded in 1798 in northern San Diego County (a few miles east of the present Oceanside), and named after King Louis IX of France. It was the largest, most prosperous, and the most beautiful mission in California. At its peak it was the home of nearly 3,000 Indians, 2,200 horses, 28,900 sheep, and 27,500 cattle.

HISTORY II

1800-1849
SPANISH AND MEXICAN DAYS

1. The main cargo loaded aboard the New England maritime merchant ships in San Diego in the late 1700s and early 1800s was the fur from what animal?

2. In the "Battle of San Diego" in 1803, the San Diegans at Fort Guijarros fired on the ship *Lelia Byrd*. To what country did that brig belong?

3. In the early 1800s, three asistencias or sub-missions were built in San Diego County; chapels remain at two of these sites. Where are they?

4. Where was the first dam in San Diego?

HISTORY II   A

1. The sea otter. Most of these animals were caught by the California Indians for the mission fathers. The Yankee merchants took them to China to exchange for silk, tea, sugar, porcelain, chests, and other wares.

2. The United States of America. The *Lelia Byrd* was attempting to smuggle out otter skins which the Spanish leaders wanted for Spanish trade only. In addition, the Americans were holding five San Diego customs guards hostage on the ship, so the cannons were ordered to be fired from the fort on Ballast Point to prevent the ship from leaving the bay. The battle caused no damage or injuries, nor did it prevent the eventual influx of American ships into Spanish waters.

3. Pala and Santa Ysabel. San Antonio de Pala was established in 1816 along the San Luis Rey River, and Santa Ysabel was established in 1818 in the back country; both still serve as places of worship for the nearby Indians. Only a few mounds remain of the third asistencia, Las Flores, built in 1823 between Oceanside and San Clemente.

4. Mission Gorge, on the San Diego River. The padres and Indians built it from 1813 to 1816, about six miles northeast of the mission. It was constructed of rocks and a cement they made by burning native lime in kilns. Soon after the dam was finished, a tile aqueduct was constructed to bring water to the mission and valley. Today the dam site is a historical landmark known as Old Mission Dam or Padre Dam.

5.   When was San Diego the capital of California?

6.   What fur trapper was the first American to arrive over-
     land in San Diego?

7.   In the days of the great California cattle ranches, from
     the 1820s through the 1840s, what was the most valu-
     able part of the cow?

8.   What father and son fur trappers were imprisoned in
     San Diego because the Mexican governor Echeandía
     was afraid of an influx of Americans?

9.   When Yankee trader ships came to San Diego from
     the 1820s through the 1840s, their goods were
     traded for hides. What were these hides commonly
     called?

10. Where were most of California's hides dried,
     cured, and stored before they were shipped around
     the Horn to Boston?

5. 1825-1831. At this time California was under Mexican rule, and included both Upper and Lower California. The capital was unofficially moved here from Monterey because Governor Echeandía liked the mild climate, and because he found the señoritas here attractive. Some say that he was particularly fond of Josefa Carrillo, daughter of one of the prominent families of San Diego.

6. Jedediah Smith. He arrived here in the winter of 1826-27 after blazing a trail through the Rocky Mountains that thousands would later follow in the westward movement to California.

7. The hide. A rancher didn't mind if someone killed his cattle for the meat, as long as he left the hide. It is estimated that anywhere from one to eight million hides were shipped out of California, mostly to Boston, with some going to England.

8. Sylvester Pattie and his son James Ohio Pattie. They had come to California in 1828 by way of the Colorado River. Sylvester died in jail and is buried on Presidio Hill, but James Ohio was released because he agreed to vaccinate the Californios (Spanish Californians) against smallpox. He claimed to have inoculated 22,000 persons, 1,000 of them in San Diego.

9. California banknotes, California dollars, or leather dollars.

10. La Playa. This area, on the bay side of Point Loma, was known as "Hide Park" and contained hide houses which had been framed in Boston and erected here. Iron pots for rendering tallow, and warehouses for tallow storage were also located here. The hides were generally shipped to Boston, and the tallow shipped to Mexico or South America to be made into soap or candles.

11. What is the name of the long-sought gold mine discovered in 1829 by Thomas L. Smith?

12. What beloved padre administered Mission San Luis Rey from its founding in 1798 until 1832, just before secularization?

13. Who was the first alcalde (mayor) of San Diego under Mexican rule?

14. What prominent resident of early San Diego was the last Mexican governor of California?

15. Where was the United States flag first officially raised in San Diego?

16. What new name was the fort on Presidio Hill given in November 1846?

11. The lost Pegleg Mine. Thomas L. "Pegleg" Smith found black nuggets of gold near three buttes as he was crossing the desert from Yuma to Los Angeles. He was later picked up in a delirium and could never again find the spot. A monument commemorating the mine is located in Borrego Springs, and is the site of the annual Pegleg Smith Liar's Contest.

12. Father Antonio Peyri. The Indians were devastated at his departure and ran after him to try to persuade him to stay. He did not want to witness the downfall of the mission he loved, however, so he returned to Spain.

13. Juan María Osuna. Thirteen voters showed up to vote at the election, and Señor Osuna took office in 1835. He carried a silver-tipped cane as the symbol of his authority, and it is said that he never appeared in public without it.

14. Pío Pico. He made Los Angeles his government headquarters during his term from 1845 to 1846.

15. Old Town Plaza. The flag was raised July 29, 1846, by Lt. Stephen C. Rowan, U.S.N., who had come in on the sloop-of-war USS *Cyane*. A large boulder at the plaza bears a plaque commemorating this event.

16. Fort Stockton. It was named by Commodore Robert Stockton, commander of the American Pacific Squadron. An earthworks had been built there in 1838 and reinforced in 1846. Later that year Stockton and his men built walls from casks of sand and dirt, mounted twelve guns, and dug a moat. Today a flagpole, a cannon, and several monuments mark the site.

17. Who led the "Army of the West" from Fort Leaven-worth, Kansas, to Southern California in 1846 to sub-due the Californios?

18. After the Battle of San Pasqual in December 1846, what well-known frontiersman cut through enemy lines to San Diego to bring reinforcements?

19. After the Battle of San Pasqual, Kearny and his "Army of the West" were besieged by the Californios on a nearby hill. They ran out of food so had to eat their emaciated mules. What is this hill now called?

20. The longest infantry march in history, over 2000 miles, from Council Bluffs, Iowa, to San Diego, was made by what group?

17. General Stephen Watts Kearny. He met the Californios led by General Andrés Pico at San Pasqual, in what was California's bloodiest conflict. Kearny and his weary troops, armed with wet carbines, suffered many casualties, while Pico and his lancers came through almost unharmed. The story of this battle is displayed at the San Pasqual Battlefield State Historic Park Visitor Center and Museum.

18. Kit Carson. He was accompanied by naval Lt.Edward Beale and an Indian. Carson and Beale lost their shoes and had to crawl or walk barefoot thirty miles over gravel, rocks, and cactus.

19. Mule Hill. It is a historical landmark, about four miles southwest of Escondido. For many years a different hill was so honored, but in 1970 excavations uncovered evidence of the error, and a few years later this new hill was officially declared to be the true Mule Hill. It lies north of Lake Hodges and east of Highway 15, and can be viewed from Pomerado Road.

20. The Mormon Battalion. In 1846-47 they marched here to help secure California in the war with Mexico. They arrived too late to join in the fighting, but made themselves useful during their stay here by whitewashing houses, laying bricks, digging wells, and performing other tasks that made San Diego a more desirable place in which to live.

21. Captain Abraham Johnston was the first to be killed at the Battle of San Pasqual. When his body was supposedly sent home to his relatives in Ohio, what was actually in his coffin?

22. The Mormon Battalion blazed a wagon road with hand tools through what canyon in the California desert?

23. Who claimed that he was the first white man on Smith (Palomar) Mountain?

21. A stove. His body had been sent to San Francisco where it was kept in a government warehouse, along with three boxes of cast-iron stoves, until it could be shipped East. A fire swept the city in May 1850, and all items were removed from the warehouse for safekeeping. The following year the San Francisco *Herald* announced that "a most foul murder was most probably committed," because a ghastly skeleton of a man had been found in a box that was supposed to contain a stove. The mystery was soon solved when it was deduced that the stove had been sent to Ohio instead of Captain Johnston's body, where the box containing the stove had been given a proper burial.

22. Box Canyon. In 1847 the Mormon Battalion, led by Lt. Col. Philip St. George Cooke, widened this 2 1/2-mile chasm in the Anza-Borrego Desert using only crowbars and pick axes because their road-building tools had been lost. For a time Box Canyon was aptly known as Cooke's Pass.

23. Nate Harrison, a Black. He had been born a slave, and arrived here around 1848. During the 70-odd years that he lived here he would carry buckets of water to the tired horses of travelers coming up the mountain road. This old road on the west side of the mountain was called Nigger Nate Road for many years, and was later changed to Nate Harrison Grade.

HISTORY III

1850-1899
THE WILD AND WOOLLY WEST

1. When William Heath Davis and his associates tried to move the center of San Diego from Old Town to New Town on the waterfront in 1850, what did the citizens derisively call his new development?

2. In a single year San Diego County became the first county in California, San Diego became a city, and California became a state. In what year did these events take place?

3. What is the oldest park in San Diego outside of Old Town?

4. Who was the last alcalde (Mexican mayor) and first American mayor of San Diego, in 1850?

5. When San Diego County was created in 1850, what present-day California counties did it include?

6. The last Indian uprising in Southern California took place in 1851. Who led it?

HISTORY III   A

1. Davis' Folly. His development, including a wharf, warehouse, and several stores and houses, was bounded roughly by what are now Broadway, Market, Front, and the waterfront. It failed to attract enough settlers, however, due to lack of water and wood, and to resentment by Old Towners and La Playans.

2. 1850. San Diego became a county on February 18 and a city on March 27, and California became the 31st state on September 9.

3. Pantoja Park. It is located at F, G, India, and Columbia streets, a spot that was planned to be the center of New Town. It was established in 1850 and named for Don Juan Pantoja, who was the pilot for the 1782 expedition that first charted San Diego Harbor. It was also known as Plaza de Pantoja, New Town Park, or F Street Park. In the early 1870s women carried buckets of water to the park to water the newly planted trees. Today there are a number of tall old trees there, plus a statue of Benito Juárez, which was erected in 1981 as a gift from the people of Mexico.

4. Joshua H. Bean. He was a former soldier, and was the brother of "Judge" Roy Bean, famous for his "Law West of the Pecos."

5. San Diego County, Imperial County, most of Riverside and San Bernardino counties, and a large part of Inyo County. It contained 37,400 square miles, compared with 4,255 today.

6. Antonio Garra. He was a well-educated Cupeño Indian from Warner Springs. The final straw in the Indians' grievances was when they were ordered to pay high taxes on their livestock and property, even though they had no voting rights.

7. What was the popular name of James Birch's overland stagecoach line that ran between San Antonio, Texas, and San Diego from 1857 to 1861?

8. How many unmarried American girls lived in San Diego in 1855?

9. Who ran the stage line that went from St. Louis through the San Diego back country and on up to Los Angeles and San Francisco?

10. Who was the first Jewish resident of San Diego?

11. What animal was brought to the United States to carry passengers and soldiers across the deserts from Texas to California?

7. The "Jackass Mail Line." It received this name because passengers had to switch to mules to cross the sand dunes and mountains between the Colorado River and San Diego.

8. One. So notes Richard Pourade in his history *The Silver Dons*. He points out that at that time most San Diego girls could not read or write, but were good at dancing and eating.

9. John Butterfield. His Butterfield Overland Mail line ran from 1858 until 1861, when the Civil War interfered with its southern route. There were six stations in the area covered by present-day San Diego County: Carrizo Springs; Palm Spring (an animal changing station); Vallecito (now a restored station); San Felipe Valley; Warner's Ranch; and Oak Grove.

10. Louis Rose. He arrived here in 1850 and soon became an enterprising and prominent citizen. Among other things he was a retailer, hotel owner, tanner, brickyard operator, rancher, and postmaster of Old Town. He built Rose's Wharf, Rose's Hotel, Rose's Store, and Rose's Tannery, and founded and developed the area called Roseville on Point Loma, which he planned to turn into a townsite for his employees. Rose Canyon is named after him.

11. The camel. In 1855-56, seventy-eight camels including two dromedaries were brought here under the leadership of Lt. Edward Beale. They were generally better-suited to the area than horses and mules: they maneuvered better on rocky ground, thrived on the thorny bushes, carried heavier loads, stood up better in the heat, and could go longer without water. The soldiers and public, however, did not like them, and that, coupled with the success of stage travel and the political considerations of the impending Civil War, prevented camel transportation from catching on.

12. What person hanged on the site of the Whaley House in 1852 still haunts the spot, according to popular tradition?

13. When whaling became an important industry, from the 1850s to the 1880s, where were the two locations of whaling stations in San Diego?

14. What is the oldest iron merchant ship afloat?

15. What was the name of the Army camp established in San Diego County during the Civil War?

12. "Yankee" Jim Robinson. He was hanged for stealing a row-boat during a time when San Diegans were tired of the crime wave and ready to take drastic action. In 1966, when a local theater troupe presented Frances Bardacke's play *The Ballad of Yankee Jim* at the Whaley House and yard, the actors reported feeling the presence of spirits.

13. Ballast Point and North Island. Ballast Point was the prominent location in the 1850s and 1860s. There the whale blubber was boiled down for oil and then stored in barrels. The industry moved to North Island around 1871 because Ballast Point was taken over as a military reservation. At this time North Island had a small arm of water called Whaler's Bight cutting into the shore, where whaling ships would anchor. There was also a fresh water spring there known as Russian Spring or Whaler's Spring.

14. The *Star of India*. She was launched in 1863 at the Isle of Man, and circled the globe 21 times as an Australian immigrant ship. Now she is part of San Diego's Maritime Museum, and is the oldest ship of any type still able to sail, having sailed off San Diego in 1976, 1984, and 1986.

15. Camp Wright. It was established in October 1861 on Warner's Ranch, but was soon moved to Oak Grove for a more sheltered position from wind and cold. Here the California Volunteers guarded the lines of communication between California and Arizona, and patrolled the mountain passes to prevent Southern sympathizers from joining Confederate forces in Texas. The only military action between Union and Confederate troops in California took place here. The camp was named after Brigadier General George Wright, U.S. Army, and was abandoned in 1866.

16. Who is known as the "Father of San Diego"?

17. What brothers founded and developed National City?

18. For what crop is John S. Harbison (for whom Harbison Canyon is named) famous?

19. What was the name of San Diego's first firefighting company?

20. Who was largely responsible for turning San Diego from a Democratic city into a Republican one?

16. Alonzo E. Horton. In 1867 he bought most of what is now downtown San Diego and moved the center of town from Old Town to Horton's Addition, also called New Town or New San Diego. At one time he was the wealthiest person in Southern California because of his land holdings, but he gave away much of his land to persons or organizations who would help develop San Diego.

17. The Kimball brothers. Frank was the most influential, aided by Warren, and to a lesser degree by Levi and George. They bought Rancho de la Nación in 1868 and laid out the town of National City. Frank founded a number of businesses and helped establish the olive and citrus industries there.

18. Honey. He brought some of the first honey bee colonies to San Diego in 1869, and is considered to be the father of the honey industry in Southern California. By the 1880s San Diego County was one of the leading honey producers in the world, and the fine quality honey won many international prizes.

19. Pioneer Hook and Ladder Company. When it was established in 1869 it did not have a truck, but was strictly a bucket brigade. The first truck was acquired in 1872, and the first motorized one in 1909. Today San Diego's Firehouse Museum at 1572 Columbia Street is sponsored by the Pioneer Hook and Ladder Company, a non- profit corporation named after the first fire department.

20. Alonzo Horton. San Diego had been strongly Democratic since the 1850s, as many of the settlers were from the Southern states. After Horton arrived here in 1867 he was quoted as saying, "I would not employ a man unless he was a Republican. Two years after I started San Diego, I carried the city for the Republican ticket, county and state, and the city and county have remained Republican ever since."

21. When what is now downtown San Diego was laid out in the late 1860s, the streets were 80 feet wide with the exception of one, which was 100 feet wide. That street is still the widest. Which is it?

22. Where was the San Diego County gold rush of the 1870s?

23. Where was the famous gunfight of 1875, which was the last raid of an organized bandit gang in Southern California?

24. What was the name of the first hotel in El Cajon?

25. What famous frontiersman and peace officer operated three gambling halls in San Diego in the 1880s?

21. Market Street, then called H Street. For many years it was the main street in the downtown area, and Fifth and Market was the center of town.

22. Julian. It is estimated that from $4,000,000 to $13,000,000 worth of gold was taken from the mines in the area, and for a short time Julian enjoyed a tremendous boom.

23. Campo. The Gaskill Brothers, who owned the store there, shot it out with a group of Mexican border bandits who were attempting to rob them. There are many versions of what actually happened, but most of the bandits were killed or captured, and the Gaskills were never bothered again. Some say that this was the bloodiest fight in the old West—even greater than the shootout at the OK Corral.

24. The Knox Hotel. Amaziah Knox came to El Cajon in 1869. The following year gold was discovered in Julian, and hundreds of travelers slept at a bend in the road in El Cajon while en route there. In 1876 Knox built a two-story hotel at that bend, which is now the intersection of Main and Magnolia streets. For $1.00 a traveler could receive a room and feed for his animals. In 1882 a large annex was added to the hotel. After two moves the original building of the Knox Hotel was moved to its present location at Park and Magnolia streets, where it is now a museum maintained by the El Cajon Historical Society.

25. Wyatt Earp. He arrived here around 1887 and leased concessions for three gambling halls, which offered such games as faro, roulette, poker, blackjack, and keno. In addition, he bought up several pieces of property in the downtown area and Hillcrest, and he is listed in the San Diego City Directories of the time as "Capitalist." He also refereed boxing matches. (Who would disagree with his decisions?)

26. For whom was the Villa Montezuma built?

27. What San Diegan made the first controlled flight in a heavier-than-air glider?

28. Where was the first San Diego county fair held?

29. What San Diego priest was the model for Father Gaspara in the novel *Ramona*?

26. Jesse Shepard. This ornate Victorian house at 1925 K Street was financed by his wealthy admirers to entice this internationally known pianist, spiritualist, mystic, poet, composer, and author to settle in San Diego. The 1887 house has recently been restored to its former lavish splendor by the San Diego Historical Society.

27. John J. Montgomery. In 1883 he flew his homemade glider 600 feet on Otay Mesa. This was 20 years before the Wright Brothers made their more famous engine-powered flight at Kitty Hawk. Montgomery's glider *Evergreen* is now on display at the San Diego Aerospace Museum, on loan from the Smithsonian Institution. Montgomery Field was named after him, and an 80-foot-high silver wing stands in Otay Mesa's Montgomery Waller Park as a memorial to his great achievement.

28. National City. Promoted by Frank Kimball, it was held in 1880 on the site now occupied by Kimball Park. Fruits, vegetables, embroidery work, paintings, and hair, fern, and shell work were displayed. The variety and quality of the fruit were considered the best in the world.

29. Father Antonio Ubach. He officiated in San Diego from 1866 to 1907, and is considered the last of the padres. He actually did perform a marriage ceremony for a couple upon whom Helen Hunt Jackson based her characters Ramona and Alessandro.

30. Where was San Diego's first college?

31. Where in San Diego County did renowned "Historian of the West" Hubert Howe Bancroft live and write?

32. What nationality were most of the fishermen of San Diego in the 1870s and 1880s?

33. What city almost became the permanent western terminus of a transcontinental railroad in the 1860s, 1870s, and 1880s, and would then have overtaken San Diego in size and importance?

30. Pacific Beach.   It was the San Diego College of Letters (sometimes called San Diego College of Arts and Letters), located on what is now Garnet between Lamont and Kendall streets. Harr Wagner, publisher of *The Golden Era* magazine, started it. The college opened in 1888 with one completed building out of a promised five, and with a faculty of fourteen. One more building was soon completed, but the project folded when the land boom broke, and the buildings and grounds were sold in October 1891.

31. Spring Valley. The adobe house in which he lived and wrote some of his 39 volumes of history was the first home in Spring Valley to have been built by a white man (Judge A. S. Ensworth, in 1863). In 1885 Bancroft purchased it and the surrounding ranch where he raised olives and fruit. Now known as "The Bancroft Ranch House," it is a museum and a state and national historic landmark.

32. Chinese. Their junks dotted the harbor, and they lived in the southern downtown area called "Chinatown" and in Roseville on Point Loma. The Chinese are credited with starting San Diego's fishing industry, which was later taken over by the Italians, the Portuguese, and eventually the Japanese.

33. National City. Developer Frank Kimball offered land subsidies to several railroad companies to entice them to build railroads to his city, but the plans did not work out or were short-lived.

34. What wooden side-wheel steamer brought the majority of settlers and visitors from San Francisco to San Diego from the 1860s through the 1880s?

35. Where did the Salvation Army hold its first public meeting in San Diego?

36. What city "seceded" from San Diego in 1890?

37. Who was the first U.S. President to visit San Diego?

38. What San Diego County supervisor had to decide whether to resign or live in his barn?

34. The *Orizaba*. Being able to say that one's family came to San Diego on the *Orizaba* was almost as prestigious as saying that one's ancestors came over on the *Mayflower*. The best-known commander was Captain Henry James Johnson, who purchased 65 acres of land in what is now Mission Hills. In 1887 his daughter built her house, the "Villa Orizaba," there, using pieces from the recently dismantled vessel. Later the street on which the house stands was renamed Orizaba Avenue.

35. Horton Plaza. There is a plaque in the center walk there commemorating their first meeting in San Diego, which was held March 31, 1888. Horton Plaza was at that time the center of community activities such as concerts, political rallies, public speeches, and town meetings.

36. Coronado. The citizens there objected to paying San Diego city taxes while receiving no municipal benefits, so they voted to separate on October 6, 1890. On December 9 of that year the city of Coronado officially came into being.

37. Benjamin Harrison. San Diego was one of the stops on his 1891 tour from the South to the Pacific Coast and back. He arrived here April 23, and was given a reception at the Hotel del Coronado. Afterwards he was taken on a parade through the city and honored at a massive rally at Horton Plaza.

38. J. P. M. Rainbow (for whom the town of Rainbow is named). In 1890 he was elected a San Diego County supervisor, but in 1893 the new county line divided his property: his house was now in Riverside County and his barn in San Diego County. If he continued to live in his house he would no longer be eligible to hold a San Diego County office. He chose to resign.

39. What was the name of San Diego's "red-light district" that flourished from the 1880s through 1912?

40. What was the nickname of the steam train that linked San Diego to La Jolla around the turn of the century?

41. Who was San Diego's most famous madam?

42. Where in San Diego County were there Bigfoot sightings in the late 1800s?

39. Stingaree. It was named for the stingray which was common in San Diego Bay until the 1950s. The district extended approximately from First to Sixth and from Market to the bay, and in its heyday boasted 71 saloons, 120 bawdy houses, plus numerous opium dens, dance halls, and gambling houses.

40. The "Abalone Limited." It was officially named the San Diego, Pacific Beach, and La Jolla Railway Co., and operated from 1894 through 1917. Abalone hunters would ride this train from San Diego to La Jolla Cove where abalone were plentiful.

41. Ida Bailey. In her heyday around the turn of the century she was known as "Queen of the Stingaree." Her pale yellow brothel, Canary Cottage, offered the finest food, drink, and girls in town, and catered only to gentlemen, including many town leaders. Two large rubber trees near the windows provided a quick exit in case of a raid. Ida Bailey's Restaurant in the Horton Grand Hotel now stands on the site of Canary Cottage.

42. Deadman's Hole. This spot between Warner Springs and Oak Grove was named for the mysterious murders that took place there. Rumors of a wild man spread, and in 1876 and 1888 there were reported sightings of a man covered with long coarse black hair and having enormous feet. These reports have not been substantiated, but to this day Bigfoot trackers search the vicinity for this elusive creature.

43. Who was the last lighthouse keeper at the Old Point Loma Lighthouse?

44. What was the honorary title of San Diego resident Ah Quin?

45. Where was San Diego County's first watch factory?

43. Robert D. Israel. He began as assistant keeper in 1871, and in 1873 was appointed principal keeper, a position which he held until 1891. During his term he lived at the lighthouse with his wife and four children. It had long been realized that the light was too high to be seen by ships when there were low clouds or fog, so in March 1891 a new lighthouse on the lower coast began operation. For a while Mr. Israel was principal keeper there.

44. Mayor of Chinatown. This enterprising young man came to San Diego around 1879 and was the first Chinese to establish a family here. He helped hundreds of Chinese find work on the railroad, ran a successful general merchandise store on lower Fifth Avenue, and owned real estate, including farm land and a mine. These endeavors brought him wealth and made him a respected leader and spokesman for the Chinese in San Diego.

45. Otay. The Otay Watch Works, said to be the first watch factory west of the Mississippi, began operation in early 1890 in a large three-story brick building. On May 17 the first watch was completed and publicly celebrated. It was expected that the future development of the South Bay area would revolve around this enterprise, but by November of the same year the factory closed for lack of funds.

HISTORY IV

EARLY 1900s

1. What was the name of the summer resort on the Silver Strand in the early 1900s?

2. The large granite obelisk at Fort Rosecrans National Cemetery on Point Loma is a memorial to whom?

3. Who is known as the "Mother of Balboa Park"?

4. What mayor of San Diego took office by climbing a ladder and breaking a window in order to begin his term?

1. Tent City. It opened in 1900 just southeast of the Hotel del Coronado, and began to flourish in 1902 when the hotel was closed temporarily for repairs. This summer life style was so popular that Tent City was continued every summer through 1938. In addition to the square-shaped tents, the resort also featured an indoor swimming plunge, a huge dance pavilion, floating casino, lending library, concession stands, shooting gallery, bandstand, bathhouse, boat house, shops, restaurant, bowling alley, programs of music and vaudeville, and a nearby Japanese tea garden.

2. The victims of a boiler explosion on the USS *Bennington*. Sixty men were killed when the boiler exploded in San Diego Harbor on July 21, 1905. Most of the victims are buried at Fort Rosecrans.

3. Kate Sessions. This horticulturist was largely responsible for the landscaping of Balboa Park, as well as many other areas of San Diego. Prior to the 1890s the park was a barren wasteland. Then in 1892 Miss Sessions leased 30 acres in the northwest corner of the park for a nursery, in return for which she agreed to plant 100 trees in the park each year and also to give 300 ornamental trees to the city.

4. John L. Sehon, in 1905. After he was elected mayor some of his opponents challenged his right to hold office because he was still on government payroll as a retired Army captain. To avoid service of legal papers he went into hiding until the early morning before his term was to begin, at which time he climbed up a ladder, shattered the glass of his new office, and entered. When his opponents arrived at City Hall he was already in firm command.

5.   The ferry *Berkeley*, now part of San Diego's Maritime Museum, helped evacuate persons from what disaster?

6.   In August 1906 *Collier's Weekly* wrote an exposé entitled "The Miracle Workers" about a San Diego County product. What was this product?

7.   Who is said to have turned San Diego into a "one man town" after the turn of the century?

8.   In the early 1900s the Empress of China prized what San Diego export?

5.   The San Francisco earthquake and fire of April 1906. The *Berkeley* was launched October 17, 1898, and her usual run was from the ferry building in San Francisco to Oakland Pier. After the San Francisco earthquake she carried thousands of refugees to Oakland.

6   Isham's California Waters of Life. Traveling salesman Alfred Huntington Isham claimed that this mineral water from a spring near Jamacha at the foot of Mt. San Miguel was a veritable fountain of youth. Testimonials abounded stating that this water would cure a great variety of diseases including cancer and rheumatism, and in particular would restore a luxurious growth of hair to a bald head. Isham sold his bottles and jugs all over the U.S. and Europe until the magazine article and bad business deals brought an end to his elixir dreams. Currently there are plans to develop the area into a resort with a museum, and an attempt is being made to have the spring (sometimes called Bald Headed Spring) declared a historical monument.

7.   John D. Spreckels. He settled in San Diego permanently in 1906, and at one time or another he owned or controlled most of Coronado and North Island, the Hotel del Coronado, the *San Diego Union* and *Evening Tribune*, the local transit system, the water company, various oil, rubber, and lumber companies, Hotel San Diego, the Spreckels Theatre Building, the First National Bank of San Diego, the San Diego and Arizona Railway, Mission Beach Amusement Park, the wharf, the Union Building, ranch properties, the ferry system, and the San Diego Gas and Electric Company.

8.   Tourmaline, especially the pink variety. She and other wealthy Chinese purchased great quantities of this gem from San Diego mines. They then had the tourmaline carved into figurines and ornaments. When the dynasty fell in 1912 the trade ended.

9. What was the name of the utopian colony near San Ysidro which was founded by William Smythe in the early 1900s?

10. What San Diegan was known as the "Purple Mother"?

11. Who was known as the "damned old crank"?

12. What was the name of the park overlooking Mission Valley that was one of San Diego's most popular attractions from the 1890s through the 1920s?

9. Little Landers. It was an experiment in back-to-the-soil living in which owners cultivated their little plots of land to raise enough food for their families and to have surplus to sell. Their motto was "A little land and a living." The colony was successful for a number of years, until the flood of 1916 destroyed most of the farms. Smythe Avenue is all that is left to remind us of this colony.

10. Madame Katherine Tingley. She was leader of the Theosophical Society of America and the Revival of the Lost Mysteries of Antiquity, which had its headquarters on Point Loma from 1897 to 1942. She often wore purple, and was nicknamed "Purple Mother" by the press.

11. E. W. Scripps. In 1890 this fiery, outspoken newspaper magnate moved to San Diego, which he described as "a busted, broken-down boom town." Nevertheless, he liked the climate and the isolation, and he established Scripps Miramar Ranch in the north county. Here he published the *San Diego Sun*, which he is said to have run in order to irritate John D. Spreckels, owner of the *Union* and *Tribune*, with whom he had a running feud. The title and first chapter of Scripps' memoirs are entitled *Damned Old Crank*.

12. Mission Cliff Gardens (earlier called The Bluffs or Mission Cliff Park). It began as a small recreation park at the end of the cable car line, with a beer garden and merry-go-round. John D. Spreckels developed it into a spectacular botanical garden with a large pavilion, an aviary, lily pond, pergolas, a miniature Japanese garden, and an adjoining ostrich farm and deer park. Today all that remain of the park are a stone wall and rows of palm trees along Adams Avenue near Park Boulevard, plus a grassy circle that once was the lily pond.

13. Where in San Diego County did John D. Spreckels build his $100,000 mansion in 1908?

14. The son of what U.S. President built a hotel in San Diego?

15. In 1909, three of San Diego's wealthiest citizens were appointed to form a highway commission. Because their last names all began with "S" they were called the "Triple-S Commission." Who were they?

16. Where was Glenn Curtiss's flying school located?

17. On what group of speakers did the police and fire departments spray water from their firehoses on March 10, 1912?

13. Coronado. It stands on Glorietta Bay across from the Hotel del Coronado. He added a music room in 1917 to house a 40-rank pipe organ. In 1929 the house became the home of Ira C. Copley, publisher of the *San Diego Union* and *Evening Tribune,* and now it is part of the Glorietta Bay Inn.

14. Ulysses S. Grant. Son Ulysses S. Grant Jr. built the US Grant Hotel as a memorial to his father. Grant Jr. had come to San Diego in 1893 for his wife's health, and began his hotel on Broadway on the site of the old Horton Hotel. After many delays the $1.95 million structure opened in 1910. It featured a marble staircase, 426 rooms, a roof garden, two indoor plunges, and Turkish baths.

15. John D. Spreckels (the sugar prince), Albert G. Spaulding (the sporting goods magnate), and E. W. Scripps (the newspaper publisher). All three were millionaires, and all were vigorously outspoken in their usually opposing views.

16. North Island. He established it there in 1911 on land donated by John D. Spreckels. It was the first military aviation school in the United States, although civilians could be trained there as well.

17. The I.W.W. (Industrial Workers of the World) or "Wobblies." Because of problems with them and with Mexican revolutionaries, the San Diego City Council passed an ordinance prohibiting speeches in a six-square-block area. When this was violated and the crowds got out of control, the police ordered them to be sprayed.

18. On November 10, 1912, the Stingaree area was raided. One hundred thirty-eight ladies of the evening were arrested. How many promised to reform?

19. When it was incorporated in 1912, what city became the second largest in San Diego County?

20. What event did San Diego's 1915-1916 exposition celebrate?

18. Two. The next day the *San Diego Union* noted that the sanity of one of the two women was in doubt, as she had at one time been the subject of an inquiry by a lunacy commission. The raid had been prompted by the Vice Suppression Committee and by the citizens who were trying to clean up San Diego for the exposition planned for 1915. The women in the red-light district were charged with vagrancy and fined $100, which was suspended on condition that they leave town. One hundred thirty-six promised to leave the city and bought train tickets, mostly for Los Angeles. It was noticed, however, that almost all of them bought round-trip tickets.

19. East San Diego. This community developed during the land boom of the 1880s, and became a town of homes and schools. One of the first laws passed after incorporation was the prohibition of the sale or gift of liquor. East San Diego was a separate city from 1912 until 1923, when it became a part of the city of San Diego.

20. The opening of the Panama Canal. It was called the Panama-California Exposition in 1915, and the Panama-California International Exposition the following year with the addition of new exhibits from San Francisco's fair. At that time San Diego was the smallest city to host an exposition, and it was a great success.

21. Who is known in San Diego as "The Rainmaker"?

22. Where was the first large amusement park in San Diego?

23. In 1913, the Order of Panama erected a large cross in what is now Presidio Park, marking the site of Father Serra's original mission. Of what was the cross constructed?

24. What was the name of what is now the Alcazar Garden in Balboa Park when it was created for the 1915 exposition?

25. What national historic treasure was exhibited for three days at the Panama- California Exposition?

21. Charles M. Hatfield. He was hired as a rainmaker by the city of San Diego in 1916 to end a long drought. The drought ended, sure enough, with disastrous floods: two dams overflowed and a third one burst, causing considerable damage and some loss of life. Hatfield demanded his $10,000, and the city offered to pay it if he would settle the lawsuits for damages. He declined. (It is often claimed that N. Richard Nash based the main character of his play *The Rainmaker* on Charles Hatfield, but the author declares that there is no connection.)

22. Ocean Beach. Called Wonderland, it boasted the largest roller coaster on the West Coast, a dance pavilion, menagerie, fun zone with 40 attractions, roller skating rink, children's playground, and 22,000 lights outlining the buildings. Wonderland was in operation from 1913 to 1916, when it was destroyed by high tides.

23. Tiles from the original presidio. This 28-foot-high cross stands near the site of California's first mission and presidio.

24. Montezuma Garden (or Los Jardines de Montezuma). At that time the garden was surrounded by a vine-covered pergola. For the 1935 exposition the garden was redesigned by Richard Requa who patterned it after the gardens surrounding the Alcazar Castle in Seville, Spain.

25. The Liberty Bell. It arrived here in November 1915, amid much fanfare. William Randolph Hearst was instrumental in bringing it here, as he had been favorably impressed with our exposition.

26. What was the name of the midway section of the 1915-16 Panama-California Exposition?

27. Who was the founder of the San Diego Zoo?

28. San Diego County had many military camps during World War I and World War II. Which one of the following was built for World War I: Camp Elliott, Camp Kearny, Camp Callan, Camp Pendleton, or Camp Lockett?

29. What San Diego vessel returned from duty in World War I with two gold stars on her stack?

26. The Isthmus. This fun zone, named for the Isthmus of Panama, featured nearly a mile of "clean amusements" including the longest roller coaster in the world (6,000 feet), Chinatown, Mexican Village, Southern Plantation, Japanese Village, Hawaiian Village, War of the Worlds exhibit, a working model of the Panama Canal, a model gem mine, an ostrich farm, a candy factory, an aquarium, animal cages, and concessions of food, novelties, and games. The general area of the Isthmus was what is now the zoo parking lot.

27. Dr. Harry Wegeforth. This local physician started the zoo in 1916 on the east side of Park Boulevard with animals left over from the Panama-California Exposition and Wonderland. It was moved to its present location in 1922. Dr. Wegeforth was president of the Zoological Society until his death in 1941, and one of the amphitheaters in the zoo bears his name.

28. Camp Kearny. It was built for the U.S. Army in Linda Vista, and was one of the best training grounds in the country.

29. The *Venetia*. This was John D. Spreckels' private steam yacht, which the government commandeered for service as a naval auxiliary cruiser. She earned her gold stars for the submarines she destroyed, one of which was thought to have been the submarine that sank the *Lusitania*. The *Venetia* was the only vessel from the Pacific Coast to earn a gold star.

30. At the Organ Pavilion in Balboa Park there is a brass plaque honoring what gold star mother?

31. What was the nickname of the Fortieth Division of the Army, which was stationed at Camp Kearny during World War I?

32. Before Easter sunrise services were held regularly on Mt. Helix beginning in 1917, on what nearby mountain were they held?

33. Who drove the golden spike marking the completion of the San Diego and Arizona Railway?

30. Madame Ernestine Schumann-Heink. This famed contralto sang at the dedication of the Organ Pavilion on December 31, 1914. She is remembered not only for her beautiful voice, but for her charity and patriotism. She promoted Liberty Bonds, sang at Army posts and hospitals, and opened her home to servicemen. She was known as "Mother" to all servicemen who knew her, was the official Mother of Disabled American Veterans of the World War, and was voted an honorary American Legion officer. During World War I she lost one son on the German side and one son on the American side. Her plaque calls her "A Gold Star Mother; A Star of the World."

31. "The Sunshine Division." It was named for San Diego's climate.

32. Mt. Nebo. These services were held in Prospect Park atop La Mesa's Mt. Nebo from 1914 to 1916. In 1924 architect Richard Requa was commissioned by Mary Yawkey White and Cyrus Yawkey to build a memorial to their mother, Mary C. Yawkey, on Mt. Helix. The result was an open-air theater and large cross, which were dedicated on Easter Sunday, April 12, 1925.

33. John D. Spreckels. This railroad was one of his dreams, and he had raised $18,000,000 in order to link San Diego with the East. The spike-driving ceremony took place at Carrizo Gorge November 15, 1919, and Spreckels declared that this was the happiest moment of his life. Week-long celebrations were held in San Diego and Imperial counties.

34. Where in San Diego did President Woodrow Wilson speak in 1919?

35. Besides the ferries that ran to Coronado and to North Island, there were ferries that ran from downtown San Diego to at least three other locations. Name one of these locations.

36. What member of royalty was entertained at the Hotel del Coronado in 1920 while on a goodwill tour?

37. Which famous aviation first did *not* take place at North Island?:
    1. First successful seaplane flight, 1911.
    2. First successful amphibian flight, 1911.
    3. First aerial photography from an aircraft, 1911.
    4. First radio used in an airplane, 1912.
    5. First loop-the-loop in the U.S., 1913.
    6. First night flight, 1913.
    7. First torpedo bomb dropped from an airplane, 1921.
    8. First mid-air refueling between two planes, 1923.
    9. First non-stop transcontinental flight terminus, 1923.

38. What was the first regularly scheduled year-round passenger airline in the U.S?

34. City Stadium (later called Balboa Stadium), next to San Diego High School. He was on a tour of the U.S., speaking in favor of the proposed League of Nations. An audience of 50,000 turned out to hear him here on September 19, 1919. This is thought to have been the largest crowd ever assembled up to that time to hear a U.S. President, and it was the first time that a President used an electric voice-amplifying system.

35. Point Loma, National City, and Imperial Beach. The Point Loma Land and Town Company began operating the plush steamer *Roseville* in 1888. The *Roseville* and other ferries ran until about 1919, making stops at Roseville Pier at the foot of Talbot, at La Playa, at Ft. Rosecrans, and at Ballast Point. Passengers disembarking at Roseville often walked or took the stage, horse and buggy, or rail over to Ocean Beach, because there was no easy way to reach that area by land. The *Roseville* also carried crowds of passengers to National City. The ferries *Imperial* and *McKinley Jr.* ran in the early 1900s from the foot of Market to a dredged canal near the north end of Ninth in Imperial Beach, where passengers could go the rest of the way to the town by trolley or streetcar.

36. Edward, Prince of Wales (later to become King Edward VIII of England). Legend has it that at this time he met Wallis Warfield, who would later become his wife. Though she was in the area at the same time, the two denied that they met here.

37. 7: First torpedo bomb. Because of the aviation developments that took place here, San Diego was called the "Air Capital of the United States."

38. Ryan Airlines. This San Diego company, operated by T. Claude Ryan and B. Franklin Mahoney, began regular flights between San Diego and Los Angeles in 1925.

39. Who is considered to be the benefactress of La Jolla?

40. In the first half of the 1900s, what area was considered the dairy farming capital of San Diego?

41. Before East San Diego was annexed to San Diego in 1923, what street marked the eastern end of San Diego?

42. What San Diego pier once had a ballroom at the end of it?

43. What San Diego aircraft company built the *Spirit of St. Louis*, in which Charles Lindbergh made his historic New York to Paris flight in 1927?

39. Ellen Browning Scripps. This half sister of E. W. Scripps donated part or all of the following: La Jolla Woman's Club, Bishop's School, La Jolla playground and community houses, Scripps Institution of Oceanography, La Jolla Library, nurses' home, Children's Pool, Scripps Clinic and Research Foundation, the athletic field, Torrey Pines Park, and Scripps Memorial Hospital. Her beneficence was not limited to La Jolla, but included other areas of San Diego, such as the zoo.

40. Mission Valley. From the 1880s through the 1930s 20 dairy farms were established there, but when Highway 80 was extended through the valley in 1950, it marked the beginning of the end of this way of life in the city. By 1960 there were only six dairies left, and in late 1978 the last remaining buildings of the last dairy, Ferrari Dairy, were demolished.

41. Boundary Street. This street runs in a slight northwest-southeast direction as opposed to the north-south streets around it, which were laid out later.

42. Crystal Pier, in Pacific Beach. Called the Crystal Ballroom, it was popular for dancing because of its cork-lined dance floor. The building was made of stucco and wood, with mural-covered walls, colored lights, and a glittering crystal sphere hanging from the ceiling. Carnival concessions lined the length of the pier leading to the ballroom at the end. The ballroom opened in 1927, but unfortunately lasted only three months because the pilings became infested with marine borers.

43. Ryan Airlines. The airplane was constructed in a building which had been an old fish cannery. By working day and night the company built the *Spirit* within 60 days.

44. Why was the Fireman's Ball that was to have been held November 25, 1925, cancelled?

45. What father and son were both mayor of San Diego?

46. What was the name of the late Duchess of Windsor when she lived in Coronado?

47. What naturalist and conservationist was custodian of Torrey Pines State Park from 1921 to 1933?

48. What San Diego County town won the "Better Citizenship Cup" for the best voting record in California from 1924 to 1930?

44. The building burned down. On the evening of the ball the Southern California Counties Building (also called Civic Auditorium) in Balboa Park, in which it was to have been held, caught on fire from a faulty oil furnace. Firefighters on duty, as well as those dressed for the ball, struggled to put out the flames, but the building could not be saved. The Natural History Museum was later built on the site.

45. John F. Forward Sr. (1907-09), and John F. Forward Jr. (1932-34).

46. Wallis Spencer (Mrs. Earl Spencer). She was the wife of an American naval officer, Lt. Cmdr. Earl Winfield Spencer Jr., who was stationed here. He went on to become the first Commanding Officer of the Naval Air Station at North Island. When she met the Prince of Wales in England several years later she was divorced from her second husband, Ernest Simpson.

47. Guy L. Fleming. The park trail named after him was one of his favorite walks. In addition, he was the Southern district superintendent of California State Parks, and was instrumental in the development of Anza-Borrego, Cuyamaca, Palomar, and Silver Strand state parks.

48. Ramona. Because it won three times in a row (and more), the town is the permanent holder of the cup, which is on display in the Chamber of Commerce office. In 1926 and 1928 the voter turnouts were record highs of 98.3%

49. San Diego's first traffic light was at what intersection?

50. What prominent San Diego merchant and philanthropist donated Presidio Park and the Serra Museum to San Diego?

49. Fifth Avenue and Broadway. It was installed in 1926 as a combination semaphore, bell, and light unit. In 1949 it was replaced by a modern three-light signal.

50. George White Marston. Over a period of 22 years he spent more than $392,000 in purchasing the land piece by piece. Then in 1929 he gave the park to the city as a gift.

HISTORY V

MID-1900s

1. What was the name of San Diego's second exposition, held in 1935-36?

2. Mason Street School, San Diego's first publicly owned schoolhouse, became a restaurant in the early 1900s. What was the name of the restaurant?

3. Who was the first Catholic bishop of the diocese of San Diego?

4. In 1934-35, the president of Consolidated Aircraft Corporation at Buffalo, New York, moved his factory to San Diego. What was his name?

5. Where was there a nudist colony in Balboa Park?

1. California Pacific International Exposition. It was held in order to save the buildings of the 1915-16 exposition, and to pull San Diego out of the Depression.

2. Old Town Tamale Factory. The 1865 schoolhouse had been moved to a new location on Taylor and Whitman in the late 1800s and used as a home until about 1918. It served as the tamale restaurant until the late 1940s, when it was condemned to make way for a freeway on-ramp. The San Diego County Historical Days Association saved it and had it restored and moved to its original location on Mason Street, where it is now a historical landmark and the location for adult classes in California history.

3. Bishop Charles Francis Buddy. He was installed here as bishop in 1936, and served in that capacity for 30 years. It was largely through his efforts that the University of San Diego was established here.

4. Major Reuben H. Fleet. With later mergers the company eventually became Consolidated Vultee Aircraft Corporation, called Convair, and then General Dynamics, one of the largest employers in San Diego.

5. Zoro Gardens. This was a popular attraction at the California Pacific International Exposition of 1935-36. The chief of police saw to it, however, that the women wore brassieres and G-strings, and that the men wore loincloths. The Zoro Gardens are located between what are now the Reuben H. Fleet Space Theater and the Casa de Balboa. The name was a shortened form of Zoroaster, the Persian prophet, who was erroneously believed to be a sun god.

6. On July 28, 1932, what aviation celebrity gave the main address at the dedication of the new terminal and administration building at Lindbergh Field?

7. What prominent San Diego clock stopped running when its maker died?

8. What was the name of the mining camp replica at the California Pacific International Exposition in 1935?

9. What was the name of the community festival held in Escondido on September 9 from 1908 to 1950? (Hint: It did not celebrate California Admission Day.)

6. Amelia Earhart. She also unveiled a plaque to Charles Lindbergh. Both the building and the terminal had been financed by T. C. Ryan, who leased them to others.

7. The Jessop Street Clock. This 1906 timepiece was designed by Joseph Jessop Sr., and the principal builder was Claude D. Ledger. The clock has 20 dials, 12 of which tell the time in all the nations or major cities of the world. It stood outside Jessop's Jewelry Store at 1041 Fifth Avenue from 1927 until it was moved to Horton Plaza shopping center in 1985. When Mr. Ledger died in 1935, the clock stopped; it was restarted, but it stopped again three days later — the day of his funeral. This curious incident was reported in Ripley's "Believe it or Not."

8. Gold Gulch. It was complete with general store, saloon, Chinese laundry and restaurant, iron-barred bank, sheriff's office, shooting gallery, dance hall, donkey rides, cider mill, and model mine. Gold Gulch Gertie and Flaming Fanny were popular attractions. This area, which lies to the west of the Reuben H. Fleet Space Theater, is still called Gold Gulch Canyon.

9. Grape Day. This was a large celebration in which tons of grapes, especially muscats, were given away. Festivities included a parade, games, a queen, band concerts, contests, exhibits, and speeches. From 1910 on it was held at Grape Day Park. It once rivaled Pasadena's Festival of Roses, and attracted out-of-town visitors estimated at 5,000 in 1908 and 40,000 by 1941.

10. What was the original name of the roller coaster at Belmont Park?

11. What woman began as temporary bookkeeper at the San Diego Zoo and rose to become the only female zoo director in the world?

12. What was the name of San Diego's first fire boat?

13. What was the name of the parade that was held in North Park almost every December from 1930 to 1966?

10. Mission Beach Giant Dipper (or just Giant Dipper). It was built in 1925 and is the last remaining one of its kind. In its heyday it offered a thrilling ride of 40 to 45 mph, a 49° banked turn, and a 70-foot drop. The name was changed to Rollercoaster from 1957-76, to Earthquake in 1976, and back to Mission Beach Giant Dipper in 1982. It is the only roller coaster to have National Landmark status and to be on the National Register of Historic Places. Though it has been closed since December 1976, the Save the Coaster Committee Inc. is working for its preservation.

11. Belle Benchley. She was hired in 1925, and in less than two years rose to the top position of Executive Secretary and Manager, which she held until her retirement in 1953. Under her direction the zoo grew to become one of the largest and best in the world.

12. The *Bill Kettner*. It was named after one of San Diego's prominent congressmen, and was the first gasoline-powered fire boat in the world. It was built in San Diego and commissioned June 30, 1919. In the early days the crew would wait for the alarm to ring in their headquarters on Columbia Street, and then jump into their Model A Ford roadster and rush to the waterfront, where the engineer would have the *Bill Kettner* ready to go. The boat was decommissioned in August 1961, and when last heard of was being used as a fishing boat in San Pedro.

13. The North Park Toyland Parade. It went down University Avenue every December except during the war years. In the 1940s the parade was held in the evenings, but was later moved to afternoons, where it evolved into one of the largest parades in the West. In 1967 it was cancelled, partly because of freeway construction, and was not held for many years until it was revived in 1985.

14. In March 1931, San Diegan Theodore Gildred took off from Lindbergh Field in a single-engine Ryan B-5 Brougham for a 4,200-mile goodwill flight. What was his destination?

15. What was the nickname of the passenger ferries that ran from San Diego to North Island?

16. What was the original name of the Starlight Bowl in Balboa Park?

17. What U.S. President dedicated San Diego's Civic Center on Pacific Highway?

14. Quito, Ecuador. He was one of the first men to receive a commercial pilot's license, and flew with his copilot, Captain Dean Farran, on a rugged route for the adventure and to promote international friendship. The people of Quito built their airport especially for this flight, and Gildred sold his plane *Ecuador* to them for their first airmail plane. A sister ship almost identical to it is on display at the San Diego Aerospace Museum. In 1981 Gildred's son, Theodore Jr., and copilot Wally Moore, almost exactly duplicated his flight in a 1942 single-engine Stinson, the *Ecuador II*.

15. "Nickel snatchers." These ferries were called this even after the fare had increased to 10¢ and to 15¢. In the early days two small companies, The Star and The Crescent, ran water taxis to Navy landings on the island, and in 1918 they combined. Beginning in 1942 they constructed a fleet of 62-foot diesel square-ended ferries, which included the *Juanita, Glorietta, Ramona, Point Loma, Del Mar,* and in 1952 the slightly larger *Monterey.* Before the service was ended with the opening of the San Diego-Coronado Bay Bridge in 1969, these ferries carried over 5,000 passengers a day across the bay to North Island.

16. Ford Bowl. It was built for the 1935-36 California Pacific International Exposition with labor supplied by the W.P.A. It was called the Ford Bowl during the fair because the Ford Motor Company provided the orchestra concerts which were performed there. In 1948 the name was changed to Balboa Park Bowl, and in 1977 to Starlight Bowl.

17. Franklin D. Roosevelt. The ceremony was held July 16, 1938, at the building that had been made possible by the W.P.A. Since 1964 it has been the San Diego County Administration Center. On July 11, 1988, Franklin's son James Roosevelt appeared here to mark the 50th anniversary of the dedication.

18. What was the nickname of the person who manned the information booth at Horton Plaza from 1915 to 1948?

19. What former Ryan Airlines metalsmith who had worked on the *Spirit of St. Louis* formed his own successful aircraft company in 1940?

20. Which three buildings in Balboa Park besides the Naval Hospital served as hospitals during World War II?

21. What World War II general led maneuvers in the Borrego Desert in 1942?

22. What was the name of the bomber that Consolidated (Convair) produced by the thousands for the World War II effort?

23. Before the Cabrillo Freeway (now 163) was constructed through Balboa Park in 1948, what was in its place?

18. "Information Anderson." Adolph H. Anderson was originally hired by the San Diego Electric Railway Company to answer transportation questions. The sign on his kiosk read "Ask Anderson - He Knows," and at one time it was estimated that he had answered over 22,000,000 questions on all aspects of San Diego.

19. Fred H. Rohr. The first location of Rohr Aircraft Corporation was downtown San Diego, but the following year it moved to Chula Vista where it soon became one of the largest subcontracting firms in the aerospace industry. Rohr Industries Inc. now has branches and subsidiaries in other cities and states as well as in France, and is one of the largest employers in San Diego County.

20. The Natural History Museum, the Museum of Man, and the Fine Arts Gallery (now the San Diego Museum of Art). The museum collections were moved out and stored for the duration of the war.

21. Major General George S. Patton. He trained his men there in preparation for the North African campaigns.

22. B-24 or "Liberator." The San Diego plant built 6,726 of these four-engine planes by August 1945, and they were generally considered to be the best military airplanes built in America. The British used them extensively, and they were effective in the North African and European campaigns and the D-Day operation. Later they became the main bombers covering all of the Pacific.

23. A large lake or lily pond. It was called La Laguna de Cabrillo or Laguna del Puente, and was filled with water lilies and lotus.

24. When Balboa Park was taken over by the military during World War II, what was it called?

25. Where was the first J. C. Penney store in San Diego?

26. What San Diego County aviation field was known as the "Helicopter Capital of the World" for many years?

27. What national figure turned the first spade of earth in ground-breaking ceremonies for the Linda Vista shopping center in 1942?

28. On September 4, 1944, what national magazine ran a three-page spread on the 58-year reunion of San Pasqual School's class of 1886?

24. Camp Kidd. It was named after Admiral Isaac C. Kidd who died at Pearl Harbor. Camp Kidd became the nation's foremost corpsman training center, and most of the park buildings, with the exception of the zoo and the Ford Building, were used. The Balboa Park Club became an officers' club called Captain Kidd Officers Club.

25. North Park. It opened on University Avenue and Ray Street on March 26, 1942. A sign proclaiming that it was the first in San Diego was displayed over the front door until the store closed December 31, 1986.

26. Ream Field. This field in Imperial Beach was named in 1918 after Major William Roy Ream, who was the first Army flight surgeon to be killed in an aircraft accident. The aviation field was established by the Army in 1917, and after later use by the Navy was made a regular Naval facility in 1968. For many years it was the Navy's largest helicopter base, and home base to all Pacific Fleet helicopter squadrons. In 1976 it was decommissioned, and is now known as the Outlying Landing Field (OLF), Imperial Beach.

27. Eleanor Roosevelt. This was the first community shopping center in San Diego, and was reported to be the first planned shopping center in the United States, designed to help conserve gasoline during rationing.

28. *Life* magazine. The old adobe schoolhouse was restored, and the teacher and all 13 of the 20 pupils still living came to the event. Local journalist and newscaster Harold Keen covered the reunion, and the following year he sent *Life* a picture of the 59th reunion, which was published in the August 6, 1945 issue.

29. Which San Diego mayor was a minister while holding office?

30. When San Diego tunaboats were used by the Navy during World War II, what were they called?

31. What was the slogan of Consolidated that was painted on the side of one of its buildings along Pacific Highway in the early 1940s?

32. What was the name of the twin-engine flying boat manufactured by Consolidated in the 1940s?

33. What was the lily pond in front of the Botanical Garden in Balboa Park used for during World War II?

34. When did the last electric streetcar run in San Diego?

29. Dr. Howard Bard. When he was appointed mayor in 1942 to fill the term of Percy Benbough, who had died in office, he had been minister of the First Unitarian Church for 32 years. He served as mayor through 1943 and did not give up his pastorate.

30. "Yippee Boats." The letters YP, which stood for yard patrol, preceded each boat number, so they were called the "Yippee Fleet." Forty-seven of these boats were pressed into service, and most of their skippers chose to go with them. At first they were used as patrol craft in coastal waters, but later they supplied fresh water, food, ammunition, and fuel to such places as Panama, Samoa, Hawaii, Guadalcanal, and the New Hebrides.

31. "Nothing short of right is right." Major Fleet had this 480-foot-long slogan painted on the side of the final assembly building in letters nine feet high. It was later painted out when the buildings were camouflaged.

32. PBY Catalina. San Diego's Convair built 2,160 of these PBYs (Patrol Bomber Consolidated), and they gained fame during World War II. It was a Royal Air Force Catalina that air-tracked the *Bismarck* for nine days and nights until she was sunk by the British, and it was a U.S. Navy Catalina that spotted a Japanese submarine off the entrance to Pearl Harbor.

33. A swimming pool for Naval Hospital patients. It was used primarily for therapy for those injured in the war. (During World War I it had been used for swimming as well as for boat drills and survival training.)

34. 1949. When the very last one crossed University and 40th Street in the early morning hours of April 24, a pajama-clad figure rushed out and placed a coin on the track in order to have a streetcar-flattened souvenir.

35. What popular Italian restaurant in Hillcrest had large mounted fish on the walls in the 1940s and 1950s?

36. What was the Navy's first non-ship to gain a commission?

37. What was San Diego's drive-in restaurant chain that was popular from the 1940s through the early 1970s?

35. Caesar's Restaurant. The Pastore family opened a restaurant at Fifth and I streets in 1913; in 1928 it was relocated to Sixth and University. When the Natural History Museum was used as a hospital during World War II, its mounted fish were displayed at this Caesar's where they remained until the restaurant was remodeled in the 1950s. Some of the fish were record holders at the time, and were caught by such celebrities as Bing Crosby, Clark Gable, and journalist Bob Paine. A second Caesar's Restaurant opened in Grossmont in 1970, and another in Mission Valley in 1971. Shortly afterwards the one in Hillcrest closed.

36. The USS *Recruit*. It was commissioned July 27, 1949, as Training Destroyer Escort 1 (TDE-1), at the Naval Training Center along Harbor Drive. It is a mock- up of a World War II destroyer, built on two-thirds scale. The *Recruit* is designed to improve the seamanship training of recruits and to in-doctrinate them in shipboard routine. It is one of the largest training aids in the Navy, measuring 225 feet from bow to stern, and 53 feet in height. It has been periodically updated, and in 1981 it underwent an extensive renovation.

37. Oscar's. The first Oscar's Drive-in Restaurant was estab-lished here in 1941 by Robert O. Peterson. By 1958 the chain employed about 130 girl car-hops, and also provided take-out, counter, and booth service. By the mid-1960s there were 16 in San Diego County and 26 in Southern California, and they were called Oscar's Drive-in Coffee Shops.

38. In 1952, what major department store was the first to abandon its downtown San Diego location and move to the suburbs?

39. Who was San Diego's first woman judge?

40. Before the Children's Zoo opened in 1957, what was located on the site?

41. What letter of the alphabet was painted on the southwest face of Cowles Mountain from 1931 to 1971?

38. Sears, Roebuck & Co. It moved from 1101 Sixth Avenue to a ten-acre site on Cleveland Avenue in Hillcrest. The ultra-modern building contained 193,000 square feet, and there was off-street parking for 1,200 automobiles, a tremendous figure at the time.

39. Madge Bradley. She began her career in legal work in 1927 as deputy county clerk. In 1933 she was admitted to the bar, but didn't start her practice until 1940. She was appointed municipal judge by Governor Goodwin J. Knight on October 29, 1953, and served until her retirement in 1962.

40. A Japanese Tea House and Garden. These tranquil grounds, laid out and planted by Japanese gardeners for the 1915-16 Panama-California Exposition, featured goldfish ponds, arbors, stone lanterns, winding paths, and a h i g h - a r c h e d red lacquered bridge called "Bridge of Long Life." The tea house or pavilion, made in Japan, was modeled after the temple in the Katsura area of Kyoto, and during the exposition Japanese girls served tea and rice cakes there.

41. The letter "S." This 100-by-400-foot letter was limed almost every year by incoming freshmen of San Diego State College as a symbol of their school. For this reason the mountain was popularly known as "S Mountain" or "State College Mountain." When first created this was the world's largest collegiate symbol, and was visible for miles, except during World War II when it was obliterated as a security precaution. Remains of the letter can still be seen on the mountain.

42. Which of the original seven U.S. astronauts lived in Solana Beach?

43. The first Jack In The Box drive-thru restaurant in the country opened in 1951 in San Diego. On what street was it located?

44. In 1955, what San Diego store won an international gold medal for its displays?

45. What is the name of the parade that has been held in El Cajon every November since 1947?

46. What was the name of the airplane built at Convair in the 1950s that took off and landed vertically, and flew horizontally?

42. Lt. Walter M. Schirra Jr. He was a graduate of the U.S. Naval Academy at Annapolis and later became a member of the Navy Air Force. When he was chosen to be an astronaut he was stationed at Miramar Naval Air Station and lived in Solana Beach with his wife and two children.

43. El Cajon Boulevard. It was established at 6270 El Cajon Boulevard by Robert O. Peterson, who also headed the succesful chain of Oscar's Drive-ins. Within a few years there were franchised Jack In The Box restaurants throughout the county, and today there are over 900 of them in 13 states.

44. Marston's. There were only three top winners out of 3,000 contestants: a store in Stockholm, one in New York, and San Diego's Marston's at C Street between Fifth and Sixth. Marston's was well known for its beautiful floral arrangements inside the store, as well as its colorful Christmas displays in the 12 large windows along the street.

45. The Mother Goose Parade. Thomas Wigton Jr. first conceived this idea in 1946 as a way to do something special for children. Most of the floats depict Mother Goose rhymes and fairy tales, and they are accompanied by bands, clowns, and equestrians. It is held the Sunday before Thanksgiving, and is now the second-largest parade in California.

46. Pogo, or Pogo Stick, an XFY-1. It was developed for the Navy, and its first free flight was at Brown Field in November 1954. Ryan Aeronautical Company also developed a VTOL plane called the Ryan X-13, the first one of which is on display at the San Diego Aerospace Museum, on loan from the National Air and Space Museum in Washington, D.C.

47. Name at least three of the four colleges or universities that were located in Point Loma on the site of the former Theosophical Society grounds.

48. The first shopping *mall* in San Diego County was built in 1955. Which was it?

49. El Cajon woman Aileen Saunders won what national competition in 1959 and 1960?

50. What are the former and present locations of the San Diego Army and Navy Academy?

47. Balboa University; California Western University; United States International University; and Point Loma College (later Point Loma Nazarene College). Balboa University, 1950-52, was a private university which had been started in 1927 in a corner of Balboa Park. In 1952 it became "Cal Western," a Methodist-supported university that was later taken over by U.S.I.U. Point Loma College (formerly Pasadena College), sponsored by the Church of the Nazarene, was established there in 1973, and in 1983 changed its name to Point Loma Nazarene College.

48. South Bay Plaza. It stands on Highland Avenue and 10th Street in National City. It was followed by College Grove Shopping Center in 1960, Mission Valley Center and Grossmont Center in 1961, and Chula Vista Shopping Center in 1962.

49. The Powder Puff Derby (all-woman transcontinental air race). In October 1960 she was named Pilot of the Year by the National Pilots Association, and was later president of San Diego's Flying Samaritans. In 1972 Marian Banks of San Diego and Dottie Sanders, copilot from Santee, were winners in the same competition.

50. Pacific Beach and Carlsbad. The Academy was founded in 1910 at Garnet and Kendall streets in Pacific Beach by brothers Col. Thomas A. Davis and Major Lynch Davis, on the site of the old San Diego College of Letters. It was the first private school on the Pacific Coast to secure West Point accreditation and to be recognized by the U.S. Bureau of Education. In 1936 it moved to the former Red Apple Inn in Carlsbad, where it is today. The former location in Pacific Beach reopened in 1937 as Brown Military Academy, which it remained until 1958. When the buildings were razed that year the San Diego College of Letters cornerstone was uncovered and some newspapers from 1887 were removed.

51.   What was the name of the San Diego celebration held during the summers of 1956 through 1959?

52.   What San Diegan developed a polio vaccine?

53.   In 1908 Joseph Jessop presented a sun dial to the San Diego Public Library, where it stood in the yard for many years. When a new and larger library was built in the early 1950s, the sun dial was removed and placed in front of what building?

54.   In the 1950s Convair worked on the construction of what ballistic missile?

55.   What San Diego restaurant owner had his moustache insured for $50,000 with Lloyds of London?

56.   The very first American dealerships of two makes of Japanese cars were located in San Diego. Which two cars were they?

51. Fiesta del Pacifico. San Diego's Spanish heritage was celebrated, and residents and tourists were encouraged to wear Spanish-style clothes. The grand historical pageant, "The California Story," held in Balboa Stadium, was the highlight of the festivities.

52. Dr. Jonas Salk. It was developed in 1953 and officially accepted in 1955. In 1963 the Salk Institute for Biological Studies opened in La Jolla on North Torrey Pines Road, where it has become a major health-oriented research institution specializing in molecular and cellular biology and neuroscience.

53. The Natural History Museum, in Balboa Park. It is inscribed "Presented by Joseph Jessop; December 1908; I stand amid ye sommere flowers To tell ye passage of ye houres," and is accurate to the second.

54. The Atlas. The first work on it was at the plant by Lindbergh Field, but later a huge new Astronautics division of General Dynamics was built on Kearny Mesa where the work was continued. On December 17, 1957, the first Atlas built at San Diego was successfully tested at Cape Canaveral.

55. George Pernicano. In 1957 he insured his 15- inch handlebar moustache, which was his trademark. Even the door handles on his Pizza House at 3840 Sixth Avenue are in the shape of his famous moustache, which he still sports today.

56. Toyota and Datsun. The first Toyota sold in America was a Toyopet, sold here by Johnny Rose in 1957. Raymond Lemke sold the first Datsun in this country in 1958. Despite initial skepticism and prejudice, the two dealerships flourished, and became Rose Toyota and San Diego Datsun (now San Diego Nissan). They are located close to each other in Mission Valley at Mission Gorge Road and Fairmount Extension.

HISTORY VI

1960-1988

1. What city gave the citizens of San Diego the friendship bell located at the tip of Shelter Island?

2. Which San Diego County shopping center won *Redbook Magazine*'s "Shopping Center of the Year" award in 1961?

3. Where in San Diego County was Dinosaur Land?

4. The first honorary doctorate degree conferred by a California State College was awarded June 6, 1963, at San Diego State College. On whom was that degree conferred?

5. San Diegan Marilyn Mitchell held what national title in 1963?

1. Yokohama, Japan. This was a gift from San Diego's sister city as a symbol of eternal friendship. It was received in 1958 and stored until a suitable location could be found. The 2.5-ton "Bell of Friendship" was dedicated at Shelter Island December 10, 1960.

2. College Grove Shopping Center. This award was "in recognition of progressive promotion activity typifying the best qualities of shopping center management." The center was presented with a $2,700 silver cup and a 15-foot-high clock that stood on the mall until it was removed in the early 1970s.

3. Alpine . It opened on Highway 80 in 1962 with only some of the proposed attractions, which were eventually supposed to include ten full-scale animated dinosaurs, giant sea turtle rides, a dinosaur roller coaster, and facilities for swimming, picnicking, and dining. Now most of the colorful cement figures have been removed.

4. John Fitzgerald Kennedy. President Kennedy gave the commencement address at Aztec Bowl, and following that was awarded the honorary Doctorate of Laws degree, presented by Chancellor Glenn S. Dumke on behalf of the California State College System.

5. Mrs. America. She was the second San Diegan to win that title; Mrs.Frances Cloyd (later Mrs. Frances Kirchhoff) was Mrs. America of 1950. Marilyn (Mrs. R. Lyle) Mitchell, mother of three, was crowned in Miami. During her reign she traveled all over the U.S. and made many TV appearances.

6. What entertainer was made honorary mayor of Del Mar in 1963?

7. Where in San Diego County were tracks of the "Abominable Sandman" reported in 1964?

8. On June 25, 1965, what prominent TV host spent the night in the Whaley House along with a spiritualist and a "ghost hunter" in order to investigate the presence of spirits?

9. What five cities make up the San Diego Unified Port District?

10. What automobile was introduced at half time at Balboa Stadium December 26, 1965?

11. Who was the first woman on the San Diego City Council?

6. Jimmy Durante. He spent six weeks there almost every summer beginning in 1937, enjoying horse racing and surf fishing. For 13 years he made Del Mar his second home, and because of his work in community projects the Del Mar City Council named him honorary mayor. At the same time, they renamed the road and bridge leading to the fairgrounds Jimmy Durante Boulevard and Jimmy Durante Bridge.

7. Anza-Borrego Desert (near Harpers Well along Carrizo Wash). The tracks were bear-like, with five blunt digits ending in tiny claw or toenail marks. The sets of prints were seven feet apart in some places, and there were indications that the creature had climbed a tree and broken branches to a height of six feet. No satisfactory explanation has been given for these tracks.

8. Regis Philbin. He was accompanied by Sybil Leek and Hans Holzer. Their eerie findings are described in Holzer's book *Ghosts of the Golden West*.

9. San Diego, National City, Chula Vista, Imperial Beach, and Coronado. This organization was created in 1962 by an act of the state legislature in order to manage the harbor, operate the international airport at Lindbergh Field, and administer the public tidelands surrounding San Diego Bay.

10. The Dodge Charger. It was shown for the first time at the AFL championship football game between the San Diego Chargers and the Buffalo Bills.

11. Helen Cobb. She represented District 1 from 1961 until she resigned in 1971. During her terms of office she was called a "councilman."

12. What item did the officers and men from the USS *Constellation* present to Balboa Park on May 27, 1968?

13. Profiles of what two persons appear on the 1969 San Diego Bicentennial commemorative logo and medal?

14. What was the Chicken's official name before he became the San Diego Chicken?

15. When the Coronado ferries were replaced by the San Diego-Coronado Bay Bridge in 1969, there were five ferries in use. Give the names of at least three of them.

16. In the late 1960s, what UCSD professor gained national notoriety as leader of the New Left?

12. A sun dial. It is located in the north lily pond in front of the Botanical Garden. Soon after this, one like it was presented to San Diego's sister city Yokohama.

13. Father Junípero Serra and Governor Gaspar de Portolá. They both arrived here in 1769 to found what was to become the city of San Diego. The two representations were to symbolize the blending of church and state during the early years of California's settlement.

14. KGB Chicken. He made his debut as radio station KGB's mascot in April 1974, and because of his popularity at athletic events he was soon called San Diego's number one sports figure. In 1979 he left KGB to become the San Diego Chicken.

15. 1. *Coronado*, built in 1929.
    2. *San Diego*, built in 1931.
    3. *North Island*, built in 1923 and acquired in 1938. This ferry was used as a stand-by.
    4. *Silver Strand*, built in 1927 and acquired in 1944.
    5. *Crown City*, built in 1954.

16. Dr. Herbert Marcuse. He had been professor of philosophy at UCSD from 1965 to 1970. The campus radicals looked to him as their leader, and soon he was blamed for inciting riots. Community members demanded that he be fired, but Chancellor William McGill, judging him on the merits of his teaching, kept him on. His book *One-Dimensional Man* became a best seller.

17. What does Archie Moore's ABC stand for?

18. What community was known for its annual Viejas Days celebration?

19. In what year did San Diego first claim to have become the second-largest city in California?

20. Who was the first San Diegan to hold public office at the city, state, and national levels?

17. Any Boy Can. This was Archie's successful project to keep boys from using drugs and violence, and the name implies that any boy can improve himself if he wants to. He organized the San Diego Any Boy Can club in 1967, and because of his efforts to help others he was voted Mr. San Diego in 1968.

18. Alpine. Viejas is a Spanish word meaning "old women," and the 1846 land grant in the Alpine area was named Rancho Valle de Las Viejas. The Viejas Days began as a horse show in 1948. Soon a Viejas Days Parade was added preceding the show, and by 1970 the celebration had become a week-long event. In 1987, however, it was discontinued for lack of interest.

19. 1969. Every year the state estimates the population of the cities as the basis for distribution of state-collected taxes. The October 1969 estimate showed us ahead of San Francisco for the first time, so Mayor Frank Curran sent a telegram to San Francisco's Mayor Alioto offering his personal condolences. However, the official 1970 census and the estimated 1971 census surprisingly showed that San Francisco was still ahead. In late 1971 we renewed our claim, stating that the Naval population based in San Diego had not been included in the count. By the 1980 official census we were way ahead of San Francisco, 875,504 to 678,974.

20. Clair W. Burgener. He served 24 years in elected public office: City Councilman 1953-57; State Assemblyman 1963-67; State Senator 1967-73; and U.S. Representative 1973-83. For his work with the developmentally disabled and other charitable work he was named Mr. San Diego of 1987. Since then, Senator Pete Wilson has also held public office at all three levels: State Assemblyman, Mayor of the City of San Diego, and current U.S. Senator.

21. What was the name of the lounge located in Mission Valley's Stardust Hotel that had an underwater mermaid show?

22. For whom is Mr. A's restaurant named?

23. Who has been "Goodwill Ambassador" for the San Diego Zoo since 1970?

21. The Reef Lounge. The Stardust Country Club, which was previously called the Mission Valley Country Club, operated for a number of years in Mission Valley. In 1959 Harry Handlery built the 225-room Stardust Motor Hotel at that location. During this development the Reef Lounge was built, and for many years, until the early 1980s, underwater ballets were presented a number of times a night. There was a period of several years during the nationwide interest in topless performers when the underwater mermaids swam very discreetly topless. The public seemed to tire of under-water swimmers and ballet, though, and the room was closed several years later.

22. John Alessio. Mr. Alessio arrived in San Diego around 1920 and rose to become executive director of Caliente Racetrack in 1953, and owner of the Hotel del Coronado from 1960 to 1963. Because of his philanthropy, in 1964 he was voted Mr. San Diego, Mr. Tijuana, and Mr. Coronado. Mr. A's restaurant atop the Fifth Avenue Financial Centre opened in May 1965, and has won many culinary honors.

23. Joan Embery. Her first title was "Miss Zoofari," but she preferred the title "Goodwill Ambassador." Joan has become a nationally known television guest sharing her love for animals with millions of viewers, and she is the author of *My Wild World* and *Joan Embery's Collection of Amazing Animal Facts*.

24. In what 1970s San Diego restaurant could the diners listen by telephone to the Lindbergh Field control tower's directions to pilots?

25. Name at least two of the eight Nobel Prize laureates that have been affiliated with UCSD.

26. San Diego was called the "Unconventional City" in 1972 because what event did not take place here?

27. What downtown restaurant was compelled to open its doors to women during the lunch hour in 1972?

28. The largest state dinner ever held in San Diego County took place at the Hotel del Coronado in 1970. Who were the two main dignitaries at this event?

24. Boom Trenchard's Flare Path. The restaurant opened in 1969 at 2888 Pacific Highway, on land at the old Lindbergh Field terminal. It was named for Sir Hugh Montague "Boom" Trenchard, called the "Father of the Royal Air Force," and the top floor featured Lone Eagle Lounge honoring Charles Lindbergh. The restaurant gave a 180° view of the airport runway, and diners were surrounded inside by aviation memorabilia and airplane parts. Boom's was in operation until December 1980.

25. 1. Dr. Harold Urey, chemistry, 1934.
    2. Dr. Linus Pauling, chemistry, 1954.
    3. Dr. Francis Crick, medicine, 1962.
    4. Dr. Maria Goeppert Mayer, physics, 1963.
    5. Dr. Robert Holley, physiology-medicine, 1968.
    6. Dr. Hannes Alfven, physics, 1970.
    7. Dr. Renato Dulbecco, medicine, 1975.
    8. Dr. Roger Guillemin, medicine, 1977.

26. The Republican National Convention. President Nixon had originally selected San Diego as his choice for the convention site, but lack of adequate facilities and other factors caused it to be moved to Miami.

27. The Grant Grill, part of the US Grant Hotel. Since the 1940s the Grill displayed a sign saying "Gentlemen only until 3 o'clock" (or 5 o'clock). In 1969 seven women invaded the Grill, but it was not until a $1 million suit was filed in 1972 charging violation of the Federal Civil Rights Act that the policy was changed. The hotel management later honored the seven women with plaques in the Grant Grill.

28. President Richard M. Nixon and Mexican President Gustavo Diaz Ordaz. The dinner was held in the Crown Room, and was attended by more than 1000 guests. It was the second state dinner ever held outside the White House.

29. What slogan is painted on the police cars of the San Diego Police Department?

30. When San Diego lost the hosting of the Republican National Convention in 1972, Mayor Pete Wilson created a celebration to nullify the disappointment and to boost our spirits. What was it called?

31. What is the name of the person who is the San Diego Chicken?

32. What is the only branch library in the San Diego Public Library system to be part of an educational institution?

33. Who bought the El Cortez Hotel in 1978 for his World Evangelism Inc.?

34. What La Jollan was known as the "Father of Humanistic Psychology"?

29. "To protect and serve." This slogan was adopted in 1974.

30. America's Finest City Week. This has been a tradition ever since, and promotes San Diego. Over 100 events are scheduled, including tours, boat races, concerts, half marathons, picnics, and art festivals.

31. Ted Giannoulas. He was a journalism student at San Diego State University when he became the mascot for radio station KGB in 1974.

32. Beckwourth Branch. It opened in 1976 at 721 San Pasqual Street, and besides serving as a public library is also the library of the Educational Cultural Complex (ECC), a community college in southeast San Diego. It is named for James P. Beckwourth, a black mountain man of the Rocky Mountain region, one-time chief of the Crow Nation, and expert fur trapper, scout, Indian fighter, trader, hunter, and explorer.

33. Reverend Morris Cerullo. He turned the hotel into an international ministry school, which it remained until it was sold in 1981. The red neon sign glowing atop the building was changed to read "El Cortez Center."

34. Carl Rogers. He lived in La Jolla for 24 years, until his death in 1987. He originated non-directive "client-centered" psychotherapy, exemplified in his popular book *On Becoming a Person*, and also founded the Center for Studies of the Person in La Jolla.

35. What area resident is "America's only practicing caped crusader"?

36. As of July 1, 1988, how many toll booths are there on the San Diego-Coronado Bay Bridge?

37. What former ASB President of San Diego High School was held hostage in Iran for 444 days?

38. Where is the Pacific Southwest Railway Museum?

35. Captain Sticky (Richard Pesta). He is also known as DOE (Destroyer of Evil) and MMOC (Mighty Man of Carbohydrates), and he leads WOE (World Organization against Evil) in his Stickymobile or his spacecraft MARV (Mobile Attack and Reconnaissance Vehicle).

36. Seven. These are all at the Coronado end of the bridge where operators collect toll from vehicles entering Coronado. Some of the original toll collectors were former employees of the ferry operations that were discontinued with the opening of the bridge on August 3, 1969. Originally there were twelve toll booths, six for entering and six for leaving, but on January 1, 1980, the system was changed; the toll ($1.20 instead of 60¢ twice) was collected only upon entering Coronado, so the number of booths was reduced to six. On July 1, 1988, the fare was lowered to $1, and a new lane and toll booth were opened that allowed carpools, busses, and motorcycles to enter free of charge.

37. Richard Morefield. This native San Diegan was consul general of the U.S. Embassy in Iran when it was seized on November 4, 1979. While he and 51 other Americans were held hostage, his wife Dorothea became spokesman for all the families of the hostages, and was named "Headliner of the Year" by the San Diego Press Club. When Mr. Morefield arrived home January 28, 1981, he was greeted with a grand ceremony of welcome at his home in Tierrasanta, and three days later he and his wife were presented with medals of valor at a formal ceremony in Balboa Park.

38. Campo. It opened in the 1980s, and is undergoing continuous development. Here visitors can see work in progress on the restoration of many locomotives, freight cars, and passenger cars, and they can ride a 1926 cafe observation car or passenger car pulled by a restored iron horse.

39. What San Diego newspaper vendor had his own kiosk built for him in 1982 for his 90th birthday?

40. What was the area code for San Diego County before it became 619?

41. What was the name of the policeman who patrolled the Gaslamp Quarter in the early 1980s?

42. What was San Diego County's busiest non-military airport in 1985?

39. Milton Hillier, or "Milt." He has sold newspapers in San Diego for over 29 years. For the latter part of that time he stood on the corner of Seventh and Broadway, but was forced to move when the old Bank of America building was being remodeled for Home Federal Savings and Loan. Because so many of his customers were concerned about him, Charly Jennings, contractor for Home Federal, along with other local merchants, built a kiosk for him at his old corner, complete with electric lights and heater, and they inscribed it "Milton's."

40. 714. It was changed in 1982 in order to divide Southern California into more areas.

41. Clancy the Cop. Dressed in Keystone finery, Clancy (whose real name is Ben Harroll) made his first appearance October 3, 1979. He patrolled the Gaslamp district until 1986, when a store front police station opened in the area. Clancy was then able to carry out his original plans, and he now operates Paddywagon Parties from Clancy's Precinct Station and Museum at 425 F Street.

42. Montgomery Field. According to the *San Diego Economic Bulletin* of May 1987, the total traffic at that airport was 252,700. This was followed by Gillespie Field with 200,900, McClellan (Palomar) with 183,500, Lindbergh with 161,000, and Brown with 152,200. These figures for aircraft operation include air carrier, commuter/air taxi, general aviation, and military operations. The hundreds of small airplanes flying into and out of the smaller airports give them more air traffic than Lindbergh Field.

43. What was the most visited national monument in the United States in 1985?

44. In 1986, what four towns combined to form the incorporated city of Encinitas?

45. What was San Diego County's most important commodity in 1986?

46. According to the *San Diego Business Journal December 1987 Book of Lists*, what shopping center in San Diego County has the most stores?

43. Cabrillo National Monument. It was established in 1913 by President Woodrow Wilson, and at half an acre in size was the smallest national monument in the U.S. In 1959, President Eisenhower transferred 80.6 acres from the Navy to the Park Service for expansion of the Cabrillo Monument Area. For many years it was the most or the second-most visited national monument in the U.S. In 1985 it attracted 1,720,000 visitors, a figure far ahead of any other national monument. It lost its number-one status in 1986, however, to the Statue of Liberty, which was celebrating its centennial and drew 1,923,700 visitors to Cabrillo Monument's 1,754,400.

44. Encinitas, Leucadia, Olivenhain, and Cardiff-by-the-Sea. The new city encompasses 20 square miles.

45. Avocados. This crop had a value of $108,634,000, far ahead of the second-place item, indoor decorative plants at $80,345,000. That was in turn way ahead of items three and four: eggs at $48,718,000, and milk at $33,379,000.

46. North County Fair. This Escondido shopping center has 181 stores. It is followed by University Towne Centre with 176, and Mission Valley Center with 162.

SPORTS

1. What San Diegan held the world's light-heavyweight boxing title from 1952 to 1962?

2. Where in San Diego County was the race track at which Barney Oldfield set his world speed record of 65 mph in 1907?

3. In 1954, San Diego held its first annual world championship tournament for what sport?

4. On October 8, 1956, at Yankee Stadium, a historic event by a native San Diegan took place. Who was he and what did he do?

5. What 1984 Olympic event was held in San Diego County?

6. Where in San Diego County were polo tournaments held in the early 1900s?

SPORTS   A

1. Archie Moore. He has been called one of the most durable
    fighters in modern history, and the greatest light-
    heavyweight champion of all time. From 1936 through 1965
    he fought 215 professional bouts, and still holds the world's
    record for the most knockouts: 129.

2. Lakeside. The track was laid out in 1906 by John Gay, owner
    of the Lakeside Inn, and was used for horse, automobile, and
    motorcycle races. It was 60 feet wide and circled the lake.
    Oldfield drove his famous *Green Dragon*, a Peerless
    automobile, on April 21, 1907, to set the record of 51 4/5
    seconds for the mile.

3. Over-the-Line. This three-man softball game is said by some
    to have originated at Mission Beach, where the first tourna-
    ments were held. They are now held on Fiesta Island in
    mid-July, and attract over 600 teams and crowds of 50,000
    to 75,000.

4. Don Larsen pitched the only perfect game in a World Series.
    That day he led the New York Yankees to victory against the
    Brooklyn Dodgers. At Point Loma High School he was
    considered a better basketball player than baseball player,
    and in January 1947 he was chosen San Diego's Star of the
    Month for his basketball ability.

5. The equestrian endurance event. It was held at Fairbanks
    Ranch Country Club in Rancho Santa Fe.

6. Coronado. National and international polo matches were
    held on the field in the center of the Coronado Country Club
    on the west side of Coronado. At one time this city was called
    the "Polo Capital of the World." Walter Dupee, a wealthy
    Chicagoan, was largely responsible for popularizing the
    sport here, and he made his huge home on Ocean Boulevard
    the headquarters for his polo-playing friends.

7. In what year did the San Diego Padres win the National League pennant?

8. What San Diego Charger coach was the winning football coach for the San Diego State Aztecs for 12 years?

9. What level is the best in which to sit at San Diego Jack Murphy Stadium in order to catch a ball hit into the stands?

10. In 1909 and 1912, Ora C. Morningstar was world champion of what sport?

11. What is the name of the track at San Diego State University on 55th Street and Montezuma?

12. What heavyweight boxer, financed by San Diego businessmen, beat Muhammed Ali at the San Diego Sports Arena March 31, 1973?

13. In 1980, San Diego's Dennis Conner skippered what yacht to a successful defense of the America's Cup?

7. 1984. They became National League champions for the first time since they joined the majors in 1969.

8. Don Coryell. He was at San Diego State from 1961 to 1972, where he coached the Aztecs to 104 wins, 19 losses, and 2 ties, including 31 consecutive games without defeat. He was with the Chargers from mid-season 1978 until October 1986, and was the 1979 NFL Coach of the Year. He has the honor of being the first coach to win 100 games in both college and the pros.

9. The Plaza level. The *Tribune* recently conducted a ten-game study in which 191 balls entered the stands, and found that 83 of them landed in the Plaza level.

10. Billiards. In 1909 he held the title for the World 18.2 Balkline, and in 1912 for the World 18.1 Balkline. He moved to San Diego in 1914 and opened one of the world's finest billiard rooms in the Union Building downtown, with 27 tables and a billiard theater for exhibition and match games.

11. Aztrack. It was first called by that name during the 1982-83 school year.

12. Ken Norton. He broke Ali's jaw and won the bout in a two-to-one split decision before a crowd of 11,884. He was only the second fighter to defeat Ali in a professional match, the first being Joe Frazier.

13. *Freedom*. It defeated *Australia*, skippered by Jim Hardy, four to one off Newport, Rhode Island.

14. What San Diego native and graduate of Hoover High was the last baseball player to hit .400 in the majors?

15. Name at least three of San Diego's professional basketball teams of the past.

16. What native San Diegan is known as the "Father of Racquetball"?

17. San Diego has one of the few velodromes in the United States. What is a velodrome?

18. In 1892, Zulette Lamb, Lena Polhamus, Agnes Polhamus, and Caroline Polhamus founded what club?

14. Ted Williams. He achieved this in 1941 by batting .406 for the Boston Red Sox. During his baseball career he won six batting titles, and the Triple Crown in both 1942 and 1947, making him one of baseball's all-time greatest hitters. He began his professional career in 1936, playing for the minor league San Diego Padres.

15. 1. San Diego Rockets (NBA) 1967-1971.
    2. San Diego Conquistadors (ABA) 1972-1975 (called the "Qs").
    3. San Diego Sails (ABA) 1975.
    4. San Diego Clippers (NBA) 1978-1984.

16. Dr. Bud Muehleisen. This La Mesa dentist did not invent the game, but he and his friends named it and promoted it. He won 61 national and international titles, and was the first player elected to the Racquetball Hall of Fame.

17. A bicycle track. Ours was built in 1976 at the Morley Field athletic area in Balboa Park, and is one of the largest in the country. Many races are held there, and at one time the U.S. Olympic Committee considered it for the cycling events of the 1984 games.

18. ZLAC Rowing Club. The three Polhamus sisters and their best friend Zulette formed San Diego's first women's rowing club, creating its name from the initial of each girl's first name. At first they rowed in a borrowed four-oared dinghy, until 1895, when the club purchased an eight-oared rowing barge. Since then the club has grown, and now has about 600 members. It boasts many prominent rowers, including Patricia Stose Wyatt, who joined ZLAC in 1935 and was the director of rowing and canoeing for the 1984 Olympics.

19. What San Diego County native was the "Home Run King" before Babe Ruth?

20. Which five members of the Pro Football Hall of Fame have played for or coached the San Diego Chargers?

21. What San Diegan broke the world's record for swimming the English Channel in 1950?

22. Name two of the three native San Diego golfers who have won the U.S. Open.

23. When the San Diego Padres won the pennant, what Eastern Division team did they beat in the play-offs?

19. Clifford "Gavy" Cravath. This Escondidan hit 24 home runs for the Phillies in the 1915 World Series, to set a season record in the pre-World War I "dead ball" era. His 119 career homers were a modern major league record until broken by Ruth. Cravath also has the distinction of being the first San Diego County native to play for the major leagues.

20. John Unitas, David (Deacon) Jones, Ron Mix, Lance Alworth, and coach Sid Gilman.

21. Florence Chadwick. On August 8, 1950, she swam from Cape Gris Nez to Dover in 13 hours, 20 minutes, breaking the record set by Gertrude Ederle. The following year she was the first woman to swim the more difficult trip from England to France. She is the holder of 16 world records, and has been called the greatest female long distance swimmer in the world.

22. Billy Casper, in 1959 and 1966; Gene Littler, in 1961; and Scott Simpson, in 1987. Casper won 51 tour tournaments, and was voted USPGA Player of the Year in 1966 and 1970. He won the U.S. Masters in 1970 after a play-off with Littler. "Gene the Machine" Littler won the Tournament of Champions three years in a row: 1955, 1956, and 1957. Scott Simpson won two consecutive NCAA championships, in 1976 and 1977.

23. Chicago Cubs. By defeating the Cubs three games to two, they became the first National League team to come back from losing two games to win the pennant. The Padres then lost the 1984 World Series to the Detroit Tigers four games to one.

24. What were the names of the two Navy football teams headquartered in San Diego in the 1920s and 1930s?

25. What four San Diegans have pitched perfect games in the major leagues?

26. What native San Diego tennis player won the Wimbledon Ladies Crown in 1952, 1953, and 1954?

27. Two San Diegans have won Olympic gold medals for jumping. Who are they?

28. What two celebrities were the co-founders of the Del Mar Racetrack in 1937?

24. Submarine Football Team and West Coast Navy. The Submarine Teams were fleet champions from 1925 to 1931, when they disbanded. West Coast Navy (known as "Battle Force"), which played from 1931 to 1933, was called the "finest football team in U.S. fleet history." It was coached by Tom Hamilton (Rear Admiral from La Jolla), and many of its players had played on the Submarine Teams.

25. 1. Jim Wilson; Milwaukee Braves, June 12, 1954.
    2. Don Larsen; New York Yankees, October 8, 1956.
    3. Earl Wilson; Boston Red Sox, June 26, 1962.
    4. Dave Morehead; Boston Red Sox, September 16, 1965.

26. Maureen Connolly. During her short playing career she was considered to be the best women's player in the world: she was the first woman to win a Grand Slam (Australia, France, Wimbledon, and the United States), and she won 12 major international titles before the age of 20.

27. Willie Steele and Arnie Robinson. Willie Steele, graduate of Hoover High and track star at San Diego State College, was the top long jumper of the world in the 1940s. He won his gold medal in 1948 for the broad jump. Arnie Robinson, native San Diegan and graduate of Morse High and San Diego State University, was the top long jumper of the 1970s, and received his gold medal in 1976 for the long jump.

28. Bing Crosby and Pat O'Brien. The first race was held July 3, 1937. Since then the track has grown so that it now has the fourth-largest daily attendance of all thoroughbred tracks in the U.S.

29. What La Mesan was considered the world's greatest hydroplane race driver?

30. What were the two homes of the San Diego Padres before they moved to San Diego Jack Murphy Stadium?

31. What Oceanside resident was voted the world's best surfer in the 1963 *Surfer Magazine* poll?

32. What San Diegan is considered to be the world's greatest badminton player of all time?

33. In 1973, who prevented the San Diego Padres from moving to Washington, D.C., by buying the team?

29. Bill Muncey. He won 64 races, seven national championships, and eight Gold Cup titles. His Atlas Van Lines U-71, built in 1968, is on display at the San Diego Hall of Champions. On October 18, 1981, he was killed in a hydroplane race.

30. Lane Field and Westgate Park. Lane Field at the foot of Broadway, formerly called Navy Field or Sports Field, had been used for football, baseball, and motorcycle and bicycle races. It was enlarged and given its new name with the arrival in 1936 of the Pacific Coast League San Diego Padres, owned by W. H. "Bill" Lane. In 1958 it was razed and became a parking lot. Westgate Park, the Padres' home from 1958 to 1967, was at 7227 Friars Road, where Fashion Valley shopping center is now located.

31. Phil Edwards. This Oceanside High School graduate made the cover of *Sports Illustrated* in July 1966, and in that same year was inducted into the International Surfing Hall of Fame. In addition, he has earned a place in sports history as the designer of the Hobie Cat.

32. Dr. Dave Freeman. He won eight national singles championships and won the world crown on his first try. He played professionally for 14 years without losing a match, and then retired from the sport to become a neurosurgeon. The Dave Freeman Open, one of the most prestigious national badminton tournaments, is held annually in the Federal Building in Balboa Park.

33. Ray Kroc. This Chicago multimillionaire and head of the McDonald hamburger empire moved with his wife Joan to the San Diego area in 1976.

34. What two Padre pitchers have won the Cy Young award?

35. On May 13, 1973, what internationally televised sporting event took place at San Diego Country Estates in Ramona?

36. What was the name of San Diego's women's professional football team of 1975?

37. Where was the home of the Chargers before they came to San Diego?

38. Where has the famous Rough Water Swim been held since 1916?

39. What was the name of the yacht that Dennis Conner defeated in the 1987 America's Cup races?

34. Randy Jones, 1976, and Gaylord Perry, 1978. This award honors the best pitcher in baseball, and was first presented in 1956.

35. The tennis match between 55-year-old Bobby Riggs and Margaret Court. Bobby won the $10,000 match, 6-2, 6-1. It was broadcast over CBS to seven foreign countries.

36. San Diego Lobos. The Lobos were part of the National Women's Football League, which had been established the previous year. Almost 150 women tried out, and 35 were picked for the team. They played their home games at Mesa College field, and one of the games, against the Los Angeles Dandelions, was the first women's pro-football game to be nationally televised. The Lobos had a good record for the season, but folded for lack of funds.

37. Los Angeles. They had one season as the Los Angeles Chargers, 1960-61.   Before the move, the players were reportedly looking forward to the support they would receive from San Diego fans, since in Los Angeles they had to compete with the Rams for support.

38. La Jolla. This is the largest rough water swimming event in the U.S., and attracts 1,500 contestants. It has been held almost every August or September since 1916, when the first winner was noted San Diego swimmer Charles Shields and the course was from the north side of the Biological Pier to the Cove. The event was first called the Biological Pier Swim, but has been called the La Jolla Rough Water Swim since 1931.

39. *Kookaburra III*. This Australian yacht, skippered by Iain Murray, was defeated by Conner's *Stars and Stripes*, sailing for the San Diego Yacht Club.

40. How many Olympic gold medal winners has San Diego had?

41. What was the name of San Diego's semi-professional football team of 1941-1946?

42. What was the first team sport at what is now San Diego State University?

40. Twelve:
    1. Clarence Pinkston, diving, 1920.
    2. Dutch Smith, diving, 1932.
    3. Bill Miller, pole vault, 1932.
    4. George Ahlgren, eight-oared crew, 1948.
    5. Willie Steele, broad jump, 1948.
    6. Ed Sanders, boxing, 1952.
    7. Milt Campbell, decathlon, 1956.
    8. Bill McMillan, pistol, 1960.
    9. Billy Mills, 10,000 meter run, 1964.
    10. Lowell North, sailing - star class, 1968.
    11. Mike Stamm, swimming, 1972.
    12. Arnie Robinson, long jump, 1976.

41. The Bombers. They played in Balboa Stadium, and were a member of the Pacific Coast Professional Football League. Many of their players worked at Consolidated, and others were soldiers based at Camp Callan. Some were former college stars or professional football players who played here under fictitious names. The Bombers won three straight Pacific Coast championships, but could not compete with the National Football League teams for support.

42. Rowing. In 1898 the first classes of what was then San Diego State Normal School were held downtown in a building on Sixth and F. There were no facilities for sports, so rowing crews were organized because of the proximity of San Diego Bay. San Diego State Normal Rowing Association was formed, and during the first years of the school it was the center of campus social life and physical activities. In the 1920s and 1930s many of the crews turned into sororities or fraternities as other sports gained in popularity. Rowing was dropped in 1933, two years after the college moved to its present location on Montezuma Mesa, because of the increased distance from the bay. In 1960 it was started up again.

43. What was Archie Moore's nickname?

44. What was the name of the surfers' statue at Windan-sea Beach in the 1960s?

45. Where in San Diego did the Chargers play before San Diego Jack Murphy Stadium was built?

46. What San Diego State College basketball star led his team to the national collegiate title in 1941?

47. Who threw the first pitch in the opening ceremony of the Padres' first home game of the 1977 season?

43. "The Mongoose," or sometimes "The Old Mongoose," or "The Magnificent Mongoose." The mammal the mongoose is famous in India as a bold and agile snake killer. It provokes the snake into attacking, then steps back and pounces.

44. *Hot Curl.* This 400-pound steel and concrete statue of a pot-bellied beer- can-clutching surfer first appeared there in April 1963, the work of Lee Teacher of La Jolla. In July it was decapitated, but was later restored. The figure was so popular that it inspired *Hot Curl* models, decals, and key tags.

45. Balboa Stadium. This large stadium next to San Diego High School opened in 1915. It was enlarged for the Chargers when they moved to San Diego in 1961, and was demolished in 1979. The Chargers dedicated the new San Diego Stadium in Mission Valley on August 20, 1967. In 1981 the name was changed to San Diego Jack Murphy Stadium, after the longtime *San Diego Union* sports editor.

46. Milky (Milton) Phelps. He starred for San Diego State from 1938 to 1941, and is still considered the Aztecs' greatest basketball player. For three years he was picked for the Little All-American team, and was the only small-college player on Helm's 1941 All-American Team. He was killed in World War II Navy training in 1942, and in 1971 was posthumously elected to an all-time basketball team selected by the National Association of Intercollegiate Athletics.

47. The KGB Chicken. (He later became the San Diego Chicken.) The game was held April 12, 1977, at San Diego Stadium.

48. What was San Diego's first golf club?

49. What are the three colors of the San Diego Chargers?

50. What team did the San Diego Padres play for their first regular season game as a major league team in 1969?

51. What sailing cup was donated to San Diego by a titled Englishman in 1903?

52. What is the unofficial name of that section of Windansea Beach that is named after the surfer who lost his life there in a 1954 surfing accident?

48. San Diego Country Club. It was founded in 1897 at Upas and Park Boulevard. In 1913 it moved to Point Loma, and in 1920 it moved to its present location on L Street in Chula Vista. When it first opened in the 1890s the course was only sand, dirt, and weeds, and at one time sheep were used to keep the weeds under control.

49. Navy blue, white, and gold.

50. The Houston Astros. The Padres won 2 to 1 on April 8, 1969, at San Diego Stadium.

51. The Lipton Cup. L. A. Blochman, commodore of San Diego's Corinthian Yacht Club, wrote to Sir Thomas Lipton asking if his name could be used on the trophy for an area competition. In return Sir Lipton donated a 32-inch silver San Diego Lipton Cup. In 1905, the Corinthian Yacht Club combined with the San Diego Yacht Club, and in 1933 the supervision of the cup was deeded in trust to the Southern California Yachting Association. The race for the Lipton Cup has been held almost every year since 1904, and especially in the early days it was the yachting event of the year here.

52. Simmons Beach. It is named for Bob Simmons, who was killed at the north end of Windansea Beach on September 26, 1954. Besides being a renowned surfer, he is also remembered for his many innovations in the design of surfboards using plywood and Styrofoam.

53. The Del Mar Racetrack introduced what device for measuring winners on opening day, July 3, 1937?

54. What were San Diego's two major league hockey teams in the 1960s and 1970s?

55. What golfer holds the record for the lowest score at Balboa Municipal Golf Course?

56. The 1987 America's Cup races were held in the waters off what city?

57. In 1973-74 the San Diego Padres almost moved to another city. What would their new name have been?

53. The Photochart camera. It was invented by Lorenzo del Riccio, an optical engineer at Paramount Studios. The original camera is now at the Racing Hall of Fame at Saratoga, New York.

54. San Diego Gulls and San Diego Mariners. The Gulls (1966-1974) belonged to the Western Hockey League, and opened the new Sports Arena November 17, 1966. The team folded when the league folded. The Mariners (1974-1977), formerly the New Jersey Knights, belonged to the World Hockey Association. In 1977 they were sold by owner Ray Kroc and moved to Hollywood, Florida.

55. Sam Snead. On October 2, 1943, he hit 28-32-60 on the par 72 course. For many years the score card was on display at the Balboa Pro Shop in Balboa Park.

56. Fremantle, the port city of Perth, Western Australia. Here Dennis Conner won the cup for the San Diego Yacht Club in *Stars and Stripes*.

57. Washington Nationals. The sale was so close to being completed that Topps printed the San Diego Padre baseball cards as the Washington Nationals. The cards were already distributed in gum packs before Ray Kroc bought the team and kept them in San Diego. Later the error was corrected and Padres cards were printed, but both sets of cards are scarce, particularly those of the Washington Nationals.

58. What was the name of San Diego's professional tennis team in the 1970s?

59. What Lincoln High School graduate won the Heisman Trophy in 1981?

60. Broc Glover of El Cajon is a national champion of what sport?

61. What was the name of the group of surfers who hung out at the pump house at Windansea Beach in the 1960s and were immortalized in Tom Wolfe's book *The Pump House Gang*?

62. What San Diego east county team won a world championship in 1961?

58. San Diego Friars. They were in existence from 1975 through 1978, and belonged to World Team Tennis, Western Division. Though they were Western Division champions, they folded because several other teams in the league folded.

59. Marcus Allen. At Lincoln High he was star quarterback, and then became outstanding tailback at USC. In addition to winning the Heisman Trophy, which is the most prestigious award in college football, he was the first back to rush 2,000 yards in a season, with 2,342 yards. In 1982 he was voted Rookie of the Year in the NFL, and was the Most Valuable Player in Super Bowl XVIII, playing for the Los Angeles Raiders.

60. Motocross. In 1983 this Valhalla High graduate was the first rider in history to win three Super Bowls of motocross, and by the age of 25 he had won his fifth national championship.

61. Mac Meda Destruction Company. The members were known for their wild parties and beer orgies called "conventions." Mac Meda Destruction Company T-shirts and decals were popular, and decals can still be seen on local cars and trucks.

62. Northern Little League (made up of players from La Mesa and El Cajon). They became Western U.S. regional champions by winning 11 straight play-offs including seven shutouts. In August 1961 they went to the world championship games in Williamsport, Pennsylvania, where they won their final victory over the El Campo Texans 4 to 2. (It should also be noted that in 1977 the El Cajon Western Little League team became the U.S. champions. They too went to the world championships in Williamsport, where they lost to Taiwan 2 to 7.)

63. What are the three colors of the San Diego Padres?

64. What La Mesan received the 1973 James E. Sullivan award for top U.S. amateur athlete?

65. What college bowl game is played in San Diego?

66. Every New Year's Day since 1891, members of what club have dived into the cold waters of a San Diego bay?

67. What team did the San Diego Chargers play in their first AFL game?

63. Brown, orange, and gray. These colors became official in 1985; from 1969 to 1985 the colors had been brown, gold, and gray.

64. Bill Walton. This Helix High basketball star was UCLA All-American three times, and *Sporting News* College Player of the Year in 1972, 1973, and 1974. He has played professionally for the Portland Trail Blazers, San Diego Clippers, Los Angeles Clippers, and Boston Celtics, and was voted NBA Most Valuable Player for 1976-77.

65. The Holiday Bowl. This football game, first held December 22, 1978, matches the winner of the Western Athletic Conference against a nationally ranked opponent.

66. San Diego Rowing Club. This club was founded in 1888 as the Excelsior Rowing Club, and in 1891 changed its name to the present one. By the early 1900s it was the most popular and influential men's club in San Diego, and almost everyone of importance was a member. The tradition of jumping into the water on January 1st was started in order to show that in San Diego, swimming could be enjoyed as much in winter as in summer. The members jumped into San Diego Bay from their boathouse or pier at the old steamship wharf at Fifth and Harbor Drive every year except 1925, when they jumped into Mission Bay.

67. The Oakland Raiders. The Chargers defeated them 44 to 0 on September 17, 1961, at Balboa Stadium.

68. How does the Marlin Club of San Diego announce the number of marlin caught each day?

69. What was the name of the Padres before they came to San Diego?

70. What was Maureen Connolly's nickname?

71. What San Diegan is the only man to win four world championships as a Star Class sailor?

72. On August 12, 1938, what famous racehorse won the $25,000 match race against the Argentine champion Ligaroti at the Del Mar Racetrack?

68. It fires a cannon shot for each marlin. The incoming boats hoist a small blue flag for each marlin caught, so the Marlin Club will know how many shots to fire (and now the boats also radio the count in to shore). The cannon is located next to the fish racks on Shelter Island Drive.

69. Hollywood Stars. When W. H. "Bill" Lane moved his Hollywood Stars to San Diego in 1936, he held a name contest. For a while it looked as though the new name would be San Diego Dons, but in late February the name San Diego Padres was chosen.

70. "Little Mo." It was an allusion to "Big Mo," the nickname of the battleship *Missouri*, because Maureen's strokes were so powerful and accurate. She was given this nickname when she was twelve years old by *San Diego Union* sportswriter Nelson Fisher, and the name stuck.

71. Lowell North. He won his titles in 1957, 1959, 1960, and 1973. He is considered the all-time best Star Class sailor, with 4 world championships, 5 seconds, and 2 thirds, in addition to a 1968 Olympic gold medal. He also has the reputation of being the best sailmaker in the world.

72. Seabiscuit. This great thoroughbred won against the favored Ligaroti in a close race whose outcome was confirmed by the new Photochart camera.

73. Where is the Padres' spring training camp?

74. What was the former name of the Sockers when they were in San Diego in 1976?

75. Who created the San Diego Hall of Champions and Hall of Fame?

76. The San Diego Breakers played what sport?

73. Yuma, Arizona. This has been the location since the Padres' first season as a major league team. The following year the Yumans figured that having the Padres there increased their hotel and restaurant business by 30%, so they were happy to put up a $500,000 expanded training camp complete with four baseball diamonds. In March 1984 the camp was dedicated in memory of Ray Kroc.

74. San Diego Jaws. This soccer team has a long and nomadic history. The team began in 1974 as the Baltimore Comets. When interest lagged it moved to San Diego and became the San Diego Jaws for the 1976 season. Again interest was not high, and the team left to become the Las Vegas Quicksilvers in 1977. They returned in 1978 as the San Diego Sockers. By now interest in soccer had increased, and so had the ability of the team. The Sockers captured nine Western Division championships: four outdoor (1978, '79, '80, and '84) and five indoor (1982, '83, '84, '85, and '86).

75. Robert "Bob" Breitbard. Bob graduated as valedictorian of Hoover High, and was a star football player at San Diego State College when he was selected in 1940 for the All-California Collegiate Athletic Association's All-Star Team. In 1946 he created the Breitbard Athletic Foundation to give recognition to San Diego's high school, college, and amateur athletes. In addition, he was responsible for the building of the International Sports Arena, and was the owner of San Diego's professional basketball and hockey teams, the Rockets and the Gulls.

76. Volleyball. They played here from 1975 through 1979, but moved to Salt Lake City because they did not get enough support from the fans or the media in San Diego.

77. What San Diego athlete headed the San Diego Zoo's Kicks for Critters fundraisers?

78. A gym at Pine Hills Lodge in Julian was built as a training camp for what boxing champion?

79. What was the name of the U.S. Marine football team in San Diego from the 1920s through the 1960s?

77. Rolf Benirschke. He was a star kicker and leading scorer for the Chargers since 1977. In 1978 he scored on 82% of his attempts, and his longest kick was 53 yards. In Kicks for Critters, Rolf contributed $50 for every field goal he kicked, and encouraged others to pledge for his goals. The funds raised benefitted the zoo's Center for Reproduction of Endangered Species, and since originating Kicks in 1980, Rolf has helped raise over $1,014,000 to help save animals from the threat of extinction. Rolf's father, Dr. Kurt Benirschke, was Director of Research and Health Services for the San Diego Zoological Society from 1975 to 1985, and is known world-wide for his efforts to save endangered species.

78. Jack Dempsey. It was built in 1926 when he was training for his second fight with Gene Tunney. Fred A. Sutherland, the owner of Pine Hills Lodge, put in a large gymnasium, swimming pool, and ring platform for his friend Dempsey. The gym has now been made into a playhouse, and is the site of the Pine Hills Lodge Dinner Theatre.

79. San Diego Marines (nicknamed the "Devildogs"). Prior to 1917 organized football was not played by the military, but the increase in recruits brought about by World War I made the sport possible. The first Marine team of any consequence in San Diego was organized at MCRD in 1924 as the San Diego Marines. They played other military teams, as well as college and university teams and athletic clubs, and their home games were played at Balboa Stadium. Some of their best years were: 1925, when they made a total of 323 points to the opponents' 96; 1939, when they won all 10 games; and 1957 through 1959, when they were coached by Robert "Bull" Trometter. Some of their biggest games here were against the San Diego State Aztecs. 1976 was the last year this football team played.

80. What was the name of the top local sportfishing contest held from 1947 to 1973?

81. In 1972 the oldest remaining bowling alley in the state and the last to employ pin boys closed. What was its name?

82. In what city has a frog-jumping contest been held annually since 1954?

83. What teams played in the Super Bowl held in San Diego on January 31, 1988?

80. The Yellowtail Derby. It was one of the major fishing contests in the nation, and the longest-running on the Pacific coast. In 1953 there were over 60,000 participants, 60% from outside of San Diego. Yellowtail, albacore, bluefin tuna, and yellowfin tuna were some of the qualifying fish.

81. Sunshine Lanes. The alleys were on the third and fourth floors of the building on the north side of Broadway between Sixth and Seventh avenues. Mr. and Mrs. John B. Coker were the owners for 34 years, and Mr. Coker was the inventor of the automatic scorer and the electric foul detector. In addition, he funded the man who invented the automatic pinsetter, but ironically he was not able to use them in his bowling alley because they would have been too heavy for the upper floors of the building.

82. Del Mar. The Del Mar Jumping Frog Jamboree (formerly Jubilee) is an annual spring event at the Del Mar fairgrounds, sponsored by the San Dieguito Jaycees. There are as many as 1,500 entries, and persons or clubs without frogs of their own can borrow one from the Jaycees. Proceeds go to the Scripps Clinic and Research Foundation for cancer research. This is one of the largest frog-jumping contests in the world, and the winning frog goes to the international finals at Angels Camp, Calaveras County, California.

83. The Denver Broncos and Washington Redskins. The Redskins won, 42 to 10.

84. Who was the "Home Run King" of the Padres in the late 1940s?

85. What sport did the San Diego Toros play?

86. What native San Diego golfer won the Women's U.S. Open and the Ladies' Professional Golf Association tournaments four times each?

87. What former San Diego mayor has been elected to the Breitbard Hall of Fame?

84. Jack Graham. It is said that this popular outfielder and first baseman was one of the few who could pop home runs over the far-off right field wall of Lane Field, and he would sometimes hit several homers a night. In 1948 he was on his way to a new home run record when, on July 25, after hitting his 46th home run of the season, he was hit in the head by a pitch from Red Adams in Los Angeles, which put him out of commission until September.

85. Soccer. They moved here from Los Angeles in 1968, and played for one season as members of the North American Soccer League. Soccer had not yet become a popular sport in the U.S., however, and by the end of the year the Toros as well as most of the other teams in the league had disbanded.

86. Mickey (Mary Kathryn) Wright. She has been called the best woman player in the history of American professional golf. She won 82 U.S. tournaments in her career, from 1956 to 1973, and for many years (until 1982) held the LPGA record for the most tournament wins in a year, with 13 in 1963.

87. John Butler. This native San Diegan and graduate of St. Augustine High School was the first San Diego State football player to gain national recognition when he won All-Conference honors in 1933, 1934, and 1935, and was Little American guard in 1935. He became an attorney and practiced in San Diego, was deputy district attorney from 1948 to 1949, and mayor from 1951 to 1955.

88. Where in San Diego County have motocross national championships been held since the 1970s?

89. Who was the first Padre to be selected to play in a major league All-Star game?

90. What former El Cajon athlete won two gold medals at the 1984 Olympics?

91. On January 31, 1988, San Diego hosted the Super Bowl. What number was it?

88. Carlsbad. Carlsbad Raceway opened in 1964, and at first featured drag racing. Two years later motorcycle races were held there, and it became one of the first tracks in the United States to feature motocross. On September 19, 1971, the first U.S. Grand Prix of Motocross was held there, and the raceway has since been the scene of over 14 world championship races. It has the reputation for being one of the most treacherous courses in the world, with 21 turns and 10 sheer drops in 1.3 miles.

89. Chris Cannizzaro. This catcher was selected to be on the 1969 All-Star team, but unfortunately did not get a chance to play in the game. He did, however, receive a pewter mug with his name and the All-Star inscription. The following year center fielder Clarence (Cito) Gaston became the first Padre actually to play in an All-Star game, when he took over for Willie Mays in the final seven innings of a 12-inning game.

90. Greg Louganis. This Valhalla High School graduate earned his medals for springboard and platform diving, making him only the third man in Olympic history to win both events, and the first Olympic diver to earn more than 700 points in the 10-meter platform contest. (He was not a resident of San Diego at the time, so is not included in the list of local Olympic winners.) In October 1980, he was featured on the cover of *Swimming World*, and he was recipient of the Sullivan Award for top U.S. amateur athlete for 1984.

91. The 22nd (XXII). Super Bowls have been held every year since January 15, 1967, when Super Bowl I pitted the Kansas City Chiefs against the Green Bay Packers.

92. What first baseman was the star batter for the Padres during their first few years as a major league team?

93. Give at least one of the two names of San Diego's amateur ice hockey team of the 1940s.

94. What native San Diegan played in five World Series— four with the New York Yankees and one with the Padres?

95. Clairemont High School coed America Morris was featured in the March 10, 1986, issue of *People* magazine for being victorious in what sport?

92. Nate Colbert. He joined the team in 1969, and in his first four seasons hit 127 home runs. His best year was 1972, in which he hit 38 homers and drove in 111 runs. His day of glory came August 1, 1972, while playing a doubleheader against the Braves in Atlanta: he tied the record for home runs in a doubleheader (5), and broke the records for runs-batted-in (13) and total bases (22, on 7 hits in 9 times at bat).

93. San Diego Rowing Club and San Diego Skyhawks. The San Diego Rowing Club (1940-41) was started by a group of Yugoslavian fishermen from Minnesota who moved to San Diego and wanted to continue their hockey games. In 1941 the team name was changed to Skyhawks because most of the players worked at Convair. Home games were played at Glacier Gardens at Harbor Drive and Eighth Avenue. The team was a member of the Pacific Coast Hockey League until 1949-50, when it became a semi-pro team.

94. Graig Nettles. He graduated from San Diego High in 1962, and attended San Diego State College on a basketball scholarship. He played outfield with the Minnesota Twins, and third base with the Cleveland Indians, New York Yankees, San Diego Padres, and Atlanta Braves.

95. Wrestling. This 16-year-old sophomore pinned Madison High's Russell Cain for the mandatory two-second count. This was the first time in the state, and probably in the country, that a girl pinned a boy in a varsity wrestling match.

96. The national team of what sport has practiced in San
     Diego since 1981?

97. Franklin "Bud" Held was the first American to hold a
     world record in what sport?

96. Volleyball. San Diego was selected as the home base for the U.S. Men's Volleyball Team, which formerly had been practicing in Dayton, Ohio. In 1983 the team was filmed in the motion picture *Spiker*, starring Michael Parks. This movie showed the Olympic medal quest of a U.S. volleyball team, and was filmed partly at Hoover High School gym. In 1985 the U.S. Women's Volleyball Team moved to San Diego as well. Both teams hold most of their practice sessions in the Federal Building in Balboa Park.

97. Javelin throw. This Grossmont High graduate set the world record in 1955 when he threw the javelin 268′ 2 1/2″. He won a total of nine national championships, while at the same time serving as pastor of the Westminster Presbyterian Church of Point Loma. He left the pastorate after 11 years to run a javelin production plant in Lakeside.

MUSIC

1. What two brothers donated the Organ Pavilion in Balboa Park to the people of San Diego?

2. What world-famous operatic contralto and San Diego area resident sang at both of our expositions?

3. Rosalie Hamlin of Sweetwater High and Mission Bay High recorded what hit song that became number five on the hit parade in 1961?

4. Who was the founder and first conductor of the San Diego Symphony Orchestra in 1926?

5. What celebrated pianist entertained in the Circus Room of the Hotel del Coronado during the summers of 1949 and 1950?

1.   John D. and Adolph B. Spreckels. San Diego's even tempera-
      ture makes it one of the few places in the world where an
      outdoor organ is feasible. It was built for the Panama-Califor-
      nia Exposition, and dedicated December 31, 1914. The
      pavilion cost $100,000 and the 3,400-pipe organ $33,500. It
      currently has 3,600 pipes, with further additions planned, and
      remains the largest outdoor pipe organ in the world.

2.   Madame Ernestine Schumann-Heink. She starred in opera
      houses throughout the world before settling in the planned
      colony of artists in Grossmont. Her house on El Granito
      Avenue, which she called "Casa Ernestina," was the first to
      be completed there, in 1913. Later she also maintained a
      mansion in Coronado on Eighth and Orange. In addition to
      opera, she entertained in vaudeville and on the radio, and
      even made one movie. She was beloved by San Diegans, and
      performed until she was in her 70s.

3.   "Angel Baby." It was recorded by Rosie and the Originals.
      Rosie's income for 1961, at the age of 16, was expected to
      be $40,000.

4.   Nino Marcelli. When he came to San Diego in 1920 he had
      already established a reputation as a composer and conduc-
      tor. Here he was director of instrumental music in the city
      schools, and under his direction the San Diego High School
      Orchestra became one of the finest high school ensembles in
      the country. Many of the graduates of that orchestra became
      members of the new San Diego Symphony (first called
      Philharmonic Orchestra of San Diego and San Diego Civic
      Orchestra), and their first concert was held April 11, 1927, at
      the Spreckels Theatre.

5.   Liberace. His brother, George Liberace, performed at the
      Hotel San Diego.

6.   What oratorio by Dr. David Ward-Steinman premiered in San Diego in 1964, with Gregory Peck as narrator?

7.   What popular composer was the musical director for "The California Story," the pageant presented here in 1956, 1957, and 1958?

8.   Who was the youngest member to join the San Diego Symphony?

9.   What female songwriter lived in the artists' colony in Grossmont?

10. What popular singer with 21 gold records to his credit has lived in Point Loma since 1968?

6. *The Song of Moses.* Dr. Ward-Steinman was then assistant professor of music at San Diego State College, and the San Diego State Chorus and Orchestra and soloists were led by conductor Paul Anderson. Alan M. Kriegsman, music critic for the *San Diego Union,* noted at year's end that "no event of the entire year was more impressive or imbued with greater significance than the stirring oratorio *The Song of Moses* by San Diego composer David Ward-Steinman."

7. Meredith Willson. In addition, he composed the songs "The California Story" and "San Diego Waltz," the latter of which was the theme song of the 1958 Fiesta del Pacifico. While he was in San Diego he wrote parts of *The Music Man,* and also auditioned this yet unfinished work for any potential backer he could find here.

8. Karen Moe Dirks. This violinist is a native San Diegan and a second-generation symphony member, as her mother Jean Moe was a member of the cello section for 20 years. Miss Moe had just graduated from Helix High at the age of seventeen when she joined the first violin section, and she has held positions as high as Acting Concertmaster.

9. Carrie Jacobs Bond. At the turn of the century she was the country's most successful woman composer, well known for songs such as "I Love You Truly" and "A Perfect Day." Her Grossmont house, "Nest O' Rest," on Summit Circle, was built around 1916. She also had a home in Hollywood, and she maintained both residences until her death in 1946.

10. Frankie Laine. His renditions of "That's My Desire," "Moonlight Gambler," "Mule Train," and "Lucky Ol' Sun" remain favorites. He used to spend much of his free time deep-sea fishing here in his boat *My Desire,* named after his first hit record.

11. What is believed to have been the first symphony orchestra in the country to give a concert on a Navy ship?

12. What popular San Diego "speakeasy" of the 1960s had the highest attendance in the history of nightclubs in the United States?

13. Divas Joan Sutherland and Beverly Sills appeared together for the first time in what San Diego Opera Company production?

14. Who were the four year-round conductors of the San Diego Symphony from 1959 to 1987?

15. What song is played at the Del Mar Racetrack throughout the annual summer racing season?

11. The San Diego Philharmonic Orchestra. It was formed in 1950 to perform winter concerts because the previously formed San Diego Symphony was at that time a summer orchestra. The founder and first conductor was Leslie Hodge, and the Philharmonic consisted mostly of San Diego Symphony members. On April 10, 1953, conductor Werner Janssen led the Philharmonic in a concert on board the USS *Kearsarge*, which was stationed at North Island. The audience was made up of naval personnel and some invited guests, and civilians could listen from the decks of yachts.

12. Mickie Finn's. This live show, starring Fred and Mickie Finn, played to over three million persons in a converted warehouse at 1051 University Avenue, and featured honky-tonk, ragtime, Dixieland, and sing-along. In 1966 it became a network television show, and in addition had a long and successful run in Las Vegas.

13. *Die Fledermaus*. This October 1980 production of Johann Strauss's opera marked Ms. Sills' final performances, except for occasional benefit concerts.

14. 1. Earl Bernard Murray, 1959-1966.
    2. Zoltan Rozsnyai, 1967-1971.
    3. Peter Erös, 1972-1979.
    4. David Atherton, 1980-1987.

15. "Where the Turf Meets the Surf." The lyrics are by Bing Crosby and John Burke, and the music is by James V. Monaco. It is dedicated to the Del Mar Turf Club. Bing recorded the song, and it is played as the opener and closer to every racing day.

16. What San Diego mortuary-owning brothers sponsored an award-winning boys band from 1926 to 1962?

17. What classical composer known for his use of American Indian themes lived in Grossmont?

18. In 1896-98, a Colorado silver millionaire built a music hall in San Diego County in which to house his priceless collection of rare violins, and to hold chamber music concerts. What is the name of this hall?

19. What Hoover High coed had the hit single record "My Little Marine" on the top 100 charts in 1960?

20. San Diego was the home of what avant-garde composer and inventor of exotic musical instruments?

16. The Bonham Brothers (Harley L. and Berma W.Bonham). The Bonham Brothers Boys Band, made up of boys aged 10 to 16, represented San Diego in the Rose Parade many times, and won numerous competitions against college and military school bands.

17. Charles Wakefield Cadman. He composed in all musical forms, and some of his best known works are the songs "At Dawning" and "From the Land of the Sky-Blue Water." He moved to Grossmont in 1930, and in 1938 wrote *Resurrection* for the Mt. Helix Easter Sunrise Service held April 17, 1938.

18. Granger Music Hall. This National City music hall was designed by architect Irving Gill for Ralph Granger, and it contained one of the largest grand pianos in the country, as well as a 1060-pipe organ. Some of the musicians to play in the hall around the turn of the century were violinists Eugène Ysaye and Jan Kubelik, and pianists Ignace Paderewski and Rudolf Friml. The hall was moved to its present location on Fourth near Palm in 1969.

19. Jamie Horton (pseudonym for Gayla Peevey).

20. Harry Partch. He was professor in residence at UCSD from 1967 until his death in 1974. Some of his unusual instruments are the Chromelodeon (reed pump organ adapted and tuned to his 43-tone octave); Zymo-Xyl (upside-down liquor bottles above a row of wood blocks); Boo (bamboo marimba); Gourd Tree and Cone Gongs (12 Chinese temple bells bolted to 12 gourds attached to a eucalyptus bough, with 2 aluminum cone gongs made from nose cones of airplane gas tanks at the base); Mazda Marimba (rows of 24 empty light bulbs); and Spoils of War (discarded artillery shell casings plus Pyrex chemical solution jars).

21. In how many San Diego Opera Company operas has world-renowned soprano Beverly Sills performed?

22. What San Diego marine biologist is a world-acclaimed folk singer?

23. What professor of music at UCSD received the 1984 Pulitzer Prize for music?

24. What internationally acclaimed coloratura soprano retired to Rancho Santa Fe in 1948?

21. Eight:
    1. *The Tales of Hoffmann*, 1970.
    2. *Daughter of the Regiment*, 1973.
    3. *Norma*, 1976.
    4. *La Traviata*, 1977.
    5. *The Merry Widow*, 1977.
    6. *La Loca*, 1979.
    7. *Don Pasquale*, 1980.
    8. *Die Fledermaus*, 1980.

22. Sam Hinton.   He was one of the first persons to be known professionally as a folk singer, and he is highly respected as both a performer and a music scholar. He was also director of the Aquarium- Museum at Scripps Institution of Oceanography from 1946 to 1964. From 1964 to 1980 he taught classes in folklore. In addition, he has written books on marine biology and folk music, and composed the feature "The Ocean World" in the *San Diego Union* for several decades.

23. Bernard Rands.   The piece for which he was honored was *Canti del Sole* for tenor and orchestra. It is a cycle of 14 songs about the sun, set to poems by eight different poets in four languages, depicting the metaphysical interaction between the sun's cycle and the human cycle. The English-born Professor Rands has been on the faculty of UCSD since 1975.

24. Amelita Galli-Curci. She is remembered as one of the top opera and recording stars of the early part of the century. She and her accompanist husband, Homer Samuels, lived in Rancho Santa Fe in their Italian-style farmhouse called "Sul Monte Jr.," patterned after their retreat in the Catskills. In 1962 she moved to La Jolla, where she lived until her death the following year.

25. What well-known dance band leader opened a resort in north San Diego County in 1964?

26. In May 1966, when the San Diego Opera Company was preparing an English version of Gounod's *Faust*, the lead tenor became ill. A substitute was found from an opera company in Mexico City who knew the role only in French. This relatively unknown tenor consequently sang his role in French while the rest of the company sang in English. Who was he?

27. What La Jolla resident has been a jazz band leader since 1935, and is known for his group "The Bobcats"?

28. In 1983, what Rancho Bernardo composer conducted the San Diego Symphony in his own symphonic poem *Walt Whitman*?

29. What Chula Vista pianist appeared twice at age fourteen as soloist with the New York Philharmonic under Zubin Mehta?

25. Lawrence Welk. Today it features a mobile home park, condominiums, a restaurant, specialty gift shops, an 18-hole golf course, and live theater.

26. Placido Domingo. He is now one of the most famous tenors in the world.

27. Bob Crosby. He has led a major jazz band almost continuously for five decades, specializing in Dixieland, and has had his own daytime radio and television series. He and his wife June (a noted author and columnist) settled in La Jolla in 1969.

28. Paul Creston. This largely self-taught composer was one of the most widely performed American composers in the mid-1900s. He lived in Rancho Bernardo after his retirement from teaching in 1975 until his death in 1985. The San Diego Symphony has performed several other of his works, including Symphony No. 3, *Three Mysteries*, and *Two Choric Dances*.

29. Gustavo Romero. Gustavo was born in Chula Vista, and received his early music training in the San Diego area. He has performed as soloist with the Los Angeles Philharmonic, Boston Pops, San Diego Symphony, San Antonio Symphony, and Liege Philharmonic of Belgium, and has toured with Community Concerts. In 1982 he was recipient of the prestigious Avery Fisher Young Artists Career Grant, and he is winner of the Gina Bachauer Memorial Competition at Juilliard.

30. What city is the home of the famous Maytime Band Review?

31. What was the former name of Symphony Hall?

32. What San Diego music store sponsored the children's piano festivals in the Balboa Park Bowl from 1948 through the 1980s?

33. What well-known choral director was musical director and conductor of the San Diego Symphony during the summers of 1953 through 1957?

30. National City. This annual event was founded in 1947. The first competition, which was held the following year, had 11 entries including elementary, junior and senior high, and sponsored bands. By the early 1950s it had grown to over 100 entries representing the best bands in the state. The review lasted four hours, so subsequently the competition was limited to 50 bands, from junior and senior high schools only. The Maytime Band Review is considered to be one of the toughest and most prestigious band competitions in the state, and the parade draws crowds of over 30,000.

31. Fox Theatre. When this lavish Rococo-style theater on B Street opened in 1929 it was the third-largest theater in the West. It was designed for vaudeville and movies, and as late as the 1960s it was used for live productions as well as for motion pictures. In 1985 it was restored and reopened as Symphony Hall, with the entrance now on Seventh Avenue leading to the mezzanine-level lobby.

32. Thearle Music Company. This music store was established in 1887, and at one time was one of the largest music stores in the United States. At its peak the piano festival featured over 1,000 San Diego area boys and girls aged seven to seventeen, playing on over 100 pianos simultaneously. In the 1980s the festival was moved to the East County Performing Arts Center.

33. Robert Shaw. He had formerly been a resident of San Diego when his father, Rev. Shirley Shaw, was pastor of the University Christian Church. Robert gained prominence as director of the Robert Shaw Chorale, which toured internationally and made many award-winning recordings. More recently, he has been music director and conductor of the Atlanta Symphony Orchestra.

34. What is the name of the chime melody played from the California Tower in Balboa Park every quarter hour?

35. Native San Diegans Nick Reynolds and John Stewart were members of what popular 1960s singing group?

36. The same opera was picked by the San Francisco Opera Company for its very first production in San Diego, in 1952, and also by the San Diego Opera Company for its first-ever production, in 1965. What opera what it?

37. Who is the Resident Festival Composer for the Old Globe Theatre?

34. Westminster Chimes (or Westminster Quarters). This was composed by William Crotch for the Great St. Mary's Church, Cambridge, and so was originally called Cambridge Chimes. In 1859-60 it was reproduced in Big Ben of Westminster, where it gained popularity and its new name. The chimes ring every quarter hour, with the length of playing time increasing as the hour progresses, the longest sequence being on the hour or fourth quarter. The Ona May Lowe Carillon was placed in the California Tower Christmas 1946 by her son, Dr. Frank Lowe Jr., and replaced with a 100-bell Symphonic Carillon Christmas 1966. Paul D. Peery, San Diego's official carillonneur, was the only musician to play the carillon from its dedication in 1946 until his death in 1981.

35. The Kingston Trio. This group made its San Francisco debut at the Purple Onion in 1957, and soon became one of the leaders of the folk music craze in America. Originally the trio was composed of Bob Shane, Nick Reynolds, and Dave Guard, but in 1961 Guard left and was replaced by John Stewart. Both Reynolds and Stewart were born at Mercy Hospital in San Diego, though neither actually lived in the city; Reynolds lived in Coronado and graduated from Coronado High School, and Stewart lived for a short time in La Mesa.

36. *La Bohème*. Puccini's well-loved masterpiece was a popular opener on both occasions.

37. Conrad Susa. He has held this position since 1959, and has composed music for more than 75 Globe productions. He has also composed scores for television and for most leading theaters in the country. In addition, he excels in choral writing, and has also composed three frequently produced operas, including the chamber opera *Transformations*, based on texts of Anne Sexton.

38. Which are the only two theaters in San Diego that have theater pipe organs?

38. The California Theatre and Symphony Hall (formerly the Fox Theatre). The California Theatre houses a Wurlitzer Theatre Pipe Organ originally installed in a theater in Santa Rosa, California. It was relocated here in 1977, and has been steadily improved and enlarged to over 1600 pipes. The Robert Morton Organ in Symphony Hall was originally housed in the Balboa Theatre, but was transferred to the Fox and dedicated there on opening night, November 8, 1929. It has recently been restored, and with 2,478 pipes it is the largest pipe organ in a theater in California.

THEATER

1. The first outdoor Greek theater in America was built in San Diego. Where was it located?

2. What famous fan dancer performed at the California Pacific International Exposition in 1936?

3. What member of royalty unveiled the bust of Shakespeare at the new Old Globe Theatre?

4. What three movie stars founded the La Jolla Playhouse in 1947?

5. What four locations have been used for the summer productions of Starlight Opera?

1. Point Loma, on the grounds of the Theosophical Society of America. Many Shakespearean and Greek dramas were presented here under the guidance of Madame Tingley. This 1901 theater was modeled after one in Taormina, Sicily. On November 17, 1958, it collapsed after being buffeted by high winds, but was soon reconstructed.

2. Sally Rand. Here she performed her fan dance, her bubble dance, and a new creation called "Leda and the Swan."

3. Queen Elizabeth II of England. The ceremony was held on February 26, 1983.

4. Gregory Peck, Dorothy McGuire, and Mel Ferrer. It was established in order to give Hollywood actors a chance to do quality live theater without having to travel to New York. The Playhouse continued operation through 1964, and was revived in 1983. Some of the many well-known actors and actresses to play here have been Olivia de Havilland, Charlton Heston, Dame Mae Whitty, Patricia Neal, Vincent Price, Louis Jourdan, Raymond Massey, Richard Basehart, Lee Marvin, Eve Arden, Robert Ryan, and James Mason.

5. 1. Wegeforth Bowl at the San Diego Zoo: 1946-47 and 1968- 71.
    2. The bowl in Balboa Park: 1948-66 and 1974- present.
    3. Civic Theatre: 1967.
    4. California State University (now San Diego State University) Open Air Theater, called the "Greek Bowl": 1972-73.

6. What musical depicts the 1829 elopement of San Diegan Josefa Carrillo and New England sea captain Henry Fitch?

7. What actor or actress has won the most Atlas Awards?

8. What San Diego entertainer has had the longest run in show business history?

9. The San Diego Repertory Theatre has performed the same play every December since 1976. What is that play?

10. What was the first musical presented by Starlight Opera?

11. What was the name of San Diego's live theater- in-the-round of the 1960s that featured many name stars?

6. *My Cousin Josefa*. It was written by San Diegan Robert Austin, and premiered in 1969 for Starlight Opera during San Diego's bicentennial. The story is told from the point of view of narrator Pío Pico, Josefa's cousin, who helped her elope. One of the highlights of the musical is the song "San Diego," which was the official song for San Diego's 200th Anniversary. An original cast recording was made, which was the first of its kind in San Diego.

7. Lillie Mae Barr, with 15. Though she took up acting late in life, she played a total of 20 roles at the Old Globe complex of theaters, which annually presents the Atlas Awards for excellence. Ms. Barr has been called San Diego's "First Lady of Comedy," and one of her most popular roles was the title role in *Everybody Loves Opal* at the Mission Playhouse.

8. Dr. Michael Dean. His act as the "World's Foremost Hypnotist" has run in San Diego since October 8, 1963.

9. *A Christmas Carol*, based on the story by Charles Dickens.

10. *The Mikado*. This Gilbert and Sullivan operetta was Starlight's premiere presentation in 1946, at the Wegeforth Bowl in the San Diego Zoo.

11. Circle Arts Theatre. Some of the stars to appear in this theater on Kearny Mesa were Gisele MacKenzie, Pat Boone, Robert Weede, John Raitt, José Ferrer, Frankie Laine, Howard Keel, Gypsy Rose Lee, Jerry Orbach, Martha Raye, and Jayne Mansfield. The round building that was Circle Arts Theatre became the Al Bahr Shrine Temple.

12. What San Diego actress was discovered in 1941 by an agent from Warner Brothers while she was acting in *Here Today* at the Old Globe Theatre?

13. What was the first theater built in San Diego?

14. What outdoor historical pageant was presented in or near Escondido from 1927 to 1931?

15. What husband and wife team founded the San Diego Ballet Company?

16. As of the 1988 season, Starlight Opera has produced only two musicals six times. Which two are they?

12. Faye Emerson. She came to San Diego when she was a teenager, and studied dramatics at Point Loma High School and San Diego State College. After her "discovery," she appeared in several motion pictures at Warner Brothers. She later went on to fame on the Broadway stage, radio, and on television, where she had her own shows, *The Faye Emerson Show* and *Faye Emerson's Wonderful Town*.

13. Horton's Hall. Alonzo Horton built it in 1870 at Sixth and F. The lower level was at one time a roller rink and a dry goods store, and the upper level was a theater and meeting hall.

14. *Felicita.* It tells the story of an Indian maiden's love for an American soldier at the time of the Battle of San Pasqual in 1846. The play, written by Dr. Benjamin F. Sherman, was based on a book by Mrs. Elizabeth Judson Roberts, which was in turn loosely based on a true story. The pageant was successfully revived for a few years in the 1970s and 1980s.

15. Nancy Johnson and Richard Carter. They were formerly principal stars of the San Francisco Ballet Company, and came to San Diego in 1960 to be in charge of a degree course in ballet at California Western University, one of only three such courses offered in the country. The first production of the San Diego Ballet Company was Virgil Thomson's *Filling Station*, presented August 1, 1961.

16. *The King and I* and *South Pacific*. Both are by Rodgers and Hammerstein.

17. What native San Diegan and veteran actor at the Old Globe Theatre was nominated for a 1962 Academy Award?

18. What Jerry Herman/Michael Stewart musical starring Robert Preston and Bernadette Peters had its world premiere in San Diego?

19. What San Diego family had six starring roles in Starlight's 1985 production of George M?

20. What Shakespearean play was produced for the Old Globe's first Shakespeare Festival, in the summer of 1949?

21. What La Jolla Playhouse production was taken to Broadway where it earned seven Tony awards in 1984, including best musical?

17. Victor Buono. He was nominated for best supporting actor for his role in *Whatever Happened to Baby Jane?* He began his acting at St. Augustine High School and San Diego Junior Theater. At the Globe he appeared in over 20 plays, winning three Atlas Awards, and was remembered there particularly for his outstanding portrayals of Falstaff. He played many roles in movies and on television, and achieved some of his finest moments as the arch villain King Tut in *Batman*.

18. *Mack and Mabel.* This story of Mack Sennett and Mabel Normand premiered at the Civic Theatre June 17, 1974, but when it went to Los Angeles a week and a half later for an eight-week run, it was advertised as a world premiere there. This caused some animosity between the two cities, but director-choreographer Gower Champion and producer David Merrick both proclaimed that the premiere had been in San Diego.

19. The Ward family. Starlight Co-Artistic Directors Don and Bonnie Ward played Cohan's father and mother, son Kirby starred as George M. Cohan, his real-life sister Lori Ward Hermelin played his sister Josie, his brother Kelly played his partner Sam Harris and in addition was choreographer, and his wife Beverly Davis Ward played his first wife. This was the first time that the Ward family appeared on stage together professionally.

20. *Twelfth Night.* It was produced in co-operation with San Diego State College, and was the only play presented by the Old Globe that summer.

21. *Big River: The Adventures of Huckleberry Finn.* San Diego's La Jolla Playhouse director Des McAnuff won a Tony for his direction, as did Roger Miller for his original score. This was the first Tony-winning musical to originate in the non-profit theater outside of New York.

22. Cassius Carter, for whom a theater in Balboa Park is named, was a member of what profession?

23. Before Dr. Michael Dean had his show at the Gaslight Room at Midway and Rosecrans, it ran for five years at what San Diego location?

24. Every summer from 1950 through 1966, the Coronado Playhouse presented what play that was popular with San Diegans?

25. Actress Marsha Mason appeared in what Old Globe play in the summer of 1983?

26. What is the name of the annual award given for excellence for the San Diego Associated Community Theater?

22. Law. He came to San Diego in 1886, and was district attorney from 1903 to 1906. He was a brilliant Shakespearean scholar, and it has been said that if all of the bard's works were lost to the world he could have re-created them word for word. The Cassius Carter Center Stage, to which the Carter family made a substantial contribution, opened January 16, 1969.

23. The Catamaran Hotel. He began there October 8, 1963. Next he played at the Gaslight Room, until moving to the New Alamo Nite Club in September 1987.

24. *Suds in Your Eye.* It is by John Kirkland, based on the novel by Mary Lasswell. The play had not fared well on Broadway, but was a great success here for several reasons: the setting was a San Diego junkyard on Island Avenue, so there were many local references; the three lead actresses, Gwen Challacombe, Henrietta Atkins, and Lucille Parsons, were delightful; a considerable amount of beer was consumed by the characters, and the audience in the cabaret-style theater would hoist a few along with the three old girls.

25. *Twelfth Night.* She played the part of Viola in this production. Ms. Mason has been nominated for an Academy Award for best actress four times, for *Cinderella Liberty*, *The Goodbye Girl*, *Chapter Two*, and *Only When I Laugh*.

26. The Aubrey Award. It is named in honor of Aubrey Dunne who founded A.C.T. in 1964. At that time he was coaching dramatics for the La Mesa Recreation Department, and felt that the area's community theaters would benefit from a theater league. He is currently a math teacher at La Mesa Middle School.

27. What San Diego actor received the 1970 Tony award for best actor in a musical?

28. What revue concerning San Diego was a smash hit at the Old Globe from 1949 to 1956?

29. During the Depression a fund-raising production of *H.M.S. Pinafore* was staged in San Diego. What was the unusual location of the performance?

30. What was the name of the theater in Balboa Park that was on the site of the present Cassius Carter Center Stage?

27. Cleavon Little, for *Purlie*. Cleavon moved to San Diego at the age of three, attended Kearny High, and then studied at San Diego City College where he received his theater training. He graduated from San Diego State College, and in 1965 received an ABC-TV scholarship to the American Academy of Dramatic Arts in New York. He played in some off-Broadway productions, and following his success in *Purlie*, went on to star in the movie *Blazing Saddles* and the TV series *Temperatures Rising*.

28. *Caught in the Act*. This was a locally written revue of songs, dances, and skits dealing with San Diego events, places, and personalities, including historical and current foibles of the community. Each year it had timely revisions which delighted the audiences.

29. The *Star of India*. The production was to be a fund-raiser for the ship and its museum, so the *Star* was towed to B Street Pier where temporary seats were set up. This was not a financial success, however, partly because a large portion of the audience found a way to sneak in around a pier shed without paying. When all the bills were paid the show netted $4.85.

30. Falstaff Tavern. It was built for the 1935-36 exposition, and later used as a place for serving complimentary coffee during intermissions of productions at the Old Globe. Then for many years it served as a rehearsal hall and storage facility, until it was opened experimentally as a theater in 1950. Here plays more avant-garde than those at the Globe could be presented. In 1963 it was renovated and used regularly until it was replaced by the Carter in 1968-69.

31. Who is known as San Diego's "King of Burlesque"?

32. What San Diego production was the first live telecast of a stage play over PBS?

33. Who is known as the "Puppet Lady of San Diego"?

34. The Old Globe Theatre won what national award in 1984?

31. Bob Johnston. From the mid-1920s he was the owner and manager of the Hollywood Theater, San Diego's only burlesque house, and also of the Palace Sports Bar. The burlesque shows were especially popular during the war years, and boxing, baseball, and racing celebrities, as well as entertainers, were frequent visitors to the Palace Sports Bar next door. Some of the atmosphere of the old Palace Bar has been re-created at the Palace Bar area in the Horton Grand Hotel in the Gaslamp Quarter, where Mr. Johnston can often be found.

32. *The Skin of Our Teeth.* This Thornton Wilder play was an Old Globe Theatre production, broadcast January 18, 1983. All went reasonably well until the opening of Act III, when Jonathan McMurtry as the stage manager announced that seven of the actors had been taken ill and that crew members would fill in. This is in the script, of course, but at WNET in Buffalo, a technician thought that the trouble was real and cut to the station's logo.

33. Marie Hitchcock. She presented her first puppet show with her sister, Genevieve Engman, in 1948 at the San Diego Public Library, where she has performed regularly ever since. She also established shows at the Puppet Theater in Balboa Park, which was renamed the Marie Hitchcock Puppet Theater in 1986. Some of her puppets known to San Diego area children are Bum, Cinder, Sgt. Friendly, who received a 10-year service pin from the San Diego Police Department, and Murgatroyd, who was presented a savings account by San Diego Federal Savings and Loan.

34. A Tony Award. It was for "Notable achievement and continuing dedication to theatre artistry."

35.   In 1900 John C. Fisher, San Diego showman and manager of the Fisher Opera House, created a musical extravaganza with six San Diego girls. This inaugurated the era of the American showgirl. What were these girls called?

36.   What San Diego ballet director was the first American dance expert to be invited to Romania under the auspices of the State Department, in 1975?

37.   What Academy Award winner starred in the Old Globe's 1966 production of *Romeo and Juliet*?

38.   What star of England's D'Oyly Carte Opera Company was instrumental in forming the San Diego Gilbert and Sullivan Company in 1974?

35. Floradora Girls (or Floradora Sextette). Fisher felt that San Diego had performers with talent comparable or superior to the traveling professionals, so he picked six San Diego beauties to be in his show *Floradora*, which opened in New York in 1900. One of the highlights was when six men sang "Tell Me Pretty Maiden" to them. The musical was a great success, and Floradora clothes became the latest craze.

36. Maxine Mahon. This fifth generation San Diegan and graduate of Lincoln High School founded the California Ballet Company and School in 1968 with her husband Robert Mahon. Since then it has grown to become one of the largest ballet schools on the West Coast, and many of its alumni dance with the nation's leading companies. In 1975 Ms. Mahon was a cultural exhange artist in Romania where she taught, choreographed, and lectured at major cultural centers.

37. Jon Voight. With him in this star-studded production were Lauri Peters as Juliet, Anthony Zerbe as Mercutio, and Will Geer as Friar Lawrence. Voight went on to be nominated for the best actor Academy Award in 1969 for *Midnight Cowboy* and in 1985 for *Runaway Train*, and he won in 1978 for *Coming Home*.

38. Martyn Green. For over 20 years he was the principal comedian of England's famous Gilbert and Sullivan opera company. He was fascinated with the idea of forming a Gilbert and Sullivan company in San Diego, so in 1974 he directed *H.M.S. Pinafore* here, with Hollace Koman as producer and conductor. This was performed at the All Souls' Episcopal Church in Point Loma, where Ms. Koman was the new organist-choirmaster. Mr. Green died the following year, but the company he helped start still performs.

MOVIES AND TV

1. In 1911 and 1912, what town was known as the "Film Capital of the West"?

2. What 1986 movie was named after the school at Miramar Naval Air Station where the Marine and Naval Air Force pilots are trained?

3. What star of the first musical to win the Academy Award for best picture has made Coronado her long-time home?

4. Name two military movies starring James Cagney and Pat O'Brien that were filmed in San Diego.

1.   La Mesa. The American Film Manufacturing Company, popularly known as "Flying A," made its headquarters here after a brief stay in Lakeside. Director Allan Dwan wrote and directed over 100 films in La Mesa, mostly one-reel Westerns, comedies, and documentaries. He built the first sound stage in California here, a 7,500-square-foot open air structure on what is now La Mesa Boulevard. In addition, in 1912 the Essanay Film Company, known for "Broncho Billy" Anderson cowboy pictures, moved to La Mesa for a three-month stay.

2.   *Top Gun.* This is the name given to the place where the best and the brightest pilots are trained. The movie starred Tom Cruise and Kelly McGillis, and was filmed partly in San Diego. The "sleazy bar scene" was filmed at Kansas City Barbeque on West Market Street.

3.   Anita Page. The winning movie was *The Broadway Melody,* 1928/29, in which she starred with Bessie Love and Charles King. Several years later she married naval officer Herschel A. House, and retired from the screen at age 26. She and Rear Admiral House (ret.) live in Coronado, where she has been active in Coronado Community Theater.

4.   *Here Comes the Navy* and *Devil Dogs of the Air. Here Comes the Navy,* 1934, was shot on location at the U.S. Naval Training Station in San Diego. *Devil Dogs of the Air,* 1935, featured spectacular stunt flying by the Marine Air Corps, and was filmed primarily at North Island, with Navy and Marine officers as technical advisors. The world premiere of this film was held at the Spreckels Theatre January 29, 1935, and Mayor Irones proclaimed the day "Warner Brothers' Day."

5.   What movie and TV actor owned the Los Quiotes Rancho in Carlsbad?

6.   In 1944 Jon Hall, Louise Allbritton, Edward Everett Horton, Eric Blore, Buster Keaton, and Irene Ryan made a motion picture comedy about San Diego. What was the name of it?

7.   What were the two names of the ornate theater that stood on the corner of Fifth and B streets from 1924 to 1963?

8.   What was San Diego's first TV station?

9.   What motion picture director owned the Red Mountain Ranch in Fallbrook from 1939 to 1972?

5.   Leo Carrillo. This great-grandson of one of the early gover-
     nors of California, known for his role as Pancho on the TV
     series *The Cisco Kid*, rebuilt an old adobe house into a
     beautiful hacienda which he used as a working retreat. He
     named it Los Quiotes Rancho (Ranch of the Spanish Dag-
     gers) for the white yucca flowers prevalent in the area.

6.   *San Diego, I Love You.* It is a screwball comedy about an
     inventor (Horton) whose family moves to San Diego to
     promote his latest invention. The war-time problems of con-
     gestion and housing shortages provided some of the humor,
     and there were some memorable shots of the bears at the San
     Diego Zoo. The movie has been called a "minor gem," and
     the movie poster hangs in the lobby of the Ken Cinema.

7.   Pantages and Orpheum. The Pantages (1924-1934) started
     as a vaudeville house, then showed silent films, talkies, and
     live shows. The Orpheum (1934-1963) also presented
     vaudeville, and later became a very elegant first-run theater.

8.   KFMB. The first broadcast was televised Monday evening,
     May 16, 1949, from the Continental Room of Hotel San
     Diego. It was estimated that there were only 2,000 TV sets
     in the county then, and that at least 1,500 persons crowded
     around the sets that were in the downtown department,
     appliance, and music stores to watch the programs that ran
     from 8:00 to 10:00 P.M. that night.

9.   Frank Capra. He purchased the ranch in 1939, and made it
     his permanent home in 1951. It encompassed almost 1,200
     acres, and was planted in fruit, olive, and especially avocado
     trees. Capra joined in the community activities, and his
     children grew up and went to school there. Later he left
     Fallbrook and moved to the desert for his wife's health.

10. On the grounds of what building in San Diego County were many of the Zorro movies and TV shows filmed in the early 1950s?

11. In what downtown building do you find the marquee from the old Tower Theatre?

12. Who played San Diego aviator John J. Montgomery in the 1946 motion picture *Gallant Journey*?

13. Name at least three detective/police TV series that were shot in San Diego County.

14. What Coronadoan was a member of "Our Gang" comedies, and became a Hollywood song and dance man?

10. The Royal Palms Hotel in Carlsbad. It was originally the home of grocery store merchant Albert Cohn, who had it built in the 1920s. Since 1978 it has been Fidel's Norte Restaurant, at 3003 Carlsbad Boulevard.

11. Croce's Top Hat Bar and Grille (formerly San Diego Mercantile Co.). This historic building at 818 Fifth Avenue in the Gaslamp Quarter now houses several eating places on the ground floor. Decorating the inside is the authentic neon Tower Theatre marquee, which had been a glittery landmark at 605 W. Broadway from 1941 through the early 1980s.

12. Glenn Ford. The world premiere was held at the Spreckels Theatre September 4, 1946. Earlier that day the cast of the movie participated in the ground-breaking ceremony for the Montgomery Monument on Otay Mesa. Columbia Pictures gave $25,000 for rights to the story, plus a part of the profits, to the Junior Chamber of Commerce of San Diego to build and improve the Montgomery Park and Monument.

13. 1. *Manhunt*, 1956-61, starring Victor Jory and Patrick McVey.
    2. *Coronado 9*, 1960, starring Rod Cameron.
    3. *Border Patrol*, 1960, starring Richard Webb.
    4. *Harry O*, 1974-76, starring David Janssen.
    5. *Simon and Simon*, 1981-   , starring Jameson Parker and Gerald McRaney.

14. Johnny Downs. In the 1920s, '30s, and '40s he was a favorite singing and dancing screen collegian. He also did nightclub and live TV shows, and was a hit as the Tin Man in Starlight's *The Wizard of Oz* in 1962 and 1964. He resides in Coronado where he has sold real estate and has participated in charity work.

15. What native San Diegan appeared in both the 1926 and 1939 versions of the movie *Beau Geste*?

16. For many years there were two movie theaters in North Park. The North Park Theatre was on the south side of University. What was the name of the theater on the north side?

17. What two Academy Award-winning actors were born in La Jolla?

18. Archie Moore made his motion picture debut in a leading role in what 1960 movie?

19. What San Diego girl became a Mouseketeer?

15. Sheik, the first camel born at the San Diego Zoo. He was a very gentle and intelligent animal, and each time had the honor of being chosen lead camel, ridden by the star. Both movies were filmed in the sand dunes near Yuma.

16. The Ramona Theatre. It operated from around 1922 to 1930, and then reopened around 1933 as the New Ramona Theatre, at 3018 University Avenue, one-half block east of 30th Street. From 1936 until it closed in December 1957 it was again called the Ramona Theatre. The North Park Theatre, built in 1928, was the first movie theater with a full stage to be built outside of the downtown area. It is still standing, and has recently been used for church services, films, and stage productions.

17. Gregory Peck and Cliff Robertson. Gregory Peck, who won the best actor Academy Award in 1962 for *To Kill a Mockingbird*, graduated from San Diego High School. Cliff Robertson, who won his best actor award in 1968 for *Charly*, graduated from La Jolla High.

18. *The Adventures of Huckleberry Finn*. The film also starred Eddie Hodges, Tony Randall, Patty McCormack, and Neville Brand. The San Diego boxer received very favorable reviews for his portrayal of Jim, and he went on to a few more roles in motion pictures and television.

19. Linda Lu Hughes. This talented native San Diegan was a student at Garfield Elementary School and pupil of Eula Hoff School of Dancing and Gerry Tremble Baton School when she was picked in 1957 to be a Mouseketeer. In Keith Keller's 1975 book *The Mickey Mouse Club Scrapbook*, it states that Linda is married to Myron Vaughan, a teacher, and that they and their two children live in Los Angeles.

20. What actor played Don Diego at the Del Mar Fair for 37 years?

21. What San Diego theater converted to Todd-AO equipment for the showing of *Around the World in 80 Days* in 1957?

22. What supernatural TV series starring Sebastian Cabot was shot at the Hotel del Coronado in 1972?

23. What movie about San Diego did Dan Dailey, Ray McDonald, Bonita Granville, and Leo Gorcey make in 1941?

24. What was San Diego's first drive-in theater?

25. What movie actress was crowned "Fairest of the Fair" at the 1958 Del Mar Fair?

20. Tom "Tommy" Hernandez. He played Latin-type parts in films and TV programs in the U.S. for half the year, and for the remainder of the year he made movies in Spain where he had starring roles. The character of Don Diego was inspired by the real Don Diego Alvarado, who resided in Del Mar around the turn of the century.

21. The Capri Theatre. The San Diego premiere was August 1, 1957, and the film ran here until June 7, 1958. Owner Burton Jones spent $75,000 for remodeling and for the installation of the equipment, which included multi-channel sound. This was the only theater between Dallas and Los Angeles to be so equipped.

22. *Ghost Story*. Cabot played psychic host Winston Essex, and though the series didn't fare well in the ratings, the Hotel del Coronado evoked the desired ghostly Victorian atmosphere.

23. *Down in San Diego*. The plot concerned teenagers foiling a spy ring at the San Diego Naval Base.

24. The Midway Drive-in Theatre. When it was built in 1947 at 3901 Midway Drive (later Sports Arena Boulevard), it was considered to be way out in the country. On December 6, 1980, it showed its last movie.

25. Raquel Tejada, now Raquel Welch. She was then a student at La Jolla High School, where she was a cheerleader and a member of the drama society. One of her first jobs was that of weather girl for Channel 8's *Sunup*. In 1959 she played the title role in the Ramona Pageant in Hemet, California.

26. What nationally known radio and television emcee is a native San Diegan, and started his career as an announcer on KGB in San Diego?

27. What Helix High graduate was at one time being groomed for the roles originally planned for the late James Dean?

28. Give the former names of at least two of these three neighborhood theaters: Academy Cinema, Guild Theatre, and Adams Theatre.

29. What 1979 science fiction movie filmed in San Diego has been called the worst film ever made?

26. Art Linkletter. He took the job as KGB announcer while attending San Diego State College, from which he graduated in 1934. In 1935 he became program director for the California Pacific International Exposition. His *People Are Funny* show began on radio in 1942, and moved to TV from 1954 to 1961.

27 Dennis Hopper. He played with Dean in *Rebel Without a Cause* and *Giant*, went on to co-star, co-direct, and co-produce *Easy Rider* in 1969, and was Oscar-nominated for best supporting actor in *Hoosiers* in 1986. Dennis attended Grossmont High, and was in the second graduating class of Helix High School. He appeared in numerous productions at the Old Globe Theatre, and director Craig Noel is quoted as saying, "He was one of the most brilliant young actors we ever had."

28. Rio, Hillcrest, and Carteri. The Rio, at 3721 University Avenue, had that name from 1948 until late 1955; the Hillcrest, at 3827 Fifth Avenue, was called that from 1912 to November 1961; the Carteri, 3325 Adams Avenue, had its original name from 1925 to 1934. All three theaters are still standing, though only the Academy and the Guild are currently showing films.

29. *Attack of the Killer Tomatoes.* It was produced by Four Square Productions of National City, and directed by John DeBello. In the past few years it has become popular on college campuses and in video stores. A sequel, *Return of the Killer Tomatoes*, has recently been completed here.

30. What local television personality and weatherman is known for his bow tie?

31. What 1968 movie starring Christopher Jones is set against the background of the San Diego tuna fishing fleet?

32. What San Diego ship starred in movies in the 1930s, including the 1932 film *Mr. Robinson Crusoe* with Douglas Fairbanks?

33. What San Diego theater has two 20-foot-high ornamental waterfalls inside, and a tile mosaic of a 1513 ship on the entry sidewalk?

30. Bob Dale. He was with Channel 8 for 21 years, and has been with Channel 39 since 1977. He has long been one of San Diego's most popular TV personalities, with his chatty information about movies and his spot "The Lighter Side." His fans have sent him innumerable bow ties, which he wears on the air to please them.

31. *Chubasco* (which means "sudden tropical storm"). Also in the cast were Susan Strasberg, Richard Egan, Simon Oakland, and Preston Foster. It was filmed in San Diego in the late summer of 1966, and throughout the movie San Diegans can recognize their streets, B Street Pier, the bay, Point Loma, and local tuna clippers and yachts. The world premiere was held May 29, 1968, at four theaters simultaneously: the Balboa, the Aero, the Big Sky, and the Pacific.

32. The *Invader*. This 151-foot schooner with masts of 100 feet was built in 1905, and is the largest passenger schooner in America. She has been in San Diego since 1983, and is now part of Waterfront Promotions.

33. The Balboa Theatre. This large 1924 theater was designed for live productions such as plays, vaudeville, and circuses, as well as for films. The waterfalls used to operate at full force during intermissions, but when they were turned off they dripped, which was distracting to the audience. The ship in the sidewalk mosaic at Fourth and E depicts Balboa discovering the Pacific Ocean. On top of the theater is a polychrome tile dome in the style of the Santa Fe Depot's domes.

34. What silent screen comedian played leading roles in San Diego High School plays from 1911 to 1913?

35. Siegemund Lubin, sometimes called the "Father of Motion Pictures," opened the Lubin Studio in what city in San Diego County in 1915?

36. What was the name of the movie in which John Wayne starred as Coronadoan Frank W. "Spig" Wead?

34. Harold Lloyd. He moved here during his high school years and graduated from San Diego High, where he excelled in dramatics. He also played in four local stock companies, worked as stage hand at the Spreckels Theatre, and was dramatic coach of an acting school here. In the winter of 1912-13 he made his film debut in San Diego with the Edison Company, playing a Yaqui Indian. In 1913 he moved to Los Angeles where there were more acting opportunities, and went on to make over 165 shorts, 11 silent films, and 7 talkies, often starring as the small town hero in horn-rimmed glasses.

35. Coronado. Siegemund (or Sigmund) Lubin was a pioneer in the motion picture industry, beginning his work in 1897. In Coronado he erected a studio and film plant, including a theater and open-air stage. He may have made as many as 20 short films and documentaries here, but his plans for a huge film plant in Coronado failed to materialize, and his company folded in 1916.

36. *The Wings of Eagles*. This 1957 movie, directed by Wead's friend John Ford, showed him starting out as a pioneer Navy flier and winning the Schneider Cup Race while stationed here in the 1920s. Soon after this, an accident in his Coronado home left him with a broken spinal cord. During his 2 1/2-year convalescence at the Naval Hospital he began writing for pulp magazines, gradually went on to quality magazines, and then became a playwright and author of many Hollywood scenarios about military life and aviation. His play *Ceiling Zero* was produced on Broadway and made into a successful motion picture. Despite having his neck in a steel brace he volunteered for active duty in World War II, and was awarded the Legion of Merit for his work in planning Pacific air war operations.

37. What was the final name of the theater on Fifth Avenue between A and B streets that had formerly been the Queen, the Illusion, and the Kinema?

38. What dairy sponsored Johnny Downs' local children's television show?

39. What was the large neon figure on the back of the Campus Drive-in Theatre?

37. The Mission Theatre. Built in 1909 as the Queen, it was one of the city's first movie theaters. In the early years it also presented vaudeville and stage shows on a small stage. After a long life, it was razed in 1969.

38. Golden Arrow Dairy. *The Johnny Downs Show* (first called the *Johnny Downs Express*) ran on KOGO-TV Channel 10 every weekday afternoon from the mid-1950s through 1971. Johnny danced on top of a huge bottle of Golden Arrow milk, and children often called that milk "Johnny Downs Milk."

39. A majorette in Indian headdress. From 1948 to 1983 she strutted and twirled her baton in front of a neon-outlined San Diego State College campus and S Mountain at the theater on El Cajon Boulevard near College Avenue. The 100-by-80-foot-tall sign was carefully dismantled by the Save Our Neon Society, and the 50-foot-tall majorette has been installed at Marketplace at the Grove (formerly College Grove Shopping Center) facing College Grove Drive. On the former site of the Campus Drive-in now stands the Campus Plaza shopping center, which is decorated with small medallions of scenes from the old theater sign.

40. World War II movies *Guadalcanal Diary, The Outsider, Gallant Hours, Sands of Iwo Jima,* and *First to Fight* were filmed primarily at what location in San Diego County?

41. Ronald Reagan made only one movie with his wife Nancy Davis, and it was filmed partly in San Diego. What was the name of that film?

40. Camp Pendleton. When *Guadalcanal Diary* was being shot there in 1943, actors Lloyd Nolan, William Bendix, Anthony Quinn, and Preston Foster stayed at the Carlsbad Inn. In filming *The Outsider,* the 1962 movie starring Tony Curtis as Ira Hayes, several tons of crushed cinders were scattered on the beach to simulate Iwo Jima's black sand. During filming of the 1960 film *Gallant Hours,* with James Cagney playing Admiral Bull Halsey, palm trees were brought in to make Pendleton's auxiliary air strip resemble Guadalcanal's Henderson Field. Most of the outdoor action of *Sands of Iwo Jima,* starring John Wayne and directed by Allan Dwan in 1949, was filmed at Pendleton. When it was shown at an Encinitas theater, the marquee read "CAMP PENDLETON in 'SANDS OF IWO JIMA.' With John Wayne." In *First to Fight,* Chad Everett starred as a Medal of Honor winner on Guadalcanal who is transferred to Camp Pendleton to train recruits.

41. *Hellcats of the Navy.* The company spent three weeks of 1956 in San Diego, shooting at Point Loma, the Navy base, on board the submarines *Steelhead* and *Besugo,* and at the pier off the Admiral Kidd Club at NTC. Personnel from both submarines were used in the movie. The film company cast and crew were a familiar sight in San Diego because the production and time office where they checked in and out was located in the US Grant Hotel. In addition, the members of the cast took time to appear at Navy affairs, service clubs, and other civic events.

42. In 1987 the former Capri Theatre at 3812 Park Boulevard changed its name to Park Theatre. What was its previous name, before it was renovated in 1954?

43. What was the name of the television program shot at the San Diego Zoo from 1955 to 1969?

44. What was the last remaining drive-in theater in the city of San Diego?

42. The Egyptian Theatre. It was constructed in 1926 during the Egyptian craze sparked by the discovery of King Tut's tomb. The theater was in the style of an Egyptian temple, had hieroglyphic-covered columns, and is said to have been modeled after the Egyptian Theatre in Hollywood. Several other buildings in Egyptian motif still stand on both sides of the 3700 and 3800 blocks of Park Boulevard. In 1954, over $100,000 was spent on remodeling and turning the theater into a modern movie palace, renamed the Capri. A bronze sculpture by Bernard Rosenthal was created for the lobby, and murals by Matisse, Miro, and Chagall decorated the walls.

43. *Zoorama*. Filming at the zoo actually began in 1951, when KFMB-TV began the weekly program *Behind the Scenes at the Zoo*. This evolved into *Zoorama* in 1955. By 1960 the show appeared in cities throughout the United States and in foreign countries, and had a following of millions. It was later syndicated, and was shown in San Diego through 1974, and in other cities long after that.

44. The Frontier. This theater opened at 3601 Midway Drive in 1957, only a few blocks from the Midway Drive-in. In 1978 it became the Frontier 1 and 2. When it closed in 1985, it was the last drive-in theater in the city, though several still remained in the county.

45. What movie star began his acting career at San Diego County's Army and Navy Academy?

46. Who visited the Panama-California Exposition in a 1915 movie?

47. What was the name of the 1972 movie written by and starring San Diegan Holly Mascott about three young persons who live in a Victorian mansion?

48. What former San Diegan starred in the best picture of 1930, as well as a series of doctor movies?

45. Robert Walker. At the age of 13 he entered the prestigious Academy, which was located in Pacific Beach at the time. In January 1935 the drama teacher cast him as the lead in the school play, and he won the high school dramatic award for best actor in San Diego County. In 1936 the school moved to Carlsbad. That year he tied for best actor, and the following year won again. In his senior year he was class president and president of the drama department. One of his first major films was *See Here, Private Hargrove,* which was filmed at Camp Pendleton in 1944, enabling him to return to many familiar locations.

46. Fatty Arbuckle and Mabel Normand. The movie was *Fatty and Mabel at the San Diego Exposition,* a Mack Sennett short.

47. *Josie's Castle.* Ms. Mascott, a UCSD English major, expanded a story she had written into the screenplay, and starred in the movie along with Tom Fielding and George Takei. The three young persons live together here and tour the city on a bicycle-for-three and in a 1956 Citroen. Holly's father, Lawrence Mascott, produced and directed the movie on location here in September 1971, and it premiered April 26, 1972, at the California and the Pacific theaters. James Meade of the *San Diego Union* called it "a well-made motion picture that should have special appeal for young people and San Diegans."

48. Lew Ayres. He moved to San Diego in 1923, and attended San Diego High School. Later he entered the movies, and soon played the starring role in *All Quiet on the Western Front.* He went on to star in nine Dr. Kildare movies along with Lionel Barrymore and Larraine Day, and in 1948 was nominated for the best actor Oscar in *Johnny Belinda.*

49. *The Flying Fleet, Hell Divers,* and *Dive Bomber* were all shot primarily at what location in San Diego County?

50. What drive-in theater mural featured a Mexican standing beside a large cactus?

51. What Point Loma High and San Diego State College graduate played a mother in a 1974-84 TV series?

49. North Island. *The Flying Fleet,* 1929, starring Ramon Novarro, Anita Page, and Ralph Graves, portrays graduates of the Naval Academy and the Naval Flying School who successfully undertake a flight from San Diego to Honolulu. *Hell Divers,* 1931, starring Wallace Beery and Clark Gable, was shot in and around North Island, Panama, and on board the U.S. aircraft carrier *Saratoga. Dive Bomber,* 1941, starring Errol Flynn, Fred MacMurray, Ralph Bellamy, and Alexis Smith, is the story of a doctor taking a flight surgeon course at the Naval Air Station on North Island, and was the first important aviation story filmed entirely in technicolor. All three of these films were written by Coronadoan Lt. Commander Frank "Spig" Wead, U.S.N.

50. The Rancho. When it opened in 1948 at Euclid Avenue and Federal Boulevard, its neon-lighted Mexican mural with 2,000 feet of tubing was probably the largest of its kind in the country. The lights were later removed, however, because they were a fire hazard. The theater showed its last movie on October 17, 1978.

51. Marion Ross. One of her best-remembered roles is that of Mrs. Cunningham on *Happy Days.* She moved to San Diego at the age of 16, and in 1950 graduated from San Diego State College, where she was chosen outstanding actress. She performed at the Old Globe and the La Jolla Playhouse, and won an Atlas from the Globe for best actress. Since then she has appeared in a dozen movies and over 400 television shows. She maintains a second home in Cardiff-by-the-Sea, and has established a Marion Ross Scholarship for the Drama Department of San Diego State University.

52. What were the names of the two theaters that stood on Plaza Street facing Horton Plaza for seven decades?

53. *Showboat,* the large paddle-wheeler on San Diego Bay, was in what 1955 John Wayne movie?

54. In the 1950s, what local Western entertainer and children's television personality appeared in parades on his horse Comanche?

55. What 1953 science fiction classic had scenes shot at Palomar Observatory?

52. The Cabrillo and the Plaza. The Plaza, at 323 Plaza Street (formerly Witherby Street), opened in 1913, and the Cabrillo, at 329 Plaza Street, opened two years later. The Cabrillo was the larger and more ornate of the two, and originally had an intricately detailed archway, which was plastered over in the 1930s. These two old-timers were demolished in 1982 to make way for Horton Plaza shopping center.

53. *Blood Alley.* She played a stolen wood-burning stern-wheel ferryboat skippered by Wayne to take escaping villagers from Red China across the Formosa Strait. The *Showboat* was built in 1942 as a Sacramento River survey boat, and is propelled entirely by her stern paddle wheel. She has been in San Diego since 1984, and is one of the few authentic California river-boats in operation today. When *Blood Alley* opened at the Spreckels Theatre October 5, 1955, San Diego author Sid Fleischman, who had written both the novel and the screenplay, autographed copies of his book in the lobby.

54. Monte Hall. (This is not the Monty Hall who is the host of TV's *Let's Make a Deal.*) Monte Hall the Western singer ran Monte Hall's Playland in La Mesa, and appeared on the Saturday children's TV shows *Channel 8 Corral* and *Tiny Town Ranch*. He and Comanche were popular performers at schools and charity events, and Monte was often grand marshal of parades. San Diego children were saddened when he died in 1959.

55. *Invaders from Mars.* The giant dome and telescope created an eerie and majestic atmosphere in this film directed by William Cameron Menzies.

56. What 1985 Academy Award nominee used to wash dishes at the San Diego restaurant The Big Kitchen?

57. Name at least three full-length motion pictures filmed at the Hotel del Coronado.

56. Whoopi Goldberg. She came to San Diego in 1974, and was one of the founding members of the San Diego Repertory Theatre. While appearing there in productions such as *Mother Courage* (in which she had the title role), *Getting Out, Gold!, The Happy Haven,* and *Tragedy of Tragedies,* she worked as dishwasher at The Big Kitchen in Golden Hill where her signature can still be seen on the wall. She was nominated for best actress for her role in *The Color Purple,* her first film.

57. 1. *My Husband's Wives,* 1924, starring Bryant Washburn, Shirley Mason, and Evelyn Brent.
2. *The Flying Fleet,* 1929, starring Anita Page, Ramon Novarro, and Ralph Graves, and written by Coronadoan Lt. Commander Frank W. Wead, U.S.N.
3. *Coronado*, 1935, starring Johnny Downs, Betty Burgess, Jack Haley, Andy Devine, and Eddie Duchin and his orchestra.
4. *Yours For the Asking,* 1936, starring Dolores Costello Barrymore, George Raft, Ida Lupino, and Reginald Owen.
5. *Some Like it Hot*, 1959, starring Marilyn Monroe, Tony Curtis, and Jack Lemmon.
6. *$*, 1971, starring Warren Beatty and Goldie Hawn.
7. *Wicked, Wicked,* 1973, starring David Bailey, Tiffany Bolling, and Randolph Roberts (of USIU, making his film debut).
8. *The Stunt Man*, 1980, starring Peter O'Toole, Steve Railsback, and Barbara Hershey.
9. *Loving Couples,* 1980, starring Shirley MacLaine, James Coburn, Susan Sarandon, Stephen Collins, and Sally Kellerman.

(For a more complete list see *Coronado; The Enchanted Island* by Katherine Carlin and Ray Brandes.)

58. Which Francis the Talking Mule film was shot at the Naval Amphibious Base in Coronado?

59. What native San Diegan was the first female sportscaster in the Western United States?

60. What was the 1926 hit movie starring Lon Chaney that was filmed at MCRD?

58. *Francis in the Navy*. In this 1955 movie, Donald O'Conner answers a desperate plea for help from his friend Francis, who has been drafted into the Navy and is about to be auctioned off as surplus. The ferry landing and other spots in Coronado can be seen in this movie, which was the sixth in the series. It also featured Martha Hyer, Richard Erdman, and Jim Backus. Cmdr. Douglas Fame, Amphibious Base underwater demolition team expert, was technical advisor.

59. Laurie Singer. This Hoover High School graduate worked at KFMB-TV, the CBS affiliate in San Diego, from 1969 to 1976, where she made television news history in 1971 by becoming the first woman sportscaster in the Western United States. She also broke the all-male barrier in the locker room while working there. Laurie moved to New York City in 1979 where she worked as a sports producer and on-air sports reporter for the CBS Morning News with Charles Kuralt for three years. In 1984 she moved back to California to coordinate CBS News coverage of the Olympic games held in Los Angeles. Currently she is a producer in the CBS News, Miami Bureau.

60. *Tell it to the Marines*. Chaney played the tough Marine sergeant with a heart of gold, and William Haines portrayed the young kid from Kansas who joins the Marines in order to get a free ride to San Diego—and thus to Tijuana. General Smedley Butler of MCRD was advisor. It was MGM's second- biggest box office picture that year.

61. What star athlete of San Diego High School in the late 1920s and early 1930s won an Academy Award for film editing in 1964?

62. What was the first San Diego movie theater to be built outside the downtown area?

61. Irvine "Cotton" Warburton. At San Diego High he excelled in football, baseball, basketball, and track, and in 1930 he was the state high school quarter-mile champion. He went on to USC where he was chosen an All-American football player. Later he joined Walt Disney Studios and won an Academy Award as film editor for *Mary Poppins*.

62. The Hillcrest Theatre (now the Guild). It was built on Fifth Avenue in 1912. For a number of years it was not a financial success because patrons preferred to go downtown where they could see first-run films, which were too expensive for the Hillcrest to rent. In the 1920s it was renovated and given a mission-style facade, and in November 1961, it became the Guild Theatre.

LITERATURE

1.   Squibob Square in Old Town is named for one of America's first great humorists. Who was he?

2.   What famous romantic novel depicts the injustices done to the Mission Indians of San Diego and other areas of Southern California?

3.   What writer of horse stories and winner of the 1949 Newbery Medal has lived in Rancho Santa Fe for many years?

4.   What book by San Diego newspaper reporter Max Miller describing his beat was made into a movie starring Claudette Colbert and Ben Lyon?

5.   In what book does Richard Henry Dana Jr. immortalize the hide and tallow industry of San Diego?

LITERATURE

A

1. Lt. George H. Derby. He came to San Diego in 1850 to build a dike that was to turn the flow of the San Diego River from San Diego Bay into False Bay. He is better remembered, however, for his sharp wit and pranks, and his humorous writings that he wrote under the pen names of "John Phoenix" and "Squibob," among others. In 1855 his book *Phoenixiana*, a collection of humorous sketches, became a best seller, and many literary scholars consider him the forerunner of Mark Twain.

2. *Ramona*. Helen Hunt Jackson wrote this book in 1884 to call the attention of the world to the plight of the Indian, just as Harriet Beecher Stowe had done for the black with *Uncle Tom's Cabin*. *Ramona* was enormously successful, and is still read and loved today.

3. Marguerite Henry. The Newbery Medal is awarded each year for the best children's book by an American. Her award-winning book was *King of the Wind*. Some of her other books are *Brighty of the Grand Canyon, Justin Morgan had a Horse,* and *Misty of Chincoteague,* all three of which have been made into motion pictures.

4. *I Cover the Waterfront,* 1932. La Jollan Miller wrote 27 books, including several about San Diego and La Jolla.

5. *Two Years Before the Mast.* He described his stops in San Diego while sailing on the barks *Pilgrim* and *Alert* in 1835-36. In this book he gives one of the best written accounts of the hide and tallow trade in California, and at La Playa in particular.

6. What famous children's author spent the winters of 1904-1909 in Coronado and wrote some of his books there?

7. What San Diego County novelist wrote eight best sellers, including *The Winning of Barbara Worth*?

8. What author of hard-boiled detective novels lived in La Jolla from 1949 until his death in 1959?

9. What 1977 novel written by a San Diegan gives a fictional picture of the San Diego Symphony?

10. What La Jolla author was awarded a special Pulitzer Prize in 1984 for his 44 children's books?

11. What was San Diego's first newspaper?

12. What San Diego County author won the 1961 Newbery Medal for *Island of the Blue Dolphins*?

6. L. Frank Baum. He is best known for *The Wonderful Wizard of Oz*, but his lesser-known books *The Sea Fairies* and *Sky Island* were inspired by his visits to Coronado, and the two "Edith Van Dyne" books, *The Flying Girl* and *The Flying Girl and Her Chum*, were inspired by the annual San Diego air shows. The house at 1101 Star Park Circle where he stayed part of the time while in Coronado is the only house still standing in which he wrote an Oz book (probably *Road to Oz*).

7. Harold Bell Wright. He lived near Escondido on his "Quiet Hills Farm" for many years, until his death in 1944. His novel of Barbara Worth depicts the early settlement of Imperial Valley.

8. Raymond Chandler. He is the creator of Philip Marlowe, private detective of such classics as *The Big Sleep* and *Farewell, My Lovely*.

9. *Symphony*. In it, author Rev. Lawrence Waddy gives a good picture of the financial as well as the artistic problems faced by an American symphony orchestra.

10. Dr. Seuss. He is the author of such popular humorous books as *And to Think That I Saw It on Mulberry Street, If I Ran the Zoo, The Cat in the Hat*, and *How the Grinch Stole Christmas*.

11. The *Herald*. It was started by John Judson Ames, who brought his press with him across the Isthmus of Panama. He published the *Herald* from 1851 to 1860.

12. Scott O'Dell. It is based on the true story of a young Indian girl who was left alone on San Nicholas Island off the coast of Los Angeles. In 1964 the book was made into a movie.

13. The "Pump House Gang" in Tom Wolfe's 1960s book of the same name was made up of San Diegans engaged in what sport?

14. What is the name of the fictional rabbit that lives at the San Diego Wild Animal Park?

15. *Caddie Woodlawn*, the 1936 Newbery Medal winner based on the pioneer life of the author's grandmother, was written by what San Diegan?

16. What 1975 romantic novel takes place at the Hotel del Coronado?

17. When was the *San Diego Union* established?

18. Which Raymond Chandler detective novel is set in La Jolla (though the town is called Esmeralda in the book)?

19. In 1979 the *Evening Tribune* received a Pulitzer Prize for the coverage of what event?

13. Surfing. The gang congregated at the pump house at Windansea Beach in La Jolla, which is one of the best surfing spots in the area.

14. Finsterhall. He was introduced in the 1976 book *Finsterhall of San Pasqual* by San Diego author and columnist John Sinor, who also wrote the sequel *Finsterhall Goes Over the Wall*.

15. Carol Ryrie Brink. She has 27 books for both children and adults to her credit. For the last 21 years of her life she lived in La Jolla and Pacific Beach, until her death in 1981.

16. *Bid Time Return*. In it, author Richard Matheson incorporated some of the actual hotel employees. In 1980 it was made into the movie *Somewhere in Time* starring Christopher Reeve and Jane Seymour, but the location was changed to the Grand Hotel on Mackinac Island, Michigan.

17. 1868. The founders were William Gatewood and Edward Bushyhead. It began as a weekly paper on October 10, 1868, and has been a daily since 1871. The original office has been restored and is still standing on its original site in Old Town, serving as a museum.

18. *Playback*. Some of the key scenes in this 1958 book take place at the Hotel Casa del Poniente, modeled after the La Valencia Hotel, and at the Glass Room, a restaurant which bears a striking resemblance to the Marine Room.

19. The PSA jetliner crash of September 25, 1978, in North Park, in which 144 persons were killed. It was the worst air disaster in the United States up to that time.

20. What is the real name of Dr. Seuss?

21. What Chula Vista writer for young adults has had three of her books made into television specials?

22. What Spring Valley psychiatrist wrote the 1969 best seller about sex?

23. What former San Diego author is known for his tall tale children's books, including the stories of McBroom?

24. The author of *Gentlemen Prefer Blondes* graduated from Russ (San Diego) High School in 1907. Who was it?

20. Theodor "Ted" Geisel. Seuss is his middle name, and was his mother's maiden name. He also writes books for beginning readers under the pen name of Theo LeSieg, which is "Geisel" spelled backwards.

21. Joan Oppenheimer. Her 18 young adult books deal with problems such as drugs, alcohol, accidents, and broken homes, and are popular with teenagers because of their honesty and authenticity. The works *Francesca, Baby, It Isn't Easy Being a Teenaged Millionaire*, and *Which Mother is Mine?* have all been made into ABC Afterschool Specials, and the latter received two Emmys.

22. Dr. David Reuben. His book was *Everything You Always Wanted to Know About Sex, But Were Afraid to Ask*. It was followed two years later by another seller in the millions, *Any Woman Can!*, and more recently by books on nutrition. He moved to the San Diego area around 1962 and practiced psychiatry in a Spring Valley office for many years. He had to cut down his practice, however, when he became a celebrity and popular guest on many TV talk shows.

23. Sid Fleischman. He moved to San Diego at about the age of two, and graduated from San Diego State College. He was a San Diego police reporter and feature writer before writing novels, screenplays, and his popular children's books such as *McBroom Tells a Lie, McBroom and the Beanstalk, The Ghost on Saturday Night*, and 1986 Newbery Medal winner *The Whipping Boy*.

24. Anita Loos. She moved to San Diego as a teenager, and here began her screenwriting career, which led to over 100 scenarios (many written while in high school) and 200 screenplays. While in San Diego she acted in her father's stock company, The Rudwin Theatre, and once played opposite young San Diegan Harold Lloyd.

25. Which Ross MacDonald mystery is set in San Diego?

26. What Coronado author has written 18 children's picture books, usually based on folk tales from around the world?

27. What native San Diegan won both the Nebula and the Hugo awards in 1984 for his science fiction stories?

28. What is the name of the thriller by Michael Crichton (using the pseudonym John Lange) that takes place in San Diego during the 1972 Republican National Convention?

25. *The Goodbye Look.* This 1969 story leads detective Lew Archer here to uncover the secrets of a wealthy family.

26. Benjamin Elkin. Dr. Elkin, resident of Coronado since 1973, is author of such favorites as *Six Foolish Fishermen, The Big Jump and Other Stories, Loudest Noise in the World,* and *The King's Wish and Other Stories.*

27. Greg Bear. This San Diego State University graduate won both the Nebula and the Hugo awards for his story *Blood Music* (later expanded into a novel), and another Nebula award for his story *Hardfought.* His science fiction novels include the popular *Eon* and *The Infinity Concerto.*

28. *Binary.* In this story a mad right-wing millionaire attempts to wipe out all the conventioneers, and with them the entire city of San Diego. At the front of the book the author states, "This book was written before it became too embarrassing for the Republican party to hold its 1972 convention in San Diego, and I prefer not to follow the convention to Miami Beach."

ARCHITECTURE

1. What are the names of the two 1894 red cottages on Coast Boulevard across from La Jolla Cove?

2. What architect was the master planner for the 1915-16 Panama-California Exposition?

3. What 1913 San Diego hotel was designed by John Lloyd Wright, Frank's son?

4. What building material was used to build the houses in San Diego (Old Town) in the 1820s and 1830s?

5. Where in San Diego County is there an exact replica of Lord Tennyson's church in Somersby, England?

6. There are only two true suspension bridges in San Diego City. One is at the Wild Animal Park. Where is the other one?

ARCHITECTURE   A

1. "Red Roost" and "Red Rest." ("Red Roost" was originally named "Neptune.") From the late 1800s until around 1924 the houses in La Jolla had no house numbers, and were known by name only.

2. Bertram Goodhue. He had worked in Boston and New York, and was considered the world's foremost authority on Spanish-Colonial architecture. His lasting achievement here was the California Building (now the Museum of Man) with its much-photographed tower and dome.

3. The Golden West Hotel. It is located at 720 Fourth Avenue, and was originally called the Spreckels Hotel. It was financed by John D. Spreckels to be a workingman's hotel, particularly for those who worked on Spreckels' projects. John Lloyd Wright was only 19 years old at the time, and worked under the supervision of Harrison Albright.

4. Adobe (sun-dried) bricks. These thick-walled homes were warm in winter and cool in summer. Most had tile roofs, though some were thatched, and they had dirt, clay, plank, or tile floors.

5. Glen Abbey Memorial Park, in Bonita. It is called "Little Chapel of the Roses." The design in the window above the altar symbolizes his poem "Crossing the Bar."

6. Spruce Street, between Front and Brant. This footbridge was built in 1912 to give residents access to the streetcars that ran along Fourth Street. It was designed by Edwin M. Capps, city engineer and later mayor of San Diego. The bridge itself is 375 feet long and rises 70 feet above the canyon floor. The bridge on Kilimanjaro Hiking Trail at the Wild Animal Park, built in 1974, is 102 feet long and is 8 feet high at midspan.

7. Of what material is Balboa Park's Timken Art Gallery constructed?

8. In the 1920s Bert L. Vaughn built what stone structure at the southeast corner of San Diego County?

9. What San Diego architect designed the Serra Museum, Lion Clothing Store, Fox Theatre, San Diego Trust and Savings Bank, San Diego Museum of Art, Natural History Museum, and the San Diego Public Library?

10. What Balboa Park building is modeled after a Mayan palace?

11. The Horton Grand Hotel, which opened in the Gaslamp Quarter in 1986, was a reconstruction of what two historic San Diego buildings?

7. Travertine marble. The marble was imported from Italy, and the gallery is trimmed in bronze. It was designed by Frank Hope and Sons, and opened in 1965.

8. The Desert View Tower. It was dedicated to the early pioneers, and stands five miles east of Jacumba on I-8, three miles from the Mexican border. The tower is about 60 feet tall with walls four feet thick, and overlooks the Imperial Valley 3,000 feet below. During World War II it was used as an airplane spotting station.

9. William Templeton Johnson. He came to San Diego in 1912 after being trained at Columbia University and the Académie des Beaux Artes in Paris.

10. The Federal Building. It was built for the 1935-36 exposition, and was a free interpretation of the Palace of the Governor in Uxmal, Yucatán. For the exposition, Congress passed a bill appropriating funds for a permanent building that was to house a U.S. Government exhibit, and that was to be converted later into a theater. The conversion was never accomplished, however, and now the building is used primarily for badminton and volleyball.

11. The Horton Hotel and the Kahle Saddlery building (formerly Brooklyn Hotel). The Horton Hotel at 332 F Street, built in 1886, was originally named Grand Hotel. It was renamed Horton Hotel in 1907, although Alonzo Horton had no connection with it. The Kahle Saddlery building at 733 E Street was built in the 1880s as the Brooklyn Hotel. In 1912 it became known as the Kahle Saddlery, after that saddle and harness shop moved into the first floor where it remained for 66 years. Both buildings had fallen into disrepair, and were saved from demolition by being disassembled piece by piece, and reassembled in their new location at 311 Island Avenue.

12. What is the oldest adobe house still standing in San Diego?

13. The Chart House Restaurant in Coronado is located in what historical landmark?

14. What giant structure stood near the south rim of Highway 78 between Escondido and the San Pasqual Battlefield from 1930 to 1977?

15. On what building in San Diego is there an exact replica of the Old Point Loma Lighthouse tower?

12. Part of the Casa de Carrillo in Old Town (now the clubhouse of Presidio Hills Golf Course). It was built sometime between 1810 and 1820 by Don Francisco María Ruiz, comandante of the presidio, and may have been the first house in Old Town. It was also known as "Pear Garden House" because it was built next to Ruiz's pear garden. Later it was occupied by the Carrillo family, who were Ruiz's relatives. In 1931 part of the original casa was restored, and it was dedicated January 2, 1932, as the clubhouse of the Presidio Hills Golf Club.

13. The Hotel del Coronado Boat House. It was built over Glorietta Bay in 1887. Over the years it has been used as a bathhouse and bathing tank, as a laboratory for the forerunner of Scripps Institution of Oceanography, as a home to the families of the men who tended the hotel's fishing boats, and as headquarters for three yacht clubs. The Chart House acquired it in 1967, and restored and refinished it in Victorian theme.

14. A tepee or wigwam. This 50-foot-high structure was constructed of wood with steel reinforcement rings on a 60-foot concrete slab. It was built by Abraham Houghtelin, a sheep and cattle rancher from Idaho, in 1929-30. He never made it clear why he built it, and it was a curiosity visible for many miles until it was blown down in the storm of December 1977.

15. Tom Ham's Lighthouse Restaurant on Harbor Island. It has a 55-foot cupola in which there is an unmanned beacon that flashes automatically at five-second intervals on a 24-hour schedule. It is said to be the only restaurant in the world that has an official coast guard beacon.

16. On what building in San Diego is this motto inscribed: "Through science and the toil of patient men the nation's thought traverses land and air and sea"?

17. Where is "Brick Row"?

18. How many archways does the Cabrillo Bridge have?

19. What is claimed to be the largest wooden structure in the United States?

20. What is the design of the weather vane atop the California Tower in Balboa Park?

21. The Derby-Pendleton House and the Casa de Altamirano (*San Diego Union* Museum), both in Old Town, and the William Heath Davis House, now in the Gaslamp Quarter, are three of the first prefabricated wooden houses built in San Diego. Where did the wood come from?

22. What was the nickname of the old San Diego High School building that stood on the southwest corner of Balboa Park from 1907 to 1976?

16. The downtown post office at 815 E Street. It was built in 1936-38, sponsored by the W.P.A., and was the city's main post office until the new facility on Midway Drive opened in 1972.

17. National City. One whole side of the 900 block on A Avenue consists of ten individual but connected two-story row houses patterned after the row houses in Philadelphia. They were constructed in 1887 for Frank Kimball, and were to be used for the executives of the Santa Fe Railroad. There are over 240,000 bricks in the structure, many of them from Kimball's own brick kiln. This is probably the only example of row houses on the West Coast.

18. Seven. They are not true arches, however, as the bridge is a cantilever type. The bridge was built for the 1915-16 exposition, and was patterned after a bridge in Ronda, Spain.

19. The Hotel del Coronado. It was constructed largely of redwood, which is fire retarding. In 1916, 30,000 sprinkler heads were installed, giving the hotel one of the best fire insurance ratings in the world.

20. A ship. It is Spanish style, and similar to the one in which Cabrillo sailed in 1542.

21. Maine. The lumber and prefabricated frames and panels were shipped around the Horn in the 1850s, to be assembled here.

22. "The Old Gray Castle" or "The Gray Castle." The school resembled a castle with its towers, parapets, oaken doors, gargoyles, and veneer of granite. Some of the original features such as the doors and gargoyles have been incorporated into the new school.

23. What is the oldest existing brick house in San Diego?

24. The smallest train station in San Diego County is in what city?

25. What downtown restaurant has a 25-foot stained glass dome in the ceiling?

26. What is the highest bridge in San Diego County?

23. The Whaley House. Thomas Whaley built this house in Old Town in 1856-57 of bricks made at his two local brickyards. From 1869 to 1871 the house served as the San Diego County Courthouse and Hall of Records, and now is a historical landmark.

24. La Mesa. The La Mesa Depot was built in 1894 by the San Diego, Cuyamaca, and Eastern Railroad. It was used for passengers until 1928, and later for freight. In the 1950s the building was moved to Lakeside, where in 1974 it was found derelict in a field. In 1980-81 it was returned to its original site at Spring Street and La Mesa Boulevard, and restored by volunteers of the Pacific Southwest Railway Museum Association in cooperation with the La Mesa Historical Society and the City of La Mesa, where it now serves as a museum.

25. The Golden Lion Tavern. This restaurant opened at Fourth and F on January 1, 1907, and served men only. In 1915 it became the Golden Lion Tavern and Grill, and was open to ladies as well. In 1932 it moved to a new location, but recently reopened in the original location. The stained glass dome in the ceiling was constructed in Florence, Italy, in 1906, and was originally installed in the Elks Building in Stockton. Much of the original decor has been either restored or reproduced, and part of the original tile floor, once considered the "handsomest floor in the state," has also been saved.

26. Pine Valley Creek Bridge. It is on Interstate 8 between Japatul Valley Road and Pine Valley. The 1,710-foot-long cantilever structure spans a 450-foot-deep canyon, and was dedicated November 23, 1974.

27. In 1962 the first tall office building since 1928 was erected in downtown San Diego. What was it?

28. What was the first house to be moved to Heritage Park near Old Town?

29. What downtown department store had entrances on four streets?

30. If you were to enter La Jolla's La Valencia Hotel by the front door on Prospect Street, on what floor would you find yourself?

31. Where in San Diego do you find the buildings with the names Zapotec, Toltec, Tarastec, Maya, Olmeca, Zura, and Tenochca?

27. Home Federal Savings and Loan Association, or "Home Tower." This building at Seventh and Broadway is 278 1/2 feet (18 stories) tall. When it opened December 14, 1962, it was the first modern glass and steel skyscraper in San Diego. Recently its ownership changed to Great Western Bank.

28. The Sherman-Gilbert House. It was built in 1887 at Second and Fir by John Sherman, and soon after that was purchased by the Gilbert family, who lived in it until 1965. Through the years many visiting celebrities stayed there, including Anna Pavlova, Fritz Kreisler, Ignace Paderewski, Artur Rubenstein, Marian Anderson, the Trapp Family Singers, and Yehudi Menuhin. The house was saved from demolition and moved to its new location in 1971 by SOHO (Save Our Heritage Organization).

29. Whitney's. The first Whitney and Co. variety store opened in 1905. After five expansions, a grand opening preview was held December 4, 1936, at an enlarged Whitney's, where shoppers could now enter on Fifth, Broadway, Sixth, or E streets. This department store flourished until its closing in 1963.

30. The seventh. The hotel has eight floors, which were numbered four through eleven when it was built in 1928. Therefore the actual lowest floor, down the hill toward the ocean, is called number four. One year the manager changed the numbering of the floors to a more logical system, but received so many complaints that the floors were changed back to their original numbers.

31. San Diego State University campus. They are the names of the residence halls or dormitories. Most are named after early Mexican-Indian tribes.

32. For whom is the main salon of the Civic Theatre named?

33. What was the name of the auditorium of the old San Diego High School?

34. One of architect Louis Kahn's most celebrated buildings is in San Diego. What is it?

35. Where in San Diego is there a replica of the Kinkakuji Temple of Kyoto, Japan?

36. What local college is housed in what was formerly a bowling alley?

32. Beverly Sills. The Beverly Sills Grand Salon was dedicated October 18, 1980, honoring the superstar who had been a major contributor to the San Diego Opera Company's success. A watercolor of her as Juana La Loca, a role she originated here, hangs in the salon.

33. Russ Auditorium. The former name of San Diego High was Russ School, named after Joseph Russ who donated the lumber for the wooden school that opened in 1882. A new masonry building opened in 1907, and the auditorium was erected in 1926. It seated 2,500, and served as San Diego's main community theater for indoor cultural events until the Civic Theatre opened in 1965. In 1973 the Russ was demolished.

34. The Salk Institute for Biological Studies, in La Jolla. It was built in the early 1960s, and overlooks the cliffs and ocean. It is highly praised by architecture critics, and is considered Kahn's most famous work in the West.

35. Sea World, at Pacific Gardens (formerly Japanese Village). It is called the Golden Pavilion, and the exterior was covered by hand with 24 kt. gold foil. In the 16-foot-deep pool next to it, Ama divers descend to the bottom to retrieve pearl-bearing oysters.

36. Coleman College. The school was founded in 1963 at 110 West C as Automation Institute, where classes in data processing were taught. Following a move to Old Town, the college moved again in 1981 to its present site at 7380 Parkway Drive, into what had formerly been La Mesa Bowl. After taking possession of the bowling alley, the school built offices and classrooms and was ready to open within six weeks. Today it offers degrees in Information Science and Computer Electronics Technology.

37. On what building was San Diego's first aviation beacon established?

38. What was the first hotel built in Hotel Circle in Mission Valley?

39. What is the color of the roofs on most of California's Great American First Savings Banks?

40. What is the shape of Archie Moore's swimming pool?

37. San Diego Trust and Savings Bank, at Sixth and Broadway. The six-sided revolving unit with two searchlights and blue and red neon tubes flashed for the first time on July 11, 1928. These lights were in the cupola 240 feet above the sidewalk, and were visible for a radius of more than 25 miles. In December of the same year a fixed beam pointing over Lindbergh Field was added. The revolving unit was not needed for aviation when radio systems were developed, around 1931, but the beam was still used as a maritime beacon.

38. The Town and Country Hotel. In was built in 1953 by restaurateur Charles H. Brown, in what seemed to be an out-of-the-way location. At that time Mission Valley was the home of dairy and vegetable farms, horseback riding stables, and bridle paths. The location proved to be good, however. In 1970 the hotel added its Convention Center, and now Town and Country is the largest hotel in Mission Valley.

39. Blue. Great American was founded in 1885 as San Diego Building and Loan Association. It received a federal charter in 1936 as San Diego Federal Savings and Loan Association, and became Great American First Savings Bank in 1984. The blue tile roofs reflect the bank's patriotic color scheme of red, white, and blue. The familiar logo of three soaring forms was introduced in 1969 and is visible on all 61 branches in San Diego County.

40. A boxing glove. It can be seen from Highway I-15, just south of Highway 94, next to his large brick mansion.

41. What structural addition to a downtown building was featured in *Time, Life*, and *Business Week* in 1956?

42. The Casa de Estudillo adobe house built in Old Town in the mid-1820s by José Antonio de Estudillo was long known by what incorrect name?

43. In what store was San Diego's first escalator installed in 1947?

44. What restaurant is built so close to the ocean shore that the waves at high tide sometimes splash against and occasionally break the plate glass windows?

41. The glass elevator at the El Cortez Hotel. This was the first outside glass hydraulic elevator in the world. It was designed by architect C. J. Paderewski, and installed by Glass Elevator Corporation Inc. of San Diego. It officially opened to the public on May 10, 1956. As many as 16 passengers could ride up to the 15th floor of the hotel and get a panoramic view of the city through the plexiglass walls. An ice skater from the Ice Follies once skated inside it for a publicity stunt.

42. Ramona's Marriage Place (earlier Ramona's House). Although Helen Hunt Jackson made it clear that her characters Ramona and Alessandro were married in a chapel, this house became known as their marriage place, possibly because it contained a chapel. Also it was good publicity for the house to have that name because it brought many visitors to Old Town.

43. The Walker Scott store, at Fifth and Broadway. The escalator, narrow by more recent standards, carried shoppers from the street floor to the second, and from the second to the third. Walker's vacated that location in January 1985, but the escalator, though currently not in use, remains.

44. The Marine Room. It is located at La Jolla Shores at 2000 Spindrift Drive. The windows were broken by waves several times soon after it was built in the late 1930s, so shortly after World War II special 3/4 inch tempered plate glass windows were installed. All was well until the severe storm of December 1, 1982, shattered the glass.

45. The ceiling in the Hotel del Coronado's Crown Room is constructed of what type of wood?

46. Where in San Diego is there a replica of the Mukilteo Lighthouse of Everett, Washington?

47. What was the first hotel to be built at Mission Bay Park?

48. What now occupies the 1899 San Diego Rowing Clubhouse?

45. Sugar pine. The 33-foot-high arched ceiling is hand-fitted and held together with wooden pegs instead of nails. It is one of the largest support-free rooms in North America, and has no interior posts or pillars or other visible supports. Twice a year it is polished by four men lying on scaffolds. It takes them ten days to polish the wood with linseed oil, and buff it with dry mops.

46. Seaport Village. The 45-foot-high lighthouse re-creates in great detail the famous Northern Pacific lighthouse built soon after the turn of the century. It is regarded as Seaport Village's official symbol, and towers above the other buildings there.

47. The Bahia Motor Hotel (now Bahia Resort Hotel). William D. Evans started it soon after the dredging in Mission Bay had created some new points and islands. When the hotel opened in 1954 it consisted of 50 rental units, a restaurant, a pool, and a cocktail lounge.

48. The Chart House Restaurant. This old clubhouse on steamship wharf at Fifth and Harbor Drive was dedicated January 1, 1900. In 1975 it was designated Site No. 105 by the San Diego Historical Site Board, and in 1979 was chosen for the National Register of Historic Places. That year the San Diego Rowing Club moved to a new clubhouse on Mission Bay, so the future of the old clubhouse was threatened. Concerned citizens formed San Diegans For The Rowing Clubhouse Inc. in 1980 to try to preserve it. It was then bought by Chart House Inc., refurbished, and opened for business in June 1983.

49. According to the 1989 *World Almanac,* what is currently the tallest building in San Diego?

50. In what city do you find two houses in the shape of boats, side by side on a residential street?

51. What is the name of the tall tower on the old library building at San Diego State University?

52. What structure built in San Diego in 1914-15 was hailed as the world's largest municipal structure?

53. What is the only downtown building that has a revolving door?

49. First Interstate Bank. This 24-story bank building at Fourth and B tops all others here at 398 feet. It is followed by California First Bank (388 feet), First National Bank (379 feet), and The Meridian (371 feet), all three with 27 stories. Symphony Towers, currently under construction at Seventh and B, will soon lay claim to the title.

50. Encinitas. They were built in 1929 by a retired marine engineer, in the 700 block of Third Street. They are constructed of stucco and wood, and are complete with two decks and port holes.

51. Hardy Memorial Tower. This Moorish tower, the dominant feature on the campus, was built in 1931 when the college was moved to Montezuma Mesa. In 1975 it was named in memory of Dr. Edward L. Hardy, who served as the second president of San Diego State College, from 1910 to 1935. The tower is equipped with a carillon chimes system.

52. Balboa Stadium. Originally called simply Stadium or City Stadium, it was next to San Diego High School on Russ Boulevard, and was used for school, amateur, and professional sports. Twenty-five tiers of solid concrete ran around the field. When the Chargers moved here in 1961 it was enlarged with the addition of an upper deck.

53. San Diego Trust and Savings Bank. This 1928 building at Sixth and Broadway features a large bronze revolving door between two hinged doors. A tall Romanesque archway decorated with three bands of carved sandstone surrounds the doors.

54. In the late 1800s, what San Diego building became the largest structure outside of New York City to be electrically lighted?

55. Michaels (formerly Moskatel's) in Mission Valley Center West, La Mesa Post Office Carrier Annex, and San Diego Medical Health Center on Lake Murray Boulevard at Highway 8 all have a common background. What were these three buildings used for in the past?

56. What hotel still operating in San Diego County was started by a former slave?

57. How many bells are in the campanario (bell tower) of Mission San Diego?

54. The Hotel del Coronado. This phenomenon was so unfamiliar to the general public that the guest rooms displayed small signs stating: "This room is equipped with the Edison Electric Light. Do not attempt to light with a match. Simply turn key on the wall by the door. The use of electricity for lighting is in no way harmful to health, nor does it affect soundness of sleep."

55. Ice skating rinks. Michaels in Mission Valley was the Mission Valley Ice Plaza (later Mission Valley Ice Arena), an open-air rink, from 1963 to 1970. The Post Office Annex at 6055 Lake Murray Boulevard was the Iceland Ice Skating Rink from 1959 to around 1965. San Diego Medical Health Center at 5333 Lake Murray Boulevard was the La Mesa House of Ice from 1969 to April 1983. It was used by the San Diego Gulls for their practice sessions, and for games of the San Diego Amateur Hockey Association.

56. The Julian Hotel. Albert Robinson came to San Diego in the 1870s with his former master, and while working as a cook met and married Margaret Tull. They soon opened a small restaurant and bakery, and in 1897, as their reputation grew, built the Hotel Robinson. Mrs. Robinson sold it in 1921, at which time the name was changed to Julian Hotel. It is now operated as a Victorian-style bed and breakfast inn.

57. Five. After secularization of the mission in 1833 the original bells were scattered, but after a long search some were recovered and reinstated. In 1894 Father Ubach gathered up six bells that had been brought by the missionaries from New Spain, and had them melted down and recast into one large bell named "Mater Dolorosa" (Our Lady of Sorrow), which is the 1,200-pound bell on the lower right.

58. What was formerly situated on the site of the Veterans'
     War Memorial Building in Balboa Park?

59. What was the name of the Carlsbad restaurant famous
     for its family-style fried chicken dinners and for the four
     large chickens by the front corner?

58. An Indian Village. This was constructed by the Santa Fe Railroad Company for the 1915-16 Panama-California Exposition, and consisted of cliff dwellings, hogans, pueblos, and tepees. Here Zuñi, Navajo, Havasupai, Hopi, Apache, and Indians of other tribes lived and displayed their talents of weaving, pottery-making, jewelry-making, and ceremonial dancing. The whole area was called The Painted Desert. After the exposition the pueblo structures were used by the Boy Scouts, and then by the 21st Artillery during World War I. The Scouts again used it until they loaned it to the 1935-36 exposition for another Indian exhibit. Afterwards they took possession again, until the structure was declared unsafe and razed in 1946.

59. Twin Inns. In the late 1880s, leaders of the Carlsbad Land and Water Company built two large Victorian homes across the street from each other on what is now Carlsbad Boulevard at Elm Avenue. The north home was turned into a restaurant soon after the turn of the century, and was a popular stopping place for travelers between Los Angeles and San Diego or Tijuana. The four seven-foot-high chickens were a landmark since the early 1950s, and once a letter addressed to "Big Hen Inn, near Carlsbad, San Diego County" arrived there correctly when the writer could not remember the correct name. Recently the restaurant reopened as Neimans, but since customers still inquired about the removed chickens, one was returned to its spot on Carlsbad Boulevard for a short time. It will next be placed in the Village Faire shopping plaza that will be built soon behind Neimans.

60. What is the longest pier in San Diego County?

61. What was the original use of the round building in Balboa Park which is now the Centro Cultural de la Raza?

62. What San Diego County church building was once a railroad station?

63. In what San Diego County building are the three oldest existing Otis elevators still running?

64. What structure stood on the site of the present Balboa Club at Sixth and Ivy from the 1920s through the 1950s?

60. Ocean Beach Pier. It is 1,950 feet long over the ocean, plus 55 feet on stationing, giving it a total length straight out of 2,005 feet. At the end it forms a T, making the actual pier length 2,500 feet. Coming in a close second in length is Oceanside Pier at 1,942 feet.

61. A water tank. It was built during World War II to hold an auxiliary water supply for the Naval Hospital. Since 1971 it has been a center for the creation, promotion, and preservation of Mexican and Chicano art and culture. A brightly colored Mexican-American mural decorates the building, which stands on Park Boulevard south of Pepper Grove.

62. La Jolla United Methodist Church. The building was constructed in 1924 as a power substation and passenger station for the San Diego Electric Railway on what is now La Jolla Boulevard. In the early 1950s it was converted into a temporary church sanctuary, and when new structures were added it became the main chapel. The passenger waiting area has been enclosed, and serves as the church's youth center.

63. The Hotel del Coronado. The three elevators at the hotel are numbered 61, 62, and 63, and have been in operation since opening day in 1888. As far as the Otis Elevator Company can determine, these three are probably the oldest Otis elevators still in operation of the over ten million Otis elevators throughout the world.

64. An aviary. Most of the birds in the large cages there were domesticated stock. In 1960, the crosstown freeway cut off the southwest corner of Balboa Park where the Balboa Club had stood at Sixth and Date for 30 years. To take its place, a new facility was built in 1961 at Sixth and Ivy where the aviary had stood, as a place for shuffleboard, horseshoes, and card and board games.

65. What is the smallest public library in San Diego County?

66. What was the original name of the hotel that housed San Diego's famous Mississippi Room?

67. What San Diego bank had a shooting gallery on the roof?

65. The Descanso Library. This branch of the San Diego County Library System is probably the smallest free-standing building housing just a library in the whole state. At 192 square feet it was a contender for the smallest library in the U.S., but lost to an even smaller one in Ocracoke, North Carolina. The Descanso Library moved into its present white frame building in 1960. It has about 3,200 books and pamphlets, but no place for patrons to sit, and has parking space for only one car.

66. Imig Manor. This Southern mansion-style hotel was built by San Diego builder Larry Imig in 1946 on El Cajon Boulevard, when that street was the main east-west thoroughfare through the city. In its early days the hotel was a favorite vacation spot for Hollywood celebrities such as Ava Gardner and Lana Turner. In 1949 it changed ownership and became the Hotel Manor (or Manor Hotel), and in 1955 became the Lafayette Hotel and Club. For many years the Mississippi Room (next to Mississippi Street) was the favorite "hot spot" for San Diegans, and big bands led by Ted Fio Rito, Jack McLean, and Bill Green performed there. The Mississippi Room flourished until 1981 when it was converted to the Roxy West. It has since reopened as the Mississippi Room, serving as a place for banquets, receptions, and meetings.

67. San Diego Trust and Savings Bank, at Sixth and Broadway. The shooting gallery was put in when the present building was built in 1928. It was used by the bank's employees for recreation, and to discourage bank robbers. It was 75 feet deep and had a steel backstop with soundproof walls and roof. Rifles, revolvers, and ammunition were supplied by the bank. The FBI also made use of the shooting range, but when they moved out in the early 1950s, the range was converted into offices.

68. What is the only pier on the West Coast that provides lodging over the ocean?

69. What is currently the largest hotel in San Diego County?

70. What was the last operating one-room schoolhouse in San Diego County?

71. What is the name of the chapel in Balboa Park?

68. Crystal Pier. This Pacific Beach pier was dedicated in 1926. It was widened in 1935, and on April 19 of the following year the quaint Crystal Cottages with knotty pine walls and promenade decks were opened. In 1961 they were painted blue and white, and now they are part of Crystal Pier Motor Hotel.

69. The San Diego Marriott Hotel. This hotel and marina on West Harbor Drive, just east of Seaport Village, opened in 1983 as the Inter-Continental Hotel. In October 1987 it was transferred to the Marriott Coropration. With the opening of the south tower on January 1, 1988, the hotel now offers 1,364 guestrooms, including 100 suites.

70. Spencer Valley School. It was built in 1876, and lies just northwest of Julian on Highway 79 in the Wynola area. It lost its one-room status in 1986 when three additional rooms were added.

71. St. Francis Chapel. It was built for the 1915-16 Panama-California Exposition, in the Plaza de California next to what is now the south building of the Museum of Man. The interior of the chapel resembles that of an early California mission in its stark simplicity. It is highlighted by a gilded altarpiece. The non-sectarian chapel was used extensively by the Navy during World War II for weddings, and is now again being used for that purpose.

72. The house called Casa de las Joyas is located in what part of San Diego?

73. When it was built in 1911-12, what San Diego building was believed to be the largest reinforced concrete building in California?

72. La Jolla. This landmark at 2440 Torrey Pines Road was created by Herbert Palmer, English architect and natural son of Queen Victoria's son Edward (later Edward VII). He began it in 1927 and took five years to complete it. Because of its three domes, the Casa de las Joyas (House of the Jewels) is sometimes referred to as the "Little Taj Mahal." Legends have sprung up that there are hidden jewels in the house, that it once served as a harem, and that it was a bootleggers' hideaway during Prohibition. It originally was to have been the house of the president of a school of architecture, but the Depression ended that dream.

73. The Spreckels Theatre Building. This neo-baroque structure on Broadway between First and Second avenues consists of a large six-story office building, in the center of which is a lavish theater. The stage is 82 by 58 feet (one of the largest in the U.S. at the time), and three 88-foot steel trusses span the auditorium. Because of the large exits on both sides of the stage, live horses could be used easily in productions. On opening night, August 23, 1912, the audience was delighted with the acoustics as well as with the rich marble and onyx decor and mural-covered ceiling.

ART

1. What is the name of the large steel sculpture on the mall of the Federal Building at Front and E streets?

2. Who is represented by the equestrian statue located in the Plaza de Panama in Balboa Park?

3. What renowned artist was commissioned by the Hotel del Coronado to paint a picture of the old Coronado polo fields with the hotel in the background?

4. What San Diego sculptor created the *Guardian of Water* statue in front of the harbor entrance to the San Diego County Administration Center?

5. In 1975, when the San Diego Museum of Art celebrated its 50th anniversary, the Carl Skinner Memorial Gallery housing an Asian art court was dedicated. What prominent person dedicated it?

6. What famous El Cajon Western artist has works in the Cowboy Hall of Fame?

7. What is the symbol on the "Scenic Drive" signs in the city of San Diego?

1. *Excalibur.* This 32-foot by 40-foot by 60-foot structure was built by internationally known sculptress Beverly Pepper in 1976.

2. El Cid (El Cid Campeador). The statue of this eleventh-century Spanish hero was created by Anna Hyatt Huntington, and dedicated in 1930. It was made from a mold of the original statue which is in the court of the Museum of the Hispanic Society in New York. A third one is in Seville, Spain.

3. LeRoy Neiman. The large painting *Del Coronado Petit Galop*, dated April 1976, hangs in the hotel hall next to the lobby.

4. Donal Hord. The 30-ton statue, completed in 1939, was made from a block of silver grey granite from Lakeside which was shipped to his studio in Pacific Beach. The lady (sometimes called *Mother of Waters*) is 13 feet tall, and the overall height of the fountain in which she sits is 23 feet. In his day Hord was acknowledged as the foremost sculptor on the West Coast, and is the only local artist to be named a Fellow of the National Sculpture Society.

5. Betty Ford. She was First Lady of the United States at the time.

6. Olaf Wieghorst. He was a San Diego County resident from 1947 until his death in 1988. Many collectors and curators considered him to be the nation's leading painter of the American West.

7. A sea gull. Two hundred of these blue and yellow signs were placed approximately every 1/4 mile on the Scenic Drive, which has recently been extended beyond its original 52 miles.

8. French artist Françoise Gilot, author of *Life With Picasso*, married what prominent San Diegan in 1970?

9. Where is the May S. Marcy Sculpture Garden?

10. What husband and wife team created the copper decorations for the new Civic Theatre, which opened in 1965?

11. On the base of the fountain in Horton Plaza there are bronze medallions of three men important in San Diego's history. Who are they?

12. What animal is the symbol for TraveLodge?

8. Dr. Jonas Salk. They had met the previous year when Ms. Gilot was visiting a French friend whose husband worked for the Salk Institute for Biological Studies in La Jolla.

9. In Balboa Park (in part of the courtyard of the Museum of Fine Arts). Mrs. Marcy was president of the Fine Arts Society in the 1950s, and she and her husband were patrons of the museum. Some of the contemporary sculptors represented in the garden are Barbara Hepworth, Henry Moore, George Rickey, and Bernard Rosenthal.

10. Ellamarie and Jackson Woolley. Their folded and hammered copper and enamel reliefs decorated the stage and foyer areas. When the theater was redecorated in 1980 these ornaments were removed, but one sample was hung in the lobby where it may still be viewed.

11. Cabrillo, Father Serra, and Alonzo Horton. The fountain, financed by Louis Wilde, was designed by Irving Gill and modeled after the choragic monument of Lysicrates in Athens. It was the first successful attempt to combine colored lights with flowing water, and was dedicated October 15, 1910, when the US Grant Hotel opened across the street.

12. Sleepy Bear. The advertising committee for TraveLodge (an El Cajon-based company) wanted to create a symbol to represent California's state bear and also a comfortable night's sleep, so Sleepy Bear became the official trademark in 1954. Since then he has appeared on television and in parades, has been cuddled as a stuffed doll and puppet, cast as a Jim Beam bottle, and has become the basis of two clubs, including the Sleepy Bear Club for youngsters. The over 40,000 members of this club receive buttons, rings, patches, and T- shirts, plus personal letters from Sleepy Bear himself.

13. Where in San Diego is the Schweigardt Fountain, also called the *Four Corners of American Democracy* fountain?

14. What UCSD sculptor is known for his massive cubist-style wooden heads, as well as his tall slender figures made of Monterey pine branches?

15. What prominent San Diego couple is made up of a husband who is an artist and a wife who is a social journalist?

16. The three full statues and two busts on the façade of the Museum of Art in Balboa Park depict five seventeenth-century painters. Name at least three of them.

17. All but one of the founders of the Patterning and Decoration movement of the early 1970s were New Yorkers. What Encinitas artist was the West Coast member of this art movement?

13. In the Balboa Park Club, in Balboa Park. It was created by Frederick W. Schweigardt in 1935 for the California-Pacific International Exposition, in the building that was then called the Palace of Education. The four corners, represented by four figures, are Home, School, Community, and Church.

14. Italo Scanga. This Italian artist came to UCSD in 1978. He has had showings at the Whitney Museum of American Art in New York, the Los Angeles Museum of Contemporary Art, and the Los Angeles County Museum of Art.

15. Everett Gee and Eileen Jackson. Everett Gee Jackson is a distinguished painter and illustrator of fine books, and was chairman of the San Diego State College Art Department for many years, until his retirement in 1963. His wife, Eileen Jackson, has written society columns for San Diego newspapers for over 65 years, and was the first female editor of San Diego High School's newspaper, *The Russ*. The Jacksons have been married since 1926.

16. Murillo, Velásquez, and Zurbarán are the three full statues, and Ribera and El Greco are the busts. The building, originally called the Fine Arts Gallery, was designed by William Templeton Johnson, and opened February 28, 1926.

17. Kim MacConnel. As part of this revolt against minimalism, MacConnel painted floral and geometric designs on large fabric panels, and designed brightly decorated furniture. He has had exhibitions at the Holly Solomon Gallery in New York, as well as galleries in Europe. He received his BA and MFA from UCSD, and was on the faculty there from 1976 to 1978, and again beginning in 1987.

18. Name the locations of these two Donal Hord sculptures: *Montezuma* and *Spring Stirring*.

19. Name the locations of these two Donal Hord sculptures: *West Wind* and *Aztec Woman of Tehuantapec*.

20. Bernard Lansky, who graduated from San Diego High School in 1943, is the creator of what nationally syndicated cartoon?

21. What native American artisan, famous for making blackware pottery, was a part of the 1915-16 Panama-California Exposition?

18. San Diego State University, and University of California at San Diego (specifically the Institute of Geophysics and Planetary Physics branch of Scripps Institution of Oceanography). *Montezuma*, also called *Monty* or *Aztec*, was sculpted of black diorite from a quarry near Escondido in 1936-37. It was moved to its new location on the grassy entrance to the school in 1984. *Spring Stirring*, also of black diorite, was sculpted in 1947-48, and purchased and donated to Scripps Institution in 1964.

19. The San Diego Public Library, and the House of Hospitality courtyard in Balboa Park. *West Wind*, a 1953 rosewood statue, is located in the third floor Wangenheim Room of the library. *Aztec Woman*, or *La Tehuana of Tehuantapec*, made of Indiana limestone, sits in a tiled fountain in the park.

20. "Seventeen." Lansky moved to San Diego when he was 13, and contributed to *The Lit Parade*, the anthology of student writing and art at San Diego High, and the school newspaper, *The Russ*. While still in high school he had his work published in the *San Diego Union* and *Evening Tribune*. The cartoon teenager Sheldon was created for "Seventeen," which in its heyday was published in over 100 newspapers, and read by 60 million readers. Bernard's brother, Jordan Lansky, was creator of the golf comic strip "Mac Divot."

21. Maria Martinez (Maria the Potter) of San Ildefonso. She and her husband Julian were selected by Dr. Edgar L. Hewett to demonstrate their pottery-making skills within the Indian Village pueblo on the exposition grounds. It was while they were here that the couple first succeeded in making large chimney pots. Maria and Julian are credited with rediscovering the ancient San Ildefonso technique of making blackware pottery, and Maria went on to become the most famous and respected of all Pueblo Indian potters.

22. The sculpture *Tall Tale* by Kenneth Snelson is located on what college campus?

23. Arthur Putnam created three statues for E. W. Scripps that told the story of the historical periods of our country. The first two are located in Presidio Park. What are their names?

22. San Diego City College. Internationally renowned Snelson is best known for his aluminum and stainless steel cylinders supported from within by wire rope cables. Such a structure is the 1976 *Tall Tale*, which stands 20 feet high on the lawn near Twelfth and B streets.

23. *The Indian* and *The Padre*. Arthur Putnam, one of the finest sculptors of his day, spent part of his youth and adulthood in San Diego County. E. W. Scripps commissioned him to create a series of statues for his Miramar Ranch, but Putnam was able to complete only three before surgery in 1911 left him incapacitated. *The Indian* and *The Padre* (Father Junípero Serra), both bronze, have been given to the San Diego Historical Society by the descendants of E. W. Scripps. The third sculpture, *The Ploughman*, is at the Scripps Institution of Oceanography.

PLACE NAMES

1. What town in San Diego County is named after a fictional heroine?

2. What was the former name of Broadway in San Diego?

3. What was the name of the artists' colony in La Jolla that was established in the 1890s and 1900s by Anna Held?

4. Where in San Diego City is Easy Street?

5. What is the name of the largest of La Jolla's seven natural caves, named for the profile that can be seen at the cave entrance?

PLACE NAMES   A

1. Ramona. A town called Nuevo had sprung up there in the Santa Maria Valley around the 1870s. In 1884, Milton Santee surveyed and subdivided 6,000 or 7,000 acres there, and soon the name of the town was changed to Ramona, after the heroine of Helen Hunt Jackson's popular novel.

2. D Street. It was renamed Broadway in 1913 by Louis J. Wilde, businessman, banker, and later mayor of San Diego. In 1907 he purchased the Golden Hill mansion on 24th and D, now called the Quartermass-Wilde House, and wanted his residence to have an address more prestigious than D Street. Also, it is said that he wanted to be known as "The Man Who Made Broadway." Prior to this, D Street was sometimes called Spring Street because of the artesian wells that were dug there to bring water to the residents of Davis' New Town in the 1850s, and sometimes called Seventh Street as a part of New Town.

3. The Green Dragon Colony. Miss Held named it after a story by her friend Beatrice Harraden, and it became a cultural colony for artists, musicians, writers, and actors. The colony is still there, on Prospect Street, and now consists of art galleries, specialty shops, a restaurant, and residences.

4. In the Oak Park or Chollas area. It is a two-block-long street west of 54th Street.

5. Sunny Jim Cave. Visitors may enter through the La Jolla Cave and Shell Shop and descend 133 steps to see his profile. There are several stories concerning the origin of the name: Sunny Jim was a local Indian; he was a cartoon character on the box of the British breakfast cereal Force Wheat Flakes; he was "Sunny Jim" Rolph Jr., former governor of California; or he was merely a smiling face.

6. What is the name of the road that links the missions of Mexico and California?

7. What is the popular name of the residential area west of Balboa Park between First and Fourth avenues?

8. What community's streets are named for Greek and Roman gods and goddesses?

9. What is the popular name of the beach located below the Self-Realization Fellowship in Encinitas?

10. What San Diego community was once called "Mussel Beach"?

11. In the late 1880s, a group of settlers from Boston moved to the east county to raise citrus fruits and grapes. What did they call their community?

6. El Camino Real. It is variously translated as "The Royal Road," and "The King's Highway."

7. "Banker's Hill." Wealthy businessmen and prominent citizens settled here after the turn of the century because it was close to the downtown area. Houses by such prominent architects as Irving Gill, Richard Requa, and Frank Mead are found here.

8. Leucadia's. The town itself is named after a Greek Ionian Island renowned for its olive oil, currants, and wine. It was developed and named by a group of British spiritualists who came to the U.S. around 1885 seeking religious freedom. Being avid readers of the Greek classics they gave Greek and Roman names to all their streets, such as Hermes, Hygeia, Neptune, Glaucus, Hymettus, Orpheus, Vulcan, Diana, Jupiter, and Jason.

9. Swami's. The beach is called this because the Fellowship retreat overlooking it was built for Paramahansa Yogananda, and has architecture featuring large gold lotus towers.

10. Ocean Beach. It was called this or else "Mussel Beds" because of the mussels that were gathered there for Sunday picnics. It was also known by several other names: Los Medanos, meaning "The Dunes," because of the high white sand dunes there; and Palmer's Place, Palmer's Ranch, or Palmiros, names popular from the 1850s to the 1870s because of a now-forgotten Mr. Palmer.

11. Bostonia. This is now a part of the city of El Cajon. In the early days it made a name for itself with international-prize-winning raisins from one of the largest raisin ranches in Southern California.

12. What town was developed to lure summer visitors away from the heat of Imperial Valley?

13. Lots on what hill were given away to persons who purchased an encyclopedia set?

14. Name all 23 tree or vine streets in the heart of San Diego that run alphabetically from Ash to Walnut.

15. What was the original name of Belmont Park?

12. Imperial Beach. It was named around 1906 or 1908 by E. W. Peterson, manager of the South San Diego Investment Company, and was subdivided by George Chaffey. The developers hoped to induce Imperial Valley residents to build summer homes on the beach.

13. Dictionary Hill. In the early 1900s, lots on this steep hill in Spring Valley were given away free as premiums to persons who bought the 25-volume set *The Library of Universal History and Popular Science*. The hill was known as Encyclopedia Hill for a while, but soon became Dictionary Hill because that was easier to say. Many of the buyers lived in the Midwest and never saw their land, which they usually relinquished for non-payment of taxes. The engineers who made the original subdivision maps had never seen the area, and laid out the streets as though the land were flat. Consequently, the streets on this steep hill are perpendicular rather than spiral.

14. Ash, Beech, Cedar, Date, Elm, Fir, Grape, Hawthorn, Ivy, Juniper, Kalmia, Laurel, Maple, Nutmeg, Olive, Palm, Quince, Redwood, Spruce, Thorn, Upas, Vine, and Walnut.

15. Mission Beach Amusement Center (or Park). This 30-acre recreation area, which opened in 1925, included an indoor bathhouse with 1,500 dressing rooms, skating rink, fun zone, merry-go-round, ferris wheel, roller coaster, and a ballroom where some of the biggest name bands in the country performed during the big band era. John D. Spreckels spent $4,000,000 developing the amusement center, which was at the end of one of his streetcar lines. He hoped that it would draw the middle class, and that the aristocrats would continue to patronize Coronado, but Mission Beach was so successful that everyone wanted to go there.

16. In 1973, a Kearny Mesa street name was changed to Mesa College Drive because residents and students considered the old name to be too warlike. What was the former name of the street?

17. What community had a post office named "Nellie" for over 35 years?

18. What is the name of the traffic circle street that is the center of Borrego Springs?

19. What community in San Diego County, named for a seaport in Wales, has British place names for its streets?

20. What was the first name of Ballast Point, the spit of land on the lee side of Point Loma?

16. Artillery Drive. The street was named Artillery Drive in 1955 because it went past the California National Guard Armory.

17. Palomar Mountain. In 1883 Miss Nellie McQueen wrote to the postmaster general asking for a post office in her community, and offering to become postmaster. She suggested Fern Glen as the name of the post office, but the name Nellie was picked instead, and all mail for Palomar was addressed to Nellie, California. It was not until 1920 that the post office name was changed to Palomar Mountain.

18. Christmas Circle. Developers originally named the streets after cattle brand names, and the circle was named XMS. The road department interpreted this as XMAS, so it became Christmas Circle. For many years Santa Claus arrived in the grassy area that the circle encloses, to bring gifts to every child in Borrego.

19. Cardiff-by-the-Sea. The town and streets were named by Mrs. Frank Cullen, wife of the developer. She was from Cardiff, Wales, and chose streets named for English, Scottish, and Irish places, such as Manchester, Chesterfield, Oxford, Glasgow, Edinburg, Dublin, and Kilkenny.

20. Punta Guijarros, or La Punta de los Guijarros (Cobblestone Point). Vizcaíno gave it this name in 1602 because the cobblestones there made good ballast. New England ships bringing merchandise to San Diego in the 1800s sometimes sailed home with these rocks, and tradition has it that Boston's streets are lined with stones from this point. The name was changed to Ballast Point sometime in the 1830s.

21. Where is Dead Men's Point (La Punta de los Muertos)?

22. In what city in San Diego County is Cape Cod Village?

23. A five-mile stretch of Old Highway 395 leading past Lawrence Welk's Country Club village was given what new name in 1980?

24. When Palomar Observatory was being built, what was the road leading up to it called?

25. What was the original name of Mission Bay?

21. At the corner of Market Street and Pacific Highway. There
    is some uncertainty about who is actually buried there. Most
    recent historians think that this name commemorated the
    sailors who died from scurvy on the two ships that were the
    first to survey San Diego Bay, in 1782. A historical plaque to
    this effect stands on the southeast corner of the intersection,
    which incidentally was at water's edge before extensive
    filling altered the shoreline. It is unclear, however, whether
    Don Juan Pantoja, pilot of one of the survey ships, referred
    to this spot as the burial place for his men, or for those who
    had died of scurvy on the two ships arriving here in 1769 at
    the time Father Serra came overland. A plaque to *that* effect
    stands on the southwest corner of the intersection. Take your
    pick.

22. Oceanside. This village of shops, restaurants, and a facsimile
    lighthouse was built at Oceanside Harbor in 1965, and is
    reminiscent of an old whaling village.

23. Champagne Boulevard. Lawrence Welk paid for the new
    freeway signs.

24. Highway to the Stars. The road was built in 1935 as a means
    for transporting the heavy equipment used in construction of
    the observatory.   Today the official name of the road is
    Canfield Road.

25. False Bay (Puerto Falso or Bahia Falsa). There are several
    versions of how this name originated. One is that some of
    Cabrillo's crew members got lost while ashore, and ended up
    at this bay while trying to return to San Diego Bay. Another
    is that early explorers assumed that it was a good bay for
    sailing, but became mired in the mud flats and sloughs. A
    third is that it resembled San Diego Bay in shape.

26. In 1986, Market Street was temporarily renamed Martin Luther King Way. What was the name of the street immediately prior to the name Market?

27. In 1910, what area of San Diego was named after a Spanish explorer?

28. Emerald City Drive and Yellow Brick Road are streets in what town?

29. What was the old name of the extreme tip of Point Loma?

30. What is the popular name for the area west of Balboa Park around Fourth, Fifth, and Sixth avenues?

31. For what university was University Heights named?

26. H Street. The downtown streets were given letter names around 1867 by Alonzo Horton. In 1915, H Street was changed to Market Street after San Francisco's famous Market Street. Before it was Market Street, when it was a part of Davis and Gray's New Town of 1850, it was called Commercial.

27. Balboa Park. A name contest was held because the park had no name other than "City Park." The name Balboa was submitted by Mrs. Harriet Phillips in honor of the Spanish explorer who discovered the Pacific Ocean in 1513.

28. Valley Center. This is a small town northeast of Escondido.

29. Pelican Point. It was named either for pelicans there or for a rock formation shaped like a pelican. The first time this name appeared in print was in 1891, when the lower lighthouse was established there, but the name is seldom used today.

30. "Pill Hill." It is called that because of the many medical and dental offices and laboratories there.

31. San Diego College of Arts and Sciences. This was to be a branch of the Methodist-sponsored University of Southern California. Land was donated in 1886 by the College Hill Land Association, and proceeds from the sale of other land in the area were to go to the building of the school. By 1887, however, the land boom broke and the college was never built.

32. What community in north San Diego County was started by a group of Germans in 1884 as a site for fruit trees and grape vines?

33. For whom is the San Diego Community Concourse named?

34. When Laurel Street was extended through Balboa Park at the time of the 1915-16 Panama-California Exposition, what name was it given?

35. For what or whom was the city of Coronado named?

32. Olivenhain. The name chosen meant "olive grove," but rather than olive trees, hundreds of fruit trees and 30,000 grape vines were planted. Lack of water, and fraud and misrepresentation on the part of the leader unfortunately soon brought an end to these endeavors. The colonists changed their crops to grain, and then in 1905 to beans, particularly the lima bean. Olivenhain remained a farming community until the 1960s, when urbanization became predominant.

33. Charles C. Dail, mayor of San Diego from 1955-1963. The Community Concourse opened in 1964, and Dail participated in the ribbon-cutting ceremony. In May 1974, the facilities were renamed Charles C. Dail Concourse by agreement of the City Council, because during his terms of office as mayor, Dail had strongly promoted the building of the Civic Theatre and Convention Hall.

34. El Prado. Paseo del Prado is the name of one of the most fashionable promenades in Madrid, and the location of its famous museum of art, the Prado.

35. The Los Coronados Islands (Las Islas de los Coronados). They lie in Mexican waters about 15 miles below San Diego. These islands were named by Vizcaíno (or by Father Antonio de la Ascensión, the priest who sailed with him) when they were sighted on November 8, 1602. The name commemorated Los Cuatro Martires Coronados (the four crowned martyrs) who were killed for their faith in early Rome under Diocletian, and whose holy day was November 8. In 1886 Babcock and Story, the first promoters of Coronado, conducted a contest to name their new development, and selected Coronado as the winning name.

36. What subdivision of San Diego is named for the three silent movie star sisters who helped develop it?

37. What city in San Diego County is named after a town in Bohemia famed for its mineral waters?

38. What was an early name of Cabrillo Canyon in Balboa Park, where the Cabrillo Freeway now runs?

39. What prestigious city in San Diego County formerly had its post office named "Weed"?

40. What was the official name of the old coast highway that was referred to as "Suicide Highway," "Murder Row," "Slaughter Alley," and "Death Row"?

41. What was the name of the mud flats near the present MCRD and Lindbergh Field that connected Point Loma to the mainland?

36. Talmadge Park. There you find Constance Drive, Norma Drive, and Natalie Drive. The sisters lent their name and money to the development, and entertained at the dedication on January 3, 1926.

37. Carlsbad. It was named after Karlsbad, Bohemia, when it was discovered that the mineral water found here in 1883 by John A. Frazier was similar to that of Well Number Nine in Karlsbad, one of Europe's most popular spas. The name of the town was changed from Frazier's Station to Carlsbad, Americanizing the spelling.

38. Pound Canyon. It was called that because the City Pound for stray horses, cattle, and dogs was located there. It was also sometimes known as Rattlesnake Canyon because of the many rattlesnakes there.

39. Del Mar. William S. Weed, an early rancher, was appointed postmaster at Weed, a station named for him before the post office of Del Mar was established. The new name of Del Mar was suggested by Mrs. Loup, wife of another early rancher, Theodore M. Loup, because she had read a popular ballad entitled "The Fight of Paso del Mar," written by Bayard Taylor. She remembered the melodramatic verse, and suggested the name Del Mar, which became the official town name October 22, 1885.

40. Highway 101. There were so many accidents on narrow 101 that Del Mar and Solana Beach put up a white cross alongside the highway for each traffic death, in hopes that these would provide a deterrent to careless and speeding drivers.

41. Dutch Flats. No one seems to know the origin of this name. It was here that the first Ryan Field and several of T. C. Ryan's early companies were located.

42. In 1888, Harr Wagner, editor of *The Golden Era* magazine, ran a contest to choose a new name for what geographical area of San Diego?

43. What town name is usually interpreted as meaning "slimy water"?

44. Sixth Avenue on the west side of Balboa Park had what name when it was constructed in 1903?

45. On what San Diego mountain do you find Wister Drive, Virginian Lane, and Molly Woods Avenue?

46. For what lake is the town of Lakeside named?

47. What town is named for a young sheep?

42. Mission Bay (previously known as False Bay). The winner of the contest was local poetess Rose Hartwick Thorpe, famed for her poem "Curfew Must Not Ring Tonight." Characteristically, she submitted her entry in the form of a poem. The name Mission Bay didn't really catch on until the 1920s, however, when Mission Beach was developed.

43. Jamul. It is a Diegueño Indian word that can also be translated as "foam" or "antelope spring."

44. Park Avenue. When Park Boulevard was developed on the east side of the prado area of the park for the 1915-16 Panama-California Exposition, Park Avenue was changed to Sixth Street (later Avenue) to avoid confusion. "Park Ave." can still be seen marked in the sidewalks on the west side of Sixth Avenue at Fir, Grape, Hawthorn, Olive, Quince, and Spruce streets.

45. Grossmont. Owen Wister, author of *The Virginian,* was a friend of the developer, Ed Fletcher. Wister planned to live in Grossmont, and had a 3,000-square-foot redwood house built on El Granito Avenue. The death of his wife, however, changed his plans, and he used the house for brief visits only. The streets were named after Wister's most popular book and its heroine, Molly Wood.

46. Lindo Lake. In the early days it was also called Lago Lindo or Laguna Linda.

47. Borrego Springs. "Borrego" is a Spanish word for yearling sheep or lamb, and the town and desert are named for the Peninsular bighorn sheep found there. Only 750 of this subspecies are left in the U.S., about 400 of which live in the Anza-Borrego Desert State Park.

48. What city is called "The Jewel of the Hills"?

49. What was the name of the Army field established on North Island in 1917?

50. For what were Normal Heights and Normal Street named?

51. A prominent San Diegan donated land for several city and county parks; consequently there are three parks with the same name, each named after him, one in San Diego, one in La Mesa, and a third in Ramona. What is the name of all three of these parks?

52. The Mission Hills streets of Torrance, Puterbaugh, Guy, and Witherby were all named for San Diegans who held what position?

53. When the Butterfield Overland Mail line passed through the Anza-Borrego Desert, there was one spot so steep and narrow that the passengers had to get out and walk behind the stage, and sometimes had to help push it. What is this spot called?

48. La Mesa. This sobriquet can be seen on the community signs and street signs.

49. Rockwell Field. It was named after Second Lt. Lewis Rockwell, a pioneer Army aviator who was killed in a test flight in 1912. In 1935 the field was transferred to the Navy, and it is now a part of the Naval Air Station.

50. San Diego Normal School. It was built in 1897 at Campus Avenue near Normal Street. This location was to have been the site of San Diego College of Arts and Sciences, which had been proposed a decade earlier but had never been built.

51. Collier Park. They were all named for Col. David Charles Collier, a San Diego lawyer, realtor, and real estate broker, also remembered as one of the leaders of the Panama-California Exposition. A commemorative plaque in his honor has been placed on the west wall of the Plaza de California near the entrance to the Museum of Man.

52. Judge. Torrance Street was named in 1894 for Superior Court Judge Elisha Swift Torrance, but the street was misspelled as "Torrence," and not corrected until 1965. The other streets were named for Superior Court Judges George Puterbaugh and Wilfred R. Guy, and for Judge Oliver S. Witherby, known as the "Father of the San Diego Bar."

53. Foot and Walker Grade (or Pass).

54. What was the name of Fairbanks Ranch in Rancho Santa Fe when it was owned by Douglas Fairbanks Sr.?

55. What is the name of the street that marked the boundary between Rancho de la Misión San Diego de Alcalá (San Diego) and Rancho de la Nación (National City)?

56. What is the name of the main street in Coronado, which runs from the old ferry landing to the Hotel del Coronado?

57. San Diego Bay has at least two recognized nicknames. Name one.

58. In 1976, the block of 55th Street in front of Crawford High School had its name changed to what new name?

59. Casa de Oro, meaning "house of gold," is a community in Spring Valley. To what does the "Oro" or "gold" refer?

54. Rancho Zorro. Douglas Fairbanks Sr. gave it that name when he bought it in 1926. He and Mary Pickford used it as a rural hideaway through the 1930s, and raised citrus (especially Valencia oranges) and cattle there. Originally it contained 3,000 acres, and Fairbanks planned to develop it into a romanticized Spanish ranch with a fantasy hacienda, a project which he was only partially able to carry out.

55. Division Street. The street still divides the two cities of San Diego and National City, except for a section in the middle where part of National City extends north of it.

56. Orange Avenue. It was originally planted with orange trees, but they didn't last long because jackrabbits gnawed them down. In 1889 they were removed and replaced with palms, cypress, and pines.

57. Silver Gate and Harbor of the Sun. Both names have been used for many years, but their origins are unknown. Silver Gate, a name complementary to San Francisco's Golden Gate, was in print at least as early as 1889. Grossmont poet John Vance Cheney entitled his 1911 book of poems about San Diego *At the Silver Gate*. Harbor of the Sun has been used in print at least since 1909, and Max Miller used that as the title of one of his books about San Diego.

58. Colts Way. The students themselves took the necessary steps in order to change the name to their school nickname.

59. The avocado (green gold). The community began in 1929 as the development called Casa de Oro Avocado Estates, and each of the lots was planted with avocado trees.

60. In 1967, a portion of one of the streets in North Park was renamed North Park Way. What was its former name?

61. What mountain in San Diego County was named after a snail?

62. What city are you in when you are at the corner of Omar Drive and Khayyám Road?

63. What San Diego County beach area was once called Long Beach?

64. In what part of town do you find the streets named after authors Addison through Zola, and Alcott through Lytton?

60. Wightman Street. The change was made in order to benefit the North Park businesses by having the off-ramp street signs on the new 805 or Inland Freeway be indicative of the name of the commercial area.

61. Mt. Helix. It is generally acknowledged that Rufus King Porter, an early Spring Valley settler, gave Mt. Helix its name in 1872 after a visiting scientist from a coastal survey ship found the rare *Helix aspersa* snail in the area. This snail had been accidentally brought to California a few years earlier, and today is prevalent. A variation on this story is that the name was derived from the Latin word *Helix*, meaning spiral, because of the trails that wound around the mountain. These trails, it was said, suggested the shell of a snail.

62. Escondido. These short streets are near Ninth and Broadway.

63. La Jolla Shores. It was so called because of its length. In the early days it was also known as Spindrift, named for the Spindrift Inn, which was the first building on that beach, built about 1916. It is said that around the turn of the century this beach was used for smuggling Chinese men and opium.

64. Point Loma. The streets are Addison, Byron, Carleton, Dickens, Emerson, Fenelon, Garrison, Hugo, Ingelow, Jarvis, Keats, Lowell, Macaulay, Newell, Oliphant, Poe, Quimby, Russell, Sterne, Tennyson, Udall, Voltaire, Whittier, Xenophon, Yonge, and Zola; then Alcott, Browning, Curtis, Dumas, Elliott, Freeman, Goldsmith, Homer, Ibsen, James, Kingsley, and Lytton.

65. Every Christmas, one block of a Chula Vista street is transformed into "Candy Cane Lane." What is the name of that street?

66. What was the former name of Mission Valley?

67. In what part of San Diego are some of the streets named after precious or semiprecious stones?

65. Guava Avenue.Every house on both sides of Guava south of E Street is elaborately decorated with Christmas scenes and lights, and a large red and white candy cane is placed in front of each palm tree next to the curb. This tradition was started in 1956 by the Rindone and Shipley families, and that may have been the first time that a neighborhood in the United States had each house fully decorated for Christmas. As many as 40,000 cars drive by each year to see the display. Nearby "Christmas Circle" on Mankato and Whitney streets began in 1958, and offers similar decorations.

66. La Cañada de San Diego (The Glen of San Diego). Though Mission San Diego has been at its present site since 1774, the early settlers did not call the valley Mission Valley until around 1868 or 1870.

67. Pacific Beach. Here you will find streets named Agate, Turquoise, Sapphire, Tourmaline, Opal, Beryl, Chalcedony, Diamond, Emerald, Felspar, Garnet, and Hornblend, running east and west. When originally laid out, these streets had state names, but Pacific Beach's subdivision map was not filed with the county clerk right away. University Heights also had streets with state names, and even though it was subdivided later, its names were filed first. Therefore, Pacific Beach had to rename its streets, and gemstones were chosen, with only the name Missouri remaining. Unlike theme streets in some other areas of San Diego, these gem street names are not entirely in alphabetical order.

68. What is the popular name of San Diego's famous nude beach?

69. An elementary school and three streets are named for a San Diegan who had been Secretary of the Treasury. Who was he?

70. What is the popular name of the area bordered by I-5, I-805, and State Highway 52?

68. Black's Beach. Officially it is Torrey Pines City Beach. The swimsuit-optional status has been an "on-again off-again" proposition during the past two decades at this somewhat difficult-to-reach area. In 1974, the City Council voted to legalize it as a swimsuit-optional beach, making it the first legally recognized nude beach in the United States. Protesters brought the issue to the ballot in 1977, calling national attention to Black's Beach, and though nudity is no longer legal, it still remains the best-known nude beach in America.

69. Lyman Judson Gage. He had been president of the American Bankers Association for three terms when President McKinley offered him the cabinet position of Secretary of the Treasury. He held this position through the first year of Theodore Roosevelt's administration, when he resigned and became president of U.S. Trust Company of Chicago. In 1906 he retired and moved to Point Loma, where he lived until his death in 1927. In San Diego he was active as one of the directors of the Panama-California Exposition. Gage Drive, Gage Lane, and Gage Place, all in Point Loma, as well as Gage Elementary School in San Carlos, are named for him.

70. Golden Triangle. It was named for its shape, and designated "golden" because it was believed that the most significant growth in the north county through the year 2000 would take place there.

71. There are two streets in Coronado that run diagonally from the center of town to the northwest and southwest corners. What are the names of these two streets?

72. What city in San Diego County was named for a woman's first husband, and later renamed for her second husband?

71. Palm Avenue and Olive Avenue. They are 100 feet wide, and are planted with palm trees and olive trees, respectively. This configuration of streets results in many odd-shaped blocks.

72. Santee. George A. Cowles settled there in 1877, after traveling over the U.S. and Europe for four years searching for the perfect climate. He planted trees and grapevines, and was called the "Raisin King of the U.S." The town became known as Cowlestown, and raisins from there were shipped all over the world. A few years after Cowles' death in 1887, his widow, Jennie Cowles, married Milton Santee, a real estate man and surveyor, and in 1893 the citizens voted to change the name of the town to Santee.

PHYSICAL GEOGRAPHY

1. During the last ice age, the area that is now San Diego County contained three islands. What were they?

2. What is the highest point in San Diego County?

3. How many California counties border San Diego County?

4. Until 1944, Coronado and North Island were almost separated from each other by a body of water. What was this body of water called?

5. San Diego County is one of the world's richest sources of gems and minerals. Name at least three of the gemstones found here.

6. What town is considered the geographical center of San Diego County?

7. Name the two rivers that flow into San Diego Bay.

PHYSICAL GEOGRAPHY   A

1. The areas that are now Point Loma, Coronado, and North Island. Over the centuries the sediment carried by the San Diego and the Tijuana rivers connected them to the mainland.

2. Hot Springs Peak (or Hot Springs Mountain). It stands 6,533 feet high, and is part of the San Ysidro Mountains in the Peninsular Range.

3. Three. They are Orange, Riverside, and Imperial counties.

4. The Spanish Bight. The early Spaniards anchored their sailing vessels there when repairing and overhauling them. In the early 1900s the bight was used for seaplane takeoffs and landings, because the water was calm. The connecting land area was so small that at high tide North Island was really an island. The bight, approximately one mile long by two hundred yards wide, was filled in by a Navy dredging project for expansion of airfields and facilities during World War II.

5. Most important are: tourmaline, beryl, kunzite, topaz, quartz, morganite, and garnet. Other gems and minerals found here are: lepidolite, citrine, spodumene, aquamarine, mica, manganese, tungsten, rhodonite, epidote, zinnwaldite, cassiterite, stibiotantalite, herderite, axinite, ruby, sapphire, hyacinth, chrysolite, cats-eye, moon stone, chrysoprase, dumortierite, zircon, gold, and molybdenite.

6. Ramona.

7. Sweetwater River and Otay River. The San Diego River did flow there from time to time in years past, but has been diverted. In addition, Chollas Creek, Seventh Street Channel, and Paradise Creek all empty into San Diego Bay.

8. What is the average monthly temperature for San Diego City, rounded off to the nearest degree?

9. The largest state park in the continental United States is located almost entirely in San Diego County. What park is it?

10. San Diego *County* contains 4,255 square miles. How many *states* in the United States are smaller?

11. Shelter Island and Harbor Island are both man made. Which was made first?

12. What is the name of the Scripps Institution of Oceanography vessel that can assume a vertical position to study the ocean beneath the waves?

13. During World War II, an area in the Anza-Borrego Desert was the only site in the U.S. for the mining of what mineral used in gunsights and bombsights?

14. What is the highest point within San Diego city limits?

8. 64°. The official temperature according to the National Weather Service is 63.8°.

9. The Anza-Borrego Desert State Park. It lies about 100 miles northeast of the city of San Diego. The park contains 600,000 acres, 538,000 of which (841 square miles) are in San Diego County, and the remainder in Riverside and Imperial counties. The park was named for Juan Bautista de Anza, leader of the expedition that crossed the area in 1774, and for the lambs (borregos) of the area.

10. Two. Rhode Island and Delaware are both smaller.

11. Shelter Island. This piece of land, one mile long by 300 feet wide, was filled in by dredging projects from 1934 to 1950. Harbor Island, more than one mile long, was made in the 1960s.

12. FLIP (Floating Instrument Platform). This 355- foot-long ship was developed by the Marine Physical Laboratory of the University of California's Scripps Institution of Oceanography, with financial support from the Office of Naval Research. It was launched June 22, 1962. When being used for research, FLIP is towed to position, where her ballast tanks are flooded. This causes her stern to sink and her prow to rise, which puts her in a vertical position.

13. Calcite. Optical grade calcite crystals were mined in the Borrego Badlands and the Santa Rosa Mountains near Imperial County.

14. Cowles Mountain. It stands 1,591 feet high, and was named for George A. Cowles, a rancher who lived in the east county from 1877 to 1887.

15. What is the name of the rock formation that shelters La Jolla Cove on the west?

16. What is San Diego City's current average annual rainfall, to the nearest half inch?

17. What is the smallest incorporated city by area within San Diego County?

18. What is the largest inland body of water in San Diego County?

19. What are the latitude and longitude of San Diego, to the nearest degree?

20. What is considered to be the largest urban park in the United States?

21. What hurricane devastated the San Diego back country in September 1976?

15. Alligator Head (or Alligator Point). It resembled the head of an alligator until part of it broke off in a heavy storm on January 6, 1978. This made front-page news, because the rock was a popular tourist attraction, and because it was used as a landmark by divers and boaters.

16. 9.5 inches. The National Weather Service gives it as 9.32 inches.

17. Del Mar. That tiny city has an area of two square miles. There are three other cities under five square miles: Solana Beach, 3.4; Lemon Grove, 3.75; and Imperial Beach, 4.4.

18. El Capitan Reservoir. It was built from 1932 to 1934 on the San Diego River, seven miles east of Lakeside. Lake Henshaw on the San Luis Rey River used to be the largest, but its capacity has been greatly reduced.

19. 33° N and 117° W. The figures vary slightly, depending upon the actual place of measurement. The figures usually given can range from 32° 41' to 32° 44' N, and from 117° 9' to 117° 14' W.

20. Mission Trails Regional Park. The current area is 4,970.75 acres, and it includes Cowles Mountain, Lake Murray, and Old Mission Dam. The city is now in the process of acquiring an additional 724 acres, and the park is planned eventually to encompass approximately 5,800 acres.

21. Kathleen.   She destroyed dozens of roads, trestles, and bridges, and put the San Diego and Arizona Eastern Railroad out of commission.

22. Which is larger, Balboa Park or the Wild Animal Park?

23. What is the most valuable mineral resource of San Diego County?

24. Where in San Diego was coal mined in the 1850s?

25. How did San Diego County lose over 4,000 square miles in 1907?

26. Scripps Institution of Oceanography is one of the directors of the Deep Sea Drilling Project. What is the name of the project's drilling ship that bores holes in the ocean floor?

22. The Wild Animal Park. It contains 1,800 acres, while Balboa Park has 1,171.5 acres (of its original 1,400). This includes the San Diego Zoo's 128 acres.

23. Sand and gravel. The main production area is just north of Friars Road in Mission Valley. In 1973 alone, the latest year for which figures are available, $15,919,000 worth was produced in San Diego, to be used in such items as concrete and asphalt.

24. Point Loma. The Mormons who had arrived here with the Mormon Battalion bored several shafts on the ocean side of the point. The pits were abandoned, however, because the porous sandstone let sea water leak in. It has been only within the past few decades that the last shafts were filled in.

25. Imperial County broke off to form a separate county. The reasons for the division were that the distance and mountain range made it difficult for Imperial Valley officials to attend to government business, and also the economic bases of the two areas were quite different.

26. *Glomar Challenger.* It was named after the H.M.S. *Challenger,* which circled the globe from 1872-76. The new *Challenger,* built in 1967-68, drills into the ocean floor, and the cores that it brings up are studied in order to learn about the age of the earth and how it was formed.

PLANTS AND ANIMALS

1. Where was the first pepper tree in California planted?

2. What is the only kind of bear native to San Diego County in historic times?

3. What is the official flower of the city of San Diego?

4. What is the name of the cockatoo just inside the San Diego Zoo entrance that is the "Official Zoo Greeter"?

5. There are at least 4,000 known kinds of palm trees. How many kinds are native to San Diego County?

1. Mission San Luis Rey. It was planted in the monastery garden in 1830 by Father Peyri, from seeds or sprigs brought from Peru by a sailor. This legendary tree is still standing in the mission garden.

2. The California Grizzly Bear. The last one in the county was killed in 1908, and they are now extinct in California. In the early 1800s it was considered great sport to rope grizzlies and match them in bull and bear fights, especially in the Old Town Plaza. Today black bears are occasionally seen in the back country, but they are a recent addition from northern California.

3. The carnation. It was adopted by the City Council in 1964.

4. King Tut. This salmon-crested bird, which is native to Indonesia, was provided by Frank Buck in 1925. He was an adult when he arrived here, so his exact age is not known, but he is thought to be the oldest San Diego Zoo resident. In his younger days Tut appeared in motion pictures, on *Zoorama*, and in productions at the Old Globe Theatre and Starlight Opera. Among his talents are the ability to mimic a cat and a chicken, say a few words, and even whistle some songs. King Tut can be seen by Dryer's Flamingo Lagoon whenever the weather is not too cold.

5. One. It is the California Fan Palm (*Washingtonia filifera*), also called the Washington Fan Palm, named after George Washington. Filifera means "thread-bearing," and refers to the white strings hanging from the leaves. The tree is found in Borrego Springs Palm Canyon and other oasis and canyon areas of the desert. All the other palm trees in the county have been imported.

6.   During what season do most of the California gray whales migrate south past San Diego?

7.   What is the unusual tree with a stubby swollen trunk, puffy limbs, red sap, and blue fruit that is found in the Anza-Borrego Desert?

8.   Between March and August, what do San Diegans hunt for soon after high tide in the sand along the beach?

9.   For the 1915-16 Panama-California Exposition, Sir Thomas Lipton introduced what trees to San Diego?

6. Winter. A few, though, can be seen as early as Thanksgiving. These whales have the longest migration route of any mammal — up to 12,000 miles round trip from the Arctic Ocean to Baja California, where they give birth in the shallow bays and lagoons. They used to winter in San Diego Bay, until whalers discouraged that practice.

7. The Elephant Tree (*Bursera microphylla*). This species is found in the low deserts of Arizona and northwest Mexico, and reaches its northernmost range in our desert. The Cahuilla Indians revered these trees, and used the sap for medicinal purposes. Reports of the existence of these trees in California were noted in the early 1900s, but the "lost elephant herds" were not officially located until 1937 by an expedition from the San Diego Natural History Museum and Scripps Institution of Oceanography. An Elephant Trees Ranger Station and Elephant Trees Nature Trail have now been established in the Fish Creek area of the Anza-Borrego Desert State Park, and a new "herd" has recently been discovered in the Santa Rosa Mountains.

8. Grunion. The females of these fish are carried by waves to the beach where they dig holes in which to lay their eggs. Within a few seconds the males fertilize them, and the next wave carries them back into the ocean. The baby grunion hatch during the next high tide, about ten days later.

9. Tea trees. Two hundred young trees from his plantations in Colombo, Ceylon, were planted here for the exposition, and cared for by men and women from Ceylon. Visitors could watch the leaves being stripped, cured, and prepared, and then could enjoy a cup of tea served by girls from Ceylon.

10. What is the name of the elephant that Joan Embery trained to paint by holding a large brush in its trunk?

11. The ancient and rare Torrey Pine is native to only one location other than Torrey Pines State Reserve. What is that other location?

12. What kind of animal was the San Diego Zoo's Dudley Duplex?

13. What San Diego County resident is known as the "King of Poinsettias"?

10. Carol. This young Asian elephant and Joan appeared many times on the *Tonight Show* with Johnny Carson, and made appearances on the *Steve Allen Show* and *Truth or Consequences*. Carol's paintings sold for $100 to $500, and she can still be seen performing in other capacities at the San Diego Wild Animal Park.

11. Santa Rosa Island. This is one of the Channel Islands, 175 miles to our northwest, and about 30 miles southwest of Santa Barbara. These trees probably grew there before the glacial period, when the offshore islands were not separate from the mainland. The Torrey Pine can be distinguished from other pines by its long gray-green needles in clusters of five.

12. A two-headed snake. Actually, there have been four Dudley Duplexes at the zoo over the years. The first one, a California kingsnake, arrived there in 1953, and lived until about 1963. He probably holds the record for the longest-lived two-headed snake. Two later Dudley Duplexes were both banded California kingsnakes. One was received in December 1967 and died in July 1971, and the most recent was received in October 1969 and died in February 1975. The dates of the fourth one are not known. Two-headed snakes are not particularly unusual, but as a rule they do not live long because the heads compete with each other for food, one head usually becoming dominant.

13. Paul Ecke. The Ecke Ranch was started in Los Angeles in 1906 by Albert Ecke. His son Paul took it over in 1919, and in the mid-1920s moved the ranch to Encinitas where it developed into the largest poinsettia ranch in the world. It is now run by Paul Ecke Jr., and has an active poinsettia breeding program that produces over 10,000 new and different trial seedlings each year.

14. What is the name of the star killer whale at Sea World?

15. What are the deciduous trees that grace the center divide of the Cabrillo Freeway (163) through Balboa Park?

16. What primates are notorious for escaping from their enclosures at the San Diego Zoo?

17. What kind of tree is the large tree behind the Natural History Museum?

18. At least four cities or towns in San Diego County have claimed the title "The Avocado Capital of the World." Which are they?

19. Where in San Diego County was there a butterfly farm in the 1910s?

14. Shamu. The original 1965 Shamu was the first trained killer whale in the world. The recently opened Shamu Stadium holds more than six million gallons of filtered water, making it one of the largest marine mammal facilities ever built. Besides providing the new location for the Shamu Killer Whale Show, it also offers new opportunities for studying the killer whale's breeding and physiology.

15. Sycamore.

16. The orangutans. In the 1970s orangs Otis and Robella made some breaks, and Sheldon Campbell dubbed them "The Orangutan Escape Committee" in his 1978 book *Lifeboats to Ararat.* In the 1980s the elusive Ken Allen has taken delight in eluding his keepers, and despite close watch has escaped many times. Sometimes he acts as decoy while his mates make the move. His escapades are celebrated in the song "The Ballad of Ken Allen," written and recorded by Dennis Gersten, MD, which is available on record at the San Diego Zoo and Wild Animal Park.

17. A Moreton Bay Fig. This tree, which is native to Australia, was planted in 1915 for the exposition. Now it is more than 62 feet tall, and has a canopy 100 feet in diameter.

18. Fallbrook, Escondido, Carlsbad, and Vista. Avocados still constitute the most valuable crop of the county, and San Diego is the leading avocado-producing county in the nation.

19. Palomar Mountain. It was run by Esther Hewlett from 1913 to 1918. She collected, raised, and bred butterflies and moths, and sold them to collectors all over the country. A new variety of moth was named *Apantesis Hewletti* after her.

20. What town in San Diego County has an annual weed show?

21. What was the name of the begonia gardens on Point Loma one block east of Catalina Boulevard?

22. What whiskey-loving dog was San Diego's official Town Dog in the 1880s and 1890s?

23. San Diego has many plants called halophytes. Where do they grow?

24. What is the name of Sea World's Beluga whale?

25. From the 1890s through the early decades of the 1900s, what town was called the "Lemon Capital of the World"?

20. Julian. This festival has been held in August or September since 1961. Featured in the displays are arrangements of weeds, dried leaves, grasses, seed pods, rocks, and wood from the nearby mountain and desert areas.

21. Rosecroft Begonia Gardens. The 1½-acre gardens on Silverwood Avenue were founded in 1900 by Alfred D. Robinson, and continued by the Hunter family from 1946 until the early 1980s when the gardens began to decline. In their prime these gardens were considered to have the finest displays of begonias in the world. Other flowers such as fuchsias, azaleas, and bromeliads were raised there as well, and requests for plants or advice came from all over the world.

22. Bum. He arrived here by steamer in 1886, and soon became our mascot. One year his picture was on all San Diego dog licenses, and he has been immortalized in the 1960 book *A Dog Called Bum*, by Marie Hitchcock.

23. In salt marshes. "Halophyte" means salt-loving, and these plants grow in the mud or sand flats along our coast. At the turn of the century there were 32,000 acres of salt marshes in San Diego County, but now the total acreage is down to 3,000, mainly in the areas south of San Diego Bay and near the mouth of the Tijuana River. An exhibit on salt marshes can be viewed at the Natural History Museum.

24. Belinda. This name has been applied to several of these small white whales at Sea World.

25. Chula Vista. At one time the largest lemon orchard in the world existed here. Many of the original orchard houses remain, now surrounded by suburban developments instead of trees. Today the county's citrus crops are concentrated in the northern part of the county.

26. What is the largest flying bird native to San Diego County in recorded history?

27. What kind of tree was planted in northern San Diego County by the Santa Fe Railroad Company with the idea of using the wood for railroad ties?

28. What is the name of the botanical gardens in Encinitas?

26. The California condor. These birds weigh from 20 to 25 pounds, and their span from wing tip to wing tip can reach up to 16 feet. In the mid-1800s, quills of the larger feathers were used for storing gold dust. Though they were once fairly plentiful in the north county and along the coast, man's encroachment has brought about a rapid decline of the species, and they are now almost extinct. There was a population of condors along the San Luis Rey River until about 1910, and the last recorded sighting of a wild condor in San Diego County took place north of Palomar Mountain in August of 1933. The San Diego Wild Animal Park is currently conducting a condor breeding program, and in April 1988, Molloko, the first California condor conceived in captivity, was hatched there.

27. Eucalyptus. In the early 1900s this railroad company bought up lands of the San Dieguito Rancho, and named the area Rancho Santa Fe. Four thousand acres were planted with 3,000,000 eucalyptus seeds and seedlings, but the project did not work out as planned: the growth of the trees was slower than expected, and the wood split easily. The land was then used for cattle grazing and citrus groves, and in the late 1920s for housing developments. (Incidentally, these were not the first eucalyptus trees in the county; they had been planted in many areas since the early 1800s.)

28. Quail Botanic Gardens. The gardens are located on a 30-acre estate in Encinitas. The original land was donated by Ruth Baird Larabee in 1957, and added to in 1971 by a gift from Paul and Magdelena Ecke. The gardens serve as a horticultural center, emphasizing subtropical plants, succulents, and native chaparral, and also feature a sanctuary and feeding station for quail and other native birds.

29. What was the name of the Alaskan brown bear at the San Diego Zoo who entertained visitors from 1970 to 1985?

30. The fastest growing plant in the world is abundant in San Diego. What is it?

31. In 1987 two giant pandas were loaned to the San Diego Zoo by the People's Republic of China. What were their names?

32. Where was the first outdoor electrically lighted living Christmas tree in the United States?

29. Chester. The orphaned bear was found in the Alaskan wilds and arrived at the zoo on May 30, 1970. He was encouraged by his keeper, Jim Joiner, to perform certain behaviors for which he was rewarded with his favorite treats of bear biscuits and mackerel. On command he would lick his paws, stand on one foot while holding up the other with his front paw, or stand on his hind legs and wave. Tour bus drivers also rewarded his behavior with food, and he was a favorite with the bus passengers. Chester stood 8 1/2 feet tall, weighed 804 pounds, and was probably the most photographed and most popular animal at the zoo until his death August 6, 1985.

30. Kelp (specifically, Giant Kelp). It can grow up to two feet per day, and attains a length of 200 feet. San Diego has been called the "Kelp Capital of the World," and this crop is harvested here and used in hundreds of products such as ice cream, medicine, dental impression compounds, paint, salad dressing, beer, and cardboard.

31. Basi and Yuan Yuan (pronounced Ba-seh and Yen Yen). They were on loan from the Fuzhou Zoo, accompanied by three Chinese keepers. Basi was a seven-year-old female, and Yuan Yuan a six-year-old male, and their arrival here started an outbreak of "pandamania." There are fewer than 20 pandas in zoos outside of China, and the antics of these two delighted over two million visitors during their stay here.

32. The Hotel del Coronado. The tall Norfolk Island or Star Pine, which was first lit in 1904, still stands in front of the hotel. The custom of lighting it at Christmastime continued every year, excluding the World War II years, until the energy crisis of the 1970s. Since then the tree-lighting custom has been transferred to the large pine at Rotary Circle on Orange and Isabella avenues.

33. What town was known as the "Turkey Capital of the World" in the mid-1900s?

34. What was the location of Kate Sessions' last nursery?

35. What exploring team captured the gorillas Mbongo and Ngagi, which were residents of the San Diego Zoo until the 1940s?

33. Ramona. From the late 1920s through the mid-1960s Ramona was famous for its gobblers, and Harry Truman dined at the White House one holiday on a Ramona turkey. The town was also the top turkey egg producer in the world, and at one time 1,750,000 turkey eggs were sold annually. Ramona's famous Turkey Days were held every November from 1933 to 1940, and revived for one year in 1954. A turkey feather robe, and pictures of turkey feather jackets, hats, bathing suits, parasols, and floats from these festivities are on display at the Guy Woodward Museum there. Today in Ramona you will find chickens instead of turkeys.

34. Pacific Beach. She established it there at the foot of Mt. Soledad in 1914. The site of her sales office on Pico and Balboa is marked by a historical plaque next to a Tipuana tree that she planted from seed around 1920. Earlier she had nurseries downtown, in Coronado, in Balboa Park at the corner of Sixth and Upas, and in Mission Hills. Kate O. Sessions Elementary School and Kate O. Sessions Memorial Park are both located in Pacific Beach.

35. Martin and Osa Johnson. These gorillas, native to the Belgian Congo, were captured in 1930 by this famous wildlife photographer and collector team, and were donated to the zoo by Ellen B. and Robert Scripps. The animals weighed 618 and 635 pounds at their peaks, and died in 1942 and 1944, respectively. They are now memorialized in bronze busts near the zoo entrance, and the skeleton and stuffed form of Mbongo can be viewed at the Museum of Man.

36. What is the name of the national forest, part of which lies within San Diego County?

37. What bird is the symbol of Lake San Marcos?

38. Marston's downtown department store was famous for its spring displays of what flower?

36. Cleveland National Forest. It was created out of two reserves: Trabuco Canyon Forest Reserve, proclaimed by President Harrison in 1893, and San Jacinto Forest Reserve, proclaimed by President Cleveland in 1897. In 1908, President Theodore Roosevelt combined them, renaming them Cleveland National Forest in honor of President Cleveland, who had taken a great interest in the preservation of forests. Later most of the San Jacinto unit was transferred to San Bernardino National Forest. Today 287,861 acres of Cleveland National Forest are in San Diego County.

37. The quail. Frank Vecchio of the advertising firm of Hogan and Vecchio in Riverside was visiting this early 1960s lakeside development to plan a promotional brochure, when he was greeted by hundreds of quail. He consequently designed the three stylized quail that became the symbol of the complex. Around the lake can be found such buildings as Quails Inn Dinnerhouse, Quail Hall, and Quails Inn Motel.

38. Lilacs. In 1939, Marston's vice president Tom Hamilton saw some lilac bushes blooming in Alice and Franklin Barnes' Pine Hills garden, and brought some in for the store. They were such a success that he had Mrs. Barnes plant 1,200 bushes just for Marston's. Every spring the blossoms would be loaded into wind-protected trucks before the sun was up, and brought to the store about 4 o'clock in the morning, where they were displayed in huge baskets made by the blind.

39. What was the color of the deer that lived in Mission Hills and Presidio Park in the 1960s and 1970s?

40. What kind of tree was the first tree planted in California?

41. What insect did the San Diego Zoo trade in return for rare snakes in 1938?

42. The four topiaries at Horton Plaza shopping center are in the shape of what animal?

39. White. This gentle and elusive white fallow deer had probably escaped from a private residence, and made Presidio Park her new home. Though she remained wild she was regarded by the community as a pet, and was called Lucy by some. In an effort to prevent her from getting hurt crossing the freeway, she was shot with a tranquilizer in December 1975. This unfortunately caused her death. A monument in Presidio Park marks her burial site.

40. Palm (*phoenix dactylifera*). Legend has it that Father Serra planted several date palms from seed here in 1769. One was sent to the Chicago World's Fair in 1893. Two remaining trees were protected by a fence at the site where they stood near Taylor and Chestnut streets in Old Town, until the smaller one blew down in 1916. The last remaining one, known as the "Serra Palm," grew to over 80 feet in height, but in the 1950s became sick due to a fungus disease, drought, and musket balls and bullets that had been fired into it in the 1800s. Because of this, in June 1957 this oldest landmark in San Diego was chopped down.

41. The flea. In answer to a telegram request, Belle Benchley sent a weekly jar of fleas to New Jersey where they were used in a flea circus. Most of the fleas were obtained from the local dog pound. This was quite a switch in the status of this insect, for in the latter half of the 1800s San Diego residents and visitors alike complained bitterly about the flea problem, and San Diego was known as the "Flea Capital of the West."

42. Hippopotamus. The four dancing hippo topiaries on the main level were designed to encourage a feeling of festivity. They are created out of an ivy called creeping fig or *ficus repens* that grows from the base of the sculpture up.

43. What was the name of the rhinoceros at the San Diego Wild Animal Park who sired a record 59 rhinos?

44. What was the name of the pure white fire horse that pulled the fire chief's buggy in the early 1900s?

PLANTS & ANIMALS   A

43. Mandhla. This southern white rhinoceros arrived at the San Diego Zoo September 8, 1962, from the Natal Parks Board. In May 1971 he was transferred to the Wild Animal Park to join the rhino herd there, which consisted of 14 females and 6 young males, all recently acquired from the Natal Parks Board. Here he sired more calves than any other bull rhino in captivity, and played a large part in removing the southern white rhino from the endangered species list. In October 1983 Mandhla was transferred to another zoo, and died the following January.

44. Josh. At one time the San Diego Fire Department had 23 horses on active duty, but they were phased out gradually from 1909 to 1919. Normally the horses were sold, but Ol' Josh was placed on the pension list in December 1916, and was retired to the Municipal Farm of the City of San Diego for the remainder of his life.

A MISCELLANY

1. What denomination held the first recorded Protestant services in San Diego?

2. What is the name of the *Star of India*'s figurehead?

3. In what San Diego neighborhood do all the streets have pink sidewalks?

4. Actors Frank Morgan, Leo Carrillo, and Gale Gordon have all been honorary mayor of what San Diego town?

5. Which cross is taller — the one on Mt. Helix or the one on Mt. Soledad?

6. According to the 1980 census, the *city* of San Diego had a population of 875,504. At that time, how many *states* had smaller populations?

1. Mormon. Services were held at Mission San Diego on Sunday, January 31, 1847, for members of the Mormon Battalion.

2. Euterpe. *Euterpe*, the muse of music and lyric poetry, was the original name of the ship when she was launched in 1863. She was later bought by Alaska Packers, and they changed her name to *Star of India* in 1906, to match the names of the other "Star of..." ships they owned.

3. Burlingame. This neighborhood was developed in the early 1900s, and lies between 30th, 32nd, San Marcos Avenue, and Kalmia Street. There are other pink sidewalks in San Diego, notably in some sections of Mission Hills and areas west of Balboa Park, but they do not denote a definite neighborhood.

4. Borrego Springs. Morgan, who promoted subdivisions there, served from 1948 to 1951; Carrillo served in 1951; and Gordon, who is still a resident there, served from 1961 to 1973. In addition, Leo Carrillo was honorary sheriff of Borrego Springs in 1949, and was also honorary mayor of Vista for several years.

5. Mt. Soledad. It is the third cross to be placed there, and is 43 feet high, with an arm spread of 12 feet. This see-through concrete cross was dedicated Easter Sunday, April 18, 1954. The cross on Mt. Helix is 35 feet tall, of solid concrete, and was dedicated Easter Sunday, April 12, 1925.

6. Eight: Alaska, Wyoming, Vermont, Delaware, North Dakota, South Dakota, Montana, and Nevada.

7.   How many sister cities does San Diego have?

8.   What are the three colors of the San Diego flag?

9.   What fountain in San Diego has the tallest spout of water?

10.   Is the large 200-inch telescope on Palomar Mountain reflecting or refracting?

11.   What is the smallest incorporated city (by population) within San Diego County?

12.   There are five community colleges in San Diego County that are outside the city limits:
       1. Grossmont College.

       2. Mira Costa College.

       3. Palomar College.

       4. Southwestern College.

       5. Cuyamaca College.

Give the cities or towns in which their main campuses are located.

7. Ten: 1. Edinburgh, Scotland.
      2. Yokohama, Japan.
      3. León, Mexico.
      4. Cavite City, Philippines.
      5. Tema, Ghana.
      6. Alcalá de Henares, Spain.
      7. Jeonju, Korea.
      8. Yantai, People's Republic of China.
      9. Taichung, Republic of China.
      10. Perth, Australia.

8. Red, white, and yellow (or gold). The flag is made up of three vertical stripes with the city seal in the center of the white stripe. It was approved in 1934, but not flown until 1943.

9. The fountain in the Plaza de Balboa in Balboa Park, between the Space Theater and the Natural History Museum. It was built in 1972 and holds 25,000 gallons of water, which it spouts 50 to 60 feet into the air. There is a wind-regulator for this fountain on the roof of the Natural History Museum. As the wind gets stronger the water pressure of the fountain is lowered so that the water won't spray out over the edges.

10. Reflecting. An astronomer sits in the telescope above the mirror, which gathers light from the stars and focuses it at an observation point for examination by spectrograph.

11. Del Mar. The 1986 estimated population was 5,100.

12. 1. El Cajon.
    2. Oceanside.
    3. San Marcos.
    4. Chula Vista.
    5. El Cajon.

13. A tiny toy animal can be seen imbedded in the mechanism of the Jessop Street Clock in Horton Plaza shopping center. What animal is it?

14. What store has the oldest soda fountain in the city of San Diego?

15. San Diego State University has had that name since January 1, 1974. What were the four former names of that institution?

16. What are the numbers of the four United States House of Representative districts in San Diego County?

17. What is the second-largest city (by population) in San Diego County?

13. A bear. When the clock was on display at the Sacramento State Fair in 1907, the movement was not enclosed in glass as it is now. A child stuck a tiny carved brown bear into the pendulum ring, where it still rides today.

14. Galloway's Pharmacy. The store and fountain were built in 1924 at 2995 National Avenue, and are still in operation, though the fountain is not as popular as it was from the 1920s through the 1940s. This was the only soda fountain left in the city until Heaven Pop Cuisine and Longs Drugs recently opened in Horton Plaza. The Julian Drug Store on Main Street in Julian also has a soda fountain. It was installed in 1933 in what was then Tozer Drug Store, and it is probably the only one in the county with a marble counter.

15. 1. San Diego (State) Normal School, 1897-1921.
    2. San Diego State Teachers' College, 1921-1935.
    3. San Diego State College, 1935-1972.
    4. California State University at San Diego, 1972-1973.

16. 41, 43, 44, and 45.

17. Chula Vista. According to the 1986 estimate, Chula Vista had a population of 116,300. It was followed by Oceanside with 96,000, El Cajon with 81,800, and Escondido with 79,000. All others were at least 20,000 below this. By contrast, San Diego City had an estimated population of 1,002,900.

18. How many telescopes are there on Palomar Mountain?

19. What is the official nickname of UCSD students?

20. What San Diego merry-go-round used to be at Coney Island?

21. What is the nickname of the training ship USS *Recruit*?

22. In what San Diego hotel is the Whaling Bar?

18. Five: 1. 200-inch reflecting.
    2. 60-inch reflecting.
    3. 20-inch reflecting.
    4. 48-inch Schmidt wide-field.
    5. 18-inch Schmidt wide-field.

19. Tritons. Triton was the son of Poseidon and Amphitrite; his upper body was that of a man and his lower part the tail of a fish. He is usually depicted with a conch-shell trumpet. This mascot was picked because of the campus's proximity to the ocean, and because of its connections with Scripps Institution of Oceanography. The school colors are blue and gold.

20. The Broadway Flying Horses Carousel at Seaport Village. The animals were carved of poplar around 1890 by Charles Looff of Coney Island. Later the carousel was set up at Salisbury, Massachusetts, where it ran until the 1970s, when it was to be dismantled and the pieces sold. Seaport Village bought it and spent more than two years restoring it to its original splendor. Today people of all ages enjoy its 40 horses (with real horsehair tails), three goats, and three St. Bernard dogs, and it is the most popular of Seaport Village's special features.

21. USS *Neversail*. It is so called because it is on dry land at the Naval Training Center along Harbor Drive, firmly anchored in concrete. Even though it is landlocked, it must observe morning and evening colors and fly a commission pennant.

22. La Valencia Hotel, in La Jolla. A large tempera mural of a whale hunt was painted above the bar by Willing "Wing" Howard in 1947. In 1978 he returned to paint a new version in oils over the original.

23. In 1987, the oldest chartered private club in California closed. What was it?

24. What San Diegan claims to have had an encounter with aliens from the planet Rillispore?

25. What is the aircraft in front of the Aerospace Museum?

26. How many San Diego City Council districts are there?

27. What is the second-oldest incorporated city in San Diego County, after the city of San Diego?

28. What is the motto of the city of San Diego?

23. The Cuyamaca Club. It was started in 1887 by a group of city leaders as a luncheon club and place for discussion, conference, and comradeship. Originally it was for men only, but later took women members as well. Through the years it has occupied three locations in downtown San Diego, moving to its final site at 1055 First Avenue in 1973.

24. The Spaceman of Ocean Beach (Clint Carey). In 1957, while camping in the high desert of California, he was visited by Rillisporean aliens and taken aboard their space ship where they shared with him many secrets of the universe. Carey is a well-known figure in his community, and "Spaceman of Ocean Beach" bumper stickers adorn many cars there. He is also a respected painter, and has had shows throughout the world.

25. A Sea Dart (XF2Y-1). This experimental Convair supersonic seaplane was the world's first delta-wing jet seaplane. Five were built, but only three were ever flown. The second Sea Dart built became the first water-based aircraft to break the sound barrier. The first successful flight was over San Diego Bay April 9, 1953. On November 4, 1954, however, one exploded and crashed into San Diego Bay, and in 1956 the test project was discontinued.

26. Eight. Each council member is elected to a four-year term.

27. National City. It incorporated in 1887, and was closely followed by Oceanside and Escondido in 1888, and Coronado in 1890. All other cities were incorporated well into the twentieth century.

28. *Semper Vigilans* (Ever vigilant).

29. In what part of San Diego were the streets laid out diagonally in a northwest-southeast direction in order for the homes to receive more sunlight?

30. Until 1987 there was only one alley in downtown San Diego. Now there are none. Where was that alley?

31. What is the nickname of San Diego City College students?

32. What is the type of boat that Sea World used to operate that skimmed along the surface of the water?

33. What are the seven California State Assembly districts in San Diego County?

34. The fire hydrants in front of the First Interstate Plaza on B Street between Fourth and Fifth are covered with what material?

29. Logan Heights. The idea was that sunlight would be admitted into some room of each house during all daylight hours. The plan was not followed during later years, however, so the streets starting with Everett are diagonal, while the surrounding ones run north-south and east-west, resulting in many triangular lots.

30. From Columbia to State, parallel to Broadway on the south and C Street on the north. It is said that when Alonzo Horton laid out the streets in what is now the downtown area, he did not include alleys because he considered them to be merely places where trash accumulated. This sole alley was lost when the entire block was razed in late 1987.

31. Knights. In 1948 the Associated Student Body voted to change the nickname from Jaybirds to Knights because at that time classes were held at San Diego High School, which was known as "The Old Gray Castle." Also, the football team had recently won a championship, and it was thought that the name Knights would be more fitting.

32. Hydrofoil. These boats rise on foils to gain a speed of up to 35 miles per hour. The hull of the boat can be suspended as much as three feet above the water, resulting in a thrilling ride. Hydrofoils were in operation at Sea World until early 1988, taking 28 passengers each on a sightseeing course around Mission Bay.

33. 74, 75, 76, 77, 78, 79, and 80.

34. Brass. They were built in 1984, and were brass-plated to match the building's brass rails. Out of 19,377 fire hydrants in the city, these may be the only brass-plated ones.

35. In what city is the International Headquarters of The Rosicrucian Fellowship?

36. What are the school colors of San Diego State University?

37. How many brothers and sisters does Mayor Maureen O'Connor have?

38. At what street does Broadway widen as it goes toward the bay?

39. What annual San Diego festival held at Mission San Diego de Alcalá commemorates the founding of California's first mission?

35. Oceanside. This 40-acre site overlooking the San Luis Rey Valley was established in 1911 by Rosicrucian founder Max Heindel. The organization is based on a Christian philosophy giving an esoteric explanation of the Christian religion. At the International Headquarters there are classrooms, a complete publishing facility, a library, and a chapel.

36. Black and scarlet (or red or crimson). These colors were chosen in 1928.

37. Twelve. She has six brothers and six sisters (including twin sister Mavourneen). In 1956 the entire O'Connor family appeared on the cover of *Parade Magazine* for a Mother's Day article. Maureen and her sisters toured with the Wonderful World of Sports as the "Swimming O'Connor Sisters," and they were the first all-woman team to win the La Jolla Rough Water Swim team trophy.

38. Third Avenue. When Alonzo Horton laid out his streets they were 80 feet wide with the exception of H (Market), then the main street, which was 100 feet wide. When his hotel, the Horton House, was built in 1870 on D (Broadway) between Third and Fourth (now the site of the US Grant Hotel), it is said that he widened the street to 100 feet so the hotel guests could have a clear view to the waterfront. Another theory is that Horton made D Street wider at the west end so that it could carry commercial traffic.

39. The Festival of the Bells. It is held on the weekend in July closest to July 16, the birthday of San Diego. Each year there is a reblessing of the five mission bells.

40. What two neon signs shone alternately at the top of the El Cortez Hotel for many decades?

41. In 1980, San Diego *County* had a population of 1,861,846. How many *states* had smaller populations?

42. What three communities in San Diego City have community name signs over their main streets?

43. What two communities in San Diego City used to have community name signs?

44. Name at least one residential street in San Diego City that has a chrome-plated fire hydrant.

40. "El Cortez Hotel" and "Sky Room." The "El Cortez Hotel" sign was red, and the "Sky Room" sign, surrounded by twinkling stars, was in pastels. For many years these two signs were San Diego's most noticeable night lights.

41. Sixteen: Alaska, Wyoming, Vermont, Delaware, North Dakota, South Dakota, Montana, Nevada, New Hampshire, Idaho, Rhode Island, Hawaii, Maine, New Mexico, Utah, and Nebraska.

42. Normal Heights, Hillcrest, and Kensington. The Normal Heights sign was erected in 1951 over Felton and Adams. The Hillcrest sign went up in 1940 over Fifth and University; in 1984 an exact replica replaced the old one. The Kensington sign was put up in 1957 on Adams Avenue between Marlborough and Kensington Drive. (In addition, the Gaslamp Quarter is planning to erect two signs in the near future, at Fifth and Harbor, and Fifth and Broadway.)

43. North Park and East San Diego. The first North Park sign was erected in 1925 over 30th and University. In 1931 a new one was put up, which remained until 1966, when it was removed after a storm. In late 1987, a smaller wooden replica was placed on posts at the northeast corner of Boundary and University. East San Diego's sign was erected in 1954 over Fairmount and University, and removed in 1968 when University was widened.

44. Overlake Avenue; Nautilus Street. The addresses where these hydrants can be found are 5875 Overlake Avenue in Del Cerro, and 1205 Nautilus Street in La Jolla.

45. What is the oldest existing business in San Diego owned by one family?

46. Where is the longest free-standing outdoor public stairway in the city of San Diego?

47. What two communities within the city of San Diego have zip codes that begin with 920-- instead of 921--?

48. There is one incorporated city in San Diego County whose post office is a branch of San Diego City's, and whose zip code begins 921-- instead of 920--. What city is that?

49. In what city is the Miss Southern California Contest held?

45. San Diego Hardware Company. It was founded by Fred Gazlay in 1892, two blocks from its present location. In 1923 it relocated to its current site at 840 Fifth Avenue. It was eventually taken over by Fred's son, Wadham Gazlay, then by Wadham's nephew, Don Haynsworth, and in the early 1980s by Don's son, Bill Haynsworth. Today it is owned and operated by Bill and his partner, Rip Fleming. As far as can be determined, it is the oldest family-owned business in San Diego, and is the oldest hardware store in the county.

46. San Diego State University. One hundred fifty-one steps lead up from the lower parking lot in the northwest corner; across the road at the top there are 30 more steps. (Who needs P.E.?) A longer stairway still exists in Bachman Canyon leading up from Mission Valley to Hillcrest, but it has been closed for several years because it is unsafe. Some of the steps have crumbled, and some are overgrown with weeds, but from the top warning sign to the bottom warning sign the stairway contains 308 steps.

47. La Jolla and San Ysidro. La Jolla has the zip codes 92037 and 92038, and San Ysidro has 92073 as well as the "San Diego City" zip code of 92173.

48. Coronado. The zip code there is 92118.

49. Oceanside. It has been held there since 1934, though in the early years it was called merely "beauty contest." It was held at the outdoor Beach Stadium until 1980, when it was moved to the El Camino High School James Truax Performing Arts Theatre. This is the oldest continuous non-commercial bathing beauty contest in Southern California, and draws crowds of over 10,000.

50. In what town is the Wisteria Candy Cottage located?

51. How many fire stations in the city of San Diego have poles?

52. The *Bahia Belle* excursion boat and the Glorietta Boatique Gift Shop have what common ancestry?

53. The large stone monument replicas in the Museum of Man are from what civilization?

50. Boulevard. The Wisteria Candy Cottage was established in 1921 in Boulevard, about 65 miles east of San Diego. It features a wide variety of homemade candies, such as hand dipped chocolate creams, nut rolls, caramels, fudge, 17 kinds of divinity, and even chop suey brittle. All the candies are made at the Cottage, and will be shipped anywhere.

51. Four. There are currently 40 San Diego City fire stations in operation. The poles are located in Station 1 on Front and B, Station 4 at Eighth and J, Station 11 at 25th and Broadway, and Station 21 at Grand and Mission Boulevard. The poles in the four stations are no longer made of the traditional brass, because the brass ones were removed around 1942 for the war effort, and replaced with polished steel poles.

52. They were both "nickel snatchers" (passenger ferries which ran from San Diego to North Island). They were two of the 62-foot diesel ferries constructed for the Star and Crescent Boat Company. The *Bahia Belle* was formerly the *Juanita*, built in 1942, and converted into a cafe boat for the Bahia Hotel in 1963, and the Glorietta Boat-ique Gift Shop was the *Glorietta*, built in 1944.

53. Mayan. These copies were made from glue molds and cast in plaster during a 1914 expedition to Quirigua, Guatemala, led by Dr. Edgar L. Hewett, first director of the Museum of Man. They were on display at the 1915-16 Panama-California Exposition, and are considered to be the finest of all the reproductions that have been made of these monuments. The original stelae and the shorter zoömorphic figures were carved from hard brown sandstone between 692 and 810 AD, and are covered with intricate hieroglyphic inscriptions.

54. What is the oldest single-family-owned bakery in San Diego County?

55. What color are the street signs in the Gaslamp Quarter?

56. What is the name of the monorail that tours the San Diego Wild Animal Park?

57. How many times does the capsule on Sea World's sky tower revolve on its way up before making its descent?

58. Over the years San Diego has had many aircraft carriers based here. What are the names of the two carriers that are currently based at Naval Air Station, North Island?

54. Anderson's Bakery, in Coronado. Carl T. "Charlie" Anderson began his career as apprentice baker for the Hotel del Coronado in 1899. In 1909 he started his own business and sold bread from a horsedrawn cart. The Coronado Home Bakery building was built in 1911, and still stands behind the front display store on Orange Avenue. Charlie's sons, Clare and Bud, took over the bakery in 1936 and changed the name to Anderson Brothers Bakery. Since 1975, Clare's daughter and son-in-law, Cheryl and Jerry Johnson, have continued the business.

55. Brown. The signs are this color in order to set off the Gaslamp Quarter from the surrounding area.

56. Wgasa Bush Line monorail. This non-polluting electrically powered monorail leaves from Simba Station in Nairobi Village to take passengers on a five-mile, 50-minute safari around the park.

57. Three. The 60-passenger capsule travels 150 feet per minute up the 320- foot spire, slowly revolving to give its passengers a 360° panorama of San Diego's bays, ocean, skyline, and foothills.

58. USS *Constellation* and USS *Ranger*. The *Constellation* (CV-64) was placed in commission October 27, 1961. In 1981, President Reagan presented the Presidential Flag to this ship and proclaimed her "America's Flagship." The *Ranger* (CV-61) was commissioned August 10, 1957, and homeported at North Island June 1975. In June of 1986 she participated with ships from five nations in a major maritime exercise called RIMPAC 86. (Most recently, the USS *Kittyhawk* was homeported at North Island, from November 1, 1961, to January 3, 1986, during which time she received many awards.)

59. On what urban mountain is there a 246-step stairway leading to the top?

60. Many leading San Diego citizens of the past, such as Alonzo Horton, Elisha Babcock, George Marston, Kate Sessions, Joseph Jessop, Thomas Whaley, and Judge Oliver S. Witherby, are buried in what cemetery?

61. What is the name of the Santa Ysabel bakery that is famous for its many kinds of bread?

62. The oldest continuously operating Seventh-Day Adventist elementary school west of the Mississippi is located where in San Diego County?

59. Mt. Nebo. The stairway leads up the west side of this La Mesa mountain from Canterbury and Windsor drives to Summit Drive. It is bisected twice by streets circling the mountain. On the east side, a 185-step stairway leads up to the top from Beverly Drive.

60. Mt. Hope Cemetery. In 1869 a group of citizens under the leadership of Alonzo E. Horton met to establish a new public cemetery, and thus Mt. Hope was created. The grounds were later expanded to the 169 acres which are developed at present.

61. Dudley's Bakery. Dudley Pratt opened his first bake shop in El Cajon, and in 1963 opened Dudley's Bakery and Restaurant in Santa Ysabel, where the nearby well water imparted a good flavor to the bread. Nearly every year he traveled to a different spot in the world to bring back recipes for new kinds of bread. Since his passing in 1973 the bakery has been owned and operated by Mel Ashley. Today over 3,000 loaves of 17 varieties of bread are baked daily, the most popular being Raisin Date Nut, Danish Apple Nut, Jalapeño, Mission, and Potato.

62. San Pasqual. The little school opened in 1898, at the instigation of church elder Mr. Potts. The first teacher, Miss Eloisa Elwell, opened with ten pupils, and was paid $13 a month plus board. The original building still stands on the school grounds, and the adjoining San Pasqual Academy, a boarding high school, opened in 1949.

63. What is the oldest Chinese restaurant in the city of San Diego?

64. There are four streets in the downtown area that have horse rings embedded in the sidewalk at the curb. Name at least two of these streets.

65. What is the motto of San Diego County?

63. Wong's Nanking Cafe. It is located at 467 Fifth Avenue, in the Gaslamp Quarter. The building was built in 1913 as a carriage house, so has an unusually high ceiling. About five years later a Chinese restaurant was established there. It has had several names over the years, and has been Wong's Nanking Cafe since the early 1940s.

64. 1. Eighth Avenue (west side between Broadway and C).
    2. Fifth Avenue (west side between Hawthorn and Ivy).
    3. Columbia Street (west side between A and B).
    4. F Street (north side between Fourth and Fifth). The two rings in this block were reinstalled around 1983, when the original granite curbs were replaced with concrete ones.

65. "The noblest motive is the public good." The original Latin *Vincit amor patriae,* from Virgil's *Aeneid,* was translated into English by Steele in *The Spectator.* This motto can be seen etched on the San Diego County Administration Center building.

BIBLIOGRAPHY

Adams, H. Austin. *The Man John D. Spreckels*. San Diego: Frye & Smith, 1924.

Allen, Ann. *Borrego Springs, Yesterday, Today & Tomorrow*. San Diego, California: n.p., 1970.

Amero, Richard W. *Balboa Park, Fairy City or Country Park*. Rev. ed. San Diego, California: Author, 198-.

Andújar, Gloria. *La Jolla*. La Jolla, California: Andújar Communication Technologies, Inc., 1987.

Austin, Edward T. *Rohr: The Story of a Corporation*. Chula Vista, California: Rohr Corporation, 1969.

Bailey, Philip A. *Golden Mirages: The Story of the Lost Pegleg Mine, the Legendary Three Gold Buttes and Yarns of and by Those Who Know the Desert*. Ramona, California: Acoma Books, 1971.

A Baseball Century: The First 100 Years of the National League. New York: Macmillan, 1976.

Baumann, Thomas H. *Kensington-Talmadge, 1910-1985*. San Diego, California: Author, 1984.

Beckler, Marion F. *Palomar Mountain, Past and Present*. Palm Desert, California: Desert Magazine Press, 1958.

Benchley, Belle Jennings. *My Animal Babies*. Boston: Little, Brown & Company, 1945.

---. *My Friends, the Apes*. Boston: Little, Brown & Company, 1942.

---. *My Life in a Man-made Jungle*. Boston: Little, Brown & Company, 1940.

Berger, Dan; Jensen, Peter; and Berg, Margaret C. *San Diego: Where California Begins*. Northridge, California: Windsor Publications, Inc., 1987.

Bergstrom, Leslie. *San Diego's Scenic Drive*. San Diego, California: n.p., 1987.

Berndes, Barry, M. *San Diegan*. San Diego, California: San Diegan/San Diego Guide, 1986/87.

The Best of San Diego, a Discriminating Guide. Los Angeles, California: Rosebud Books, 1982.

Black, Samuel F. *San Diego County, California: A Record of Settlement, Organization, Progress & Achievement*. 2 v. Chicago: S.J. Clarke, 1913.

Booth, Larry; Olmstead, Roger; and Pourade, Richard F. *Portrait of a Boom Town: San Diego in the 1880s*. San Diego, California: California Historical Society, 1971.

Botts, Myrtle. *History of Julian*. Julian, California: Julian Historical Society, 1969.

Brackett, Robert W. *The History of San Diego County Ranchos*. 4th ed. San Diego, California: Union Title Insurance and Trust Company, 1951.

Brandes, Ray. *San Diego, an Illustrated History*. Los Angeles, California: Rosebud Books, 1981.

Brandes, Ray; Carrico, Susan; and Nagel, Toni. *San Diego's Chinatown and Stingaree District*. San Diego, California: n.p., 1985.

Breed, Clara. *Turning the Pages: San Diego Public Library History, 1882-1982*. San Diego, California: Friends of the San Diego Public Library, 1983.

Brennan, John Edward. *History of Ocean Beach, 1542-1900*. San Diego, California: n.p., 1960.

Britton, James N. *The Art of Living in La Jolla*. San Diego, California: California Review, 1965.

---. *You See San Diego*. San Diego: San Diego Chapter, American Institute of Architects, 1977.

Brown, Joseph E. *Cabrillo National Monument*. San Diego: Cabrillo Historical Association, 1981.

Bruns, Bill. *A World of Animals: The San Diego Zoo and The Wild Animal Park*. New York: Abrams, 1983.

Buckley, Marcie. *The Crown City's Brightest Gem: A History of the Hotel Del Coronado*. 3rd ed. Coronado: Hotel del Coronado, 1975.

Bumann, Richard. *Colony Olivenhain*. Olivenhain, California: R. Bumann, 1981.

Campbell, Sheldon. *Lifeboats to Ararat*. New York: Times Books, 1978.

Carlin, Katherine Eitzen and Brandes, Ray. *Coronado; the Enchanted Island*. Coronado, California: Coronado Historical Association, 1987.

Carrillo, Leo. *The California I Love*. Englewood Cliffs, New Jersey: Prentice-Hall, 1961.

Carroll, William. *San Marcos: A Brief History*. San Marcos, California: Coda Pub., 1975.

Chapman, Charles Edward. *A History of Calilfornia: The Spanish Period*. New York: Macmillan, 1921.

Christman, Florence. *The Romance of Balboa Park*, 4th ed., rev. San Diego, California: San Diego Historical Society, 1985.

Chula Vista Heritage, 1911-1986. Chula Vista, California: City of Chula Vista, 1986.

Chula Vista Historical Society. *Stories, Tales, Folklore of our Communities*. Chula Vista: The Society, 1984.

City of El Cajon, California: 50 Years of Progress. El Cajon, California: El Cajon Chamber of Commerce, 1962.

Cleland, Robert Glass. *A History of California: The American Period*. New York: Macmillan, 1922.

Convair Aerospace Division of General Dynamics; 50th Anniversary, 1923-1973. N.p.: n.d.

Crane, Clare B. *A Stroll Through Historic Downtown San Diego*. San Diego, California: n.p., 1972?

Crosby, June. *San Diego Fare: An Insider's Guide to San Diego Area Restaurants, With Over 70 Selected Recipes*. La Jolla, California: Crosstown Publications, 1972.

Davidson, Winifred. *Where California Began*. San Diego, California: McIntyre Publishing Company, 1929.

Davie, Theodore. *Landmark: A Commitment to San Diego.* San Diego, California: San Diego Trust and Savings Bank, 1982.

Davis, Edward J. P. *Historical San Diego, the Birthplace of California: A History of its Discovery, Settlement, and Development.* San Diego, California: Author, 1953.

Detzer, Jordan Edward. *Exploring Behind San Diego, "Bibles, Bullets, and Bullion on the Border."* N.p., 1979.

Dixon, Benjamin Franklin. *Don Diego's Old School Days: The Story of the Beginnings of Public Education in San Diego, City and County, California.* San Diego: San Diego County Historical Days Association, 1956.

---. *San Diego's Religious Heritage.* San Diego, California: Don Diego's Libreria, 1966.

Dodge, Richard V. *Rails of the Silver Gate: The Spreckels San Diego Empire.* San Marino, California: Golden West Books, 1960.

Donnelly, John Eugene. *The Old Globe Theater at San Diego, California: An Historical Survey of its Origin and Development: A Thesis.* Los Angeles: University of California, 1957.

Doyle, Harrison and Doyle, Ruth. *A History of Vista.* Vista, California: Hillside Press, 1983.

Dumke, Glenn S. *Boom of the Eighties in Southern California.* San Marino, California: Huntington Library, 1944.

Dutton, Davis. *San Diego and the Back Country.* New York: Ballantine, 1972.

Ebner, Rose Boehm. *The San Diego Companion.* San Diego, California: n.p., 1987.

Ellsberg, Helen. *Los Coronados Islands*. Glendale, California: La Siesta Press, 1970.

Embery, Joan. *My Wild World*. New York: Delacorte Press, 1980.

Engelhardt, Zephyrin, Father. *San Diego Mission*. San Francisco, California: James H. Barry, Co. 1920.

---. *San Luis Rey Mission*. San Francisco: James H. Barry Co., 1921.

Engstrand, Iris Wilson. *San Diego, California's Cornerstone*. Tulsa, Oklahoma: Continental Heritage Press, 1980.

The Exposition Beautiful: Over One Hundred Views of the Panama-California Exposition and San Diego, the Exposition City. San Diego: Pictorial Publishing Company, 1915.

Federal Writers' Project. San Diego, California. *San Diego, A California City*. San Diego, California: San Diego Historical Society, 1937.

Fodor's San Diego and Nearby Attractions. New York: Fodor's Travel Publications, 1986.

Forty, Ralph. *San Diego's South Bay Interurban*. Glendale, California: n.p., 1987.

Franks, Ray. *What's in a Nickname?: Exploring the Jungle of College Athletic Mascots*. Amarillo, Texas: R. Franks Publishing Ranch, 1982.

Fry, John. *A Short History of Crystal Pier*. San Diego, California: John Fry Productions, 1986.

---. *A Short History of Pacific Beach*. Pacific Beach, California: n.p., 1987.

Fuller, Theodore W. *San Diego Originals*. Pleasant Hill, California: California Profiles Publications, 1987.

Gary, Sally. *San Diego Connections: A Single Person's Guide and Resource Book*. San Diego, California: San Diego Connections, 1987.

Gilbert, Anna M. *La Mesa, Yesterday and Today*. La Mesa Rotary Club, 1975.

Greater San Diego Chamber of Commerce. *Demographic Profile, San Diego County*. San Diego, California: Greater San Diego Chamber of Commerce, 1987.

Green, Fred. *The San Diego Old Mission Dam and Irrigation System*. San Diego, California: n.p., 1933.

Greene, Clay M. *Venetia, Avenger of the Lusitania*. San Diego, California: n.p., 1919.

Greenwalt, Emmett A. *California Utopia: Point Loma, 1897-1942*, Rev ed. San Diego, California: Point Loma Publications, 1978.

Guideposts to History: People and Places of Historical Significance in Early La Jolla, California. La Jolla ed. N.p.: Santa Fe Federal Savings and Loan Association, 1978.

Gunn, Douglas. *Picturesque San Diego, with Historical and Descriptive Notes*. Chicago: Knight and Leonard, 1887.

Hanft, Robert M. *San Diego and Arizona: The Impossible Railroad*. Glendale, California: Trans- Angelo Books, 1984.

Harland Bartholomew and Associates. *Master Plan for Balboa Park, San Diego, California: for City of San Diego*. Saint Louis, Missouri: Harland Bartholomew and Associates, 1960.

Heilbron, Carl H. *History of San Diego County.* San Diego, California: San Diego Press Club, 1936.

Held, Ruth Varney. *Beach Town: Early Days in Ocean Beach (to 1930).* San Diego, California: Author, 1975.

Heyneman, Julie Helen. *Arthur Putnam, Sculptor.* San Francisco, California: Johnck and Seeger, 1932.

Higgins, Ethel Bailey. *Native Trees of San Diego County.* San Diego, California: San Diego Society of Natural History, 1952.

Higgins, Shelley J. *This Fantastic City, San Diego.* San Diego: City of San Diego, 1956.

Hill, Joseph John. *The History of Warner's Ranch and its Environs.* Los Angeles: Privately Printed, 1927.

Hitchcock, Marie. *A Dog Called Bum.* Chula Vista, California: Scott Printing Company, 1960.

Holland, F. Ross. *The Old Point Loma Lighthouse: Symbol of the Pacific Coast's First Lighthouses.* San Diego, California: Cabrillo Historical Association, 1968.

---. *The Origin and Development of Cabrillo National Monument.* San Diego: Cabrillo Historical Association, 1981.

Holzer, Hans. *Ghosts of the Golden West.* Indianapolis: Bobbs-Merrill, 1968.

Hopkins, Harry C. *History of San Diego: Its Pueblo Lands and Water.* San Diego: City Printing Company, 1929.

Howard-Jones, Marje. *Seekers of the Spring: A History of Carlsbad.* Carlsbad, California: Friends of the Carlsbad Library, 1982.

Hudson, Tom. *Three Paths Along a River: The Heritage of the Valley of the San Luis Rey.* Palm Desert, California: Desert-Southwest Publications, 1964.

Inside La Jolla: A Chronicle of La Jolla, 1887-1987. La Jolla, California: The Society, 1986.

Jessop, Mary Cooke. *Bicycling San Diego: Mary's Meanders.* San Diego, California: San Diego Urban..., 1976.

KGB Chicken. *From Scratch.* San Diego: Joyce Press, 1978.

Karst, Gene and Jones, Martin J. Jr. *Who's Who in Professional Baseball.* New Rochelle, New York: Arlington House, 1973.

Keller, Keith. *The Mickey Mouse Club Scrapbook.* New York: Grosset & Dunlap, 1975.

Kelsey, Harry. *Juan Rodriguez Cabrillo.* San Marino, California: Huntington Library, 1986.

Kennedy, Judy and Strada, Judi. *The Best of San Diego.* 2nd ed. Del Mar, California: Metropolitan Press, 1986.

Kettner, William B. *Why it was Done and How.* Compiled by Mary B. Steyle. San Diego: Frye and Smith, 1923.

Khteian-Keeton, T. *The Portuguese and the Port.* In Collaboration with Tony Codina. San Diego, California: F. F. Khteian-Keeton, 1978.

Knowlton, Murray. *San Diego Harbor: A Survey of San Diego Harbor, its Ships, Piers, Dredges, Plans, and People.* San Diego, California: City Schools, 1938.

Kuhn, Gerald G. and Shepard, Francis P. *Sea Cliffs, Beaches, and Coastal Valleys of San Diego County: Some Amazing Histories and Some Horrifying Implications*. Berkeley: University of California Press, 1984.

La Dow, Charles R. *The Ships, the House, and the Men: A History of the San Diego Yacht Club*. San Diego, California: Frazee Industries, 1977.

La Force, Beatrice. *Alpine, Southern California; History of a Mountain Settlement*. El Cajon, California: Sunlight Press, 1971.

Lakeside Historical Society. *Legends of Lakeside*. Lakeside, California: The Society, 1985.

Lay, Eldonna P. *Valley of Opportunity: The History of El Cajon*. El Cajon, California: E. P. Lay and Associates, 1987.

Leadabrand, Russ. *Exploring California Byways: From Kings Canyon to the Mexican Border; Trips for a Day or a Weekend*. Los Angeles: Ward Ritchie Press, 1967.

---. *Guidebook to the Mountains of San Diego and Orange Counties*. Los Angeles: Ward Ritchie Press, 1971.

League of Women Voters of San Diego. *Centre City Walking Tours*. San Diego: The League, 1977.

Lee, Robert E. *Bob Lee's Guide to Lost Mines and Buried Treasures of San Diego County*. Ramona, California: Ballena Press, 1973.

---. *Bob Lee's "Western World."* San Diego County: Author, 1983.

Leftwich, James Adolf. *La Jolla Life*. La Jolla, California: La Jolla Press, 1984.

---. *La Jolla's House of Many Legends*. La Jolla, California: La Jolla Press, 1978.

LeMenager, Charles R. *Off the Main Road: San Vicente and Barona, a History of Those Who Shaped Events in the Rancho Cañada de San Vicente y Mesa del Padre Barona*. Ramona, California: Eagle Peak Publishing Company, 1983.

Lesley, Lewis. *San Diego State College - the First Fifty Years, 1897-1947*. San Diego: San Diego State College, 1947.

Lindsay, Diana Elaine. *Our Historic Desert: The Story of the Anza-Borrego Desert, the Largest State Park in the United States of America*. San Diego, California: Copley Books, 1973.

Lindsay, Lowell and Lindsay, Diana Elaine. *The Anza-Borrego Desert Region*, 2nd ed. Berkeley, California: Wilderness Press, 1985.

Linet, Beverly. *Star-Crossed; the Story of Robert Walker and Jennifer Jones*. New York: Putnam, 1986.

Lockwood, Herbert. *Fallout From the Skeleton's Closet: A Light Look at San Diego History*. San Diego, California: San Diego Independent, 1967.

---. *Skeleton's Closet Revisited*. San Diego: Bailey and Associates, 197?

Louv, Richard, comp. *Neighborhood, the Small Towns Inside San Diego, California*. San Diego: Reader, 1977.

Lueras, Leonard. *Surfing; the Ultimate Pleasure*. New York: Workman Publishing, 1984.

McGrew, Clarence Alan. *City of San Diego and San Diego County: The Birthplace of California.* 2 v. Chicago: American Historical Society, 1922.

McKeever, Michael. *A Short History of San Diego.* San Francisco, California: Lexikos, 1985.

McMahon, Thomas Morton. *The Transformation of Downtown San Diego's Skyline, 1960-1970: A Thesis.* San Diego, California: San Diego State College, 1972.

MacMullen, Jerry. *Star of India: The Log of an Iron Ship.* Berkeley, California: Howell-North, 1961.

---. *They Came by Sea: A Pictorial History of San Diego Bay.* Los Angeles: Ward Ritchie Press/Maritime Museum Association, 1969.

McMullen, R. A. *A Study of the History of Marine Corps Football on the West Coast, 1917-1940.* N.p.: n.d.

MacPhail, Elizabeth C. *Kate Sessions: Pioneer Horticulturist.* San Diego: San Diego Historical Society, 1976.

---. *The Story of New San Diego and of its Founder Alonzo E. Horton.* 2nd ed, rev. San Diego, California: San Diego Historical Society, 1979.

---. *When the Red Lights Went Out in San Diego: The Little Known Story of San Diego's "Restricted" District.* San Diego, California: San Diego Historical Society, 1974.

Marquis, Harold H. *Fallbrook, Yesterday and Today.* Fallbrook, California: Friends of the Fallbrook Library, 1968.

Marston, Mary Gilman. *George White Marston, a Family Chronicle.* 2 v. Los Angeles: Ward Ritchie Press, 1956.

Mendel, Carol. *San Diego by Bike and Car*. San Diego, California: Mendel, 1974.

---. *San Diego on Foot*. San Diego, California: The Author, 1973.

Meyer, Ruth. *Some Highlights of the Natural History of San Diego County*. Ramona, California: Ramona Pioneer Historical Society, 1981.

Miller, Max. *Harbor of the Sun: The Story of the Port of San Diego*. New York: Doubleday, Doran, 1940.

Mills, James Robert. *Historical Landmarks of San Diego County*. San Diego: San Diego Historical Society, 1960.

---. *San Diego -- Where California Began*. 5th ed. rev. San Diego, California: San Diego Historical Society, 1985.

Moore, Archie and Pratt, Leonard B. *Any Boy Can: The Archie Moore Story*. Englewood Cliffs, New Jersey: Prentice-Hall, 1971.

Morgan, Neil Bowen. *Crosstown....* San Diego, California: Crosstown, 1953.

---. *My San Diego*. San Diego, California: Frye and Smith, 1951.

---. *San Diego: The Unconventional City*. San Diego: Morgan House, 1972.

Morgan, Neil Bowen and Blair, Tom. *Yesterday's San Diego*. Miami, Florida: E. A. Seeman Publishing, Inc., 1976.

Morrow, Thomas J. and Sullivan, William. *Hotel del Coronado*. Coronado, California: Hotel del Coronado, 1984.

Moyer, Cecil C. *Historic Ranchos of San Diego*. San Diego, California: Union-Tribune Publishing Company, 1969.

Nash, Jay Robert. *The Motion Picture Guide*. Chicago, Illinois: Cinebooks, 1985.

National Park Statistical Abstract 1986. United States Department of Interior/National Park Service, n.d.

Nelson, Ruth R. *Rancho Santa Fe, Yesterday and Today*. Encinitas, California: Coast Dispatch, 1947.

Neuhaus, Eugen. *The San Diego Garden Fair*. San Francisco: P. Elder, 1916.

O'Dell, Scott. *Country of the Sun: Southern California, an Informal History and Guide*. New York: Crowell, 1959.

Odens, Peter. *The Desert's Edge*. Benson, Arizona: Border-Mountain Press, 1977.

Oliver, Lawrence. *Never Backward: The Autobiography of Lawrence Oliver, a Portuguese-American*. San Diego, California: Neyenesch, 1972.

O'Neal, Lulu Rasmussen. *The History of Ramona, California, and Environs*. Ramona: Ballena Press, 1975.

Palmer, Lillian Pray. *A Book of Memories for the Ages*. San Diego, California: L. D. Gregory, 1925.

Palomar Mountain Views. vols. 1 & 2. N.p., 1982-83.

Parker, Horace. *Anza-Borrego Desert Guide Book: Southern California's Last Frontier*. rev. ed. Borrego Springs, California: Anza-Borrego Desert Natural History Association, 1979.

Peet, Mary Rockwood. *San Pasqual, a Crack in the Hills*, new ed. Ramona, California: Ballena Press, 1973.

Peik, Leander. *Discover San Diego*, 14th ed. San Diego, California: Peik's Enterprises, 1987.

Peterson, J. Harold. *The Coronado Story*, 2nd ed. Coronado, California: Coronado Federal Savings and Loan, 1959.

Phillips, Irene. *The Chula Vista Story, 1868-1968*. National City, California: South Bay Press, 1968.

---. *Development of the Mission Olive Industry and Other South Bay Stories*. National City, California: South Bay Press, 1960.

---. *National City Story*. National City, California: South Bay Press, 1960.

---. *San Diego Land & Town Company, 1880-1927*. National City, California: South Bay Press, 1959.

---. *The San Diego Story*. National City, California: South Bay Press, 1963.

Pourade, Richard F. *Anza Conquers the Desert: The Anza Expeditions From Mexico to California and the Founding of San Francisco, 1774 to 1776*. San Diego, California: Union-Tribune Publishing Company, 1971.

---. *The Call to California: The Epic Journey of the Portolá-Serra Expedition in 1769*. San Diego, California: Union-Tribune Publishing Company, 1968.

---. *City of the Dream*. La Jolla, California: Copley Books, 1977.

---. *The Explorers*. San Diego, California: Union-Tribune Publishing Company, 1960.

---. *The Glory Years*. San Diego, California: Union-Tribune Publishing Company, 1964.

---. *Gold in the Sun.* San Diego, California: Union-Tribune Publishing Company, 1965.

---. *The Rising Tide....* San Diego, California: Union-Tribune Publishing Company, 1967.

---. *The Silver Dons.* San Diego, California: Union-Tribune Publishing Company, 1963.

---. *Time of the Bells.* San Diego, California: Union-Tribune Publishing Company, 1961.

Price, Peter. *The Battle at San Pasqual: December 6, 1846.* San Diego, California: Author, 1975.

Pryde, Philip R., ed. *San Diego, an Introduction to the Region.* 2nd ed. Dubuque, Iowa: Kendall/Hunt Publishing Company, 1984.

El Pueblo de San Diego: Alta California: La Primera Ciudad. San Diego, California: Junior League of San Diego, 1968.

Pumphrey, Margaret Blanche. *Under Three Flags.* Caldwell, Idaho: Caxton, 1939.

Quinn, Charles Russell. *Mesa Grande Country: Some Observations About the Quiet Life and Times on a High Plateau in the San Diego Back Country.* Downey, California: E. Quinn, 1962.

Randolph, Howard. *La Jolla: Year by Year.* San Diego, California: Library Association of La Jolla, 1955.

Reichler, Joseph L, ed. *The Baseball Encyclopedia*, 6th ed. New York: Macmillan Publishing Company, 1985.

Richards, Elizabeth W. *Del Mar Decades.* Del Mar, California: Santa Fe Federal Savings & Loan Asssociation, 1974.

Robertson, Deane and Robertson, Peggy. *Camels in the West.* Sacramento, California: Arcade House, 1979.

Rolle, Andrew. *American in California: The Biography of William Heath Davis, 1822-1909.* Huntington Library, 1956.

Ruland, Skip. *Backpacking Guide to San Diego County,* 4th ed. Spring Valley, California: California Backpacking Co., 1983.

Rush, Philip Scott. *Some Old Ranchos and Adobes.* San Diego, California: Neyenesch Printers, 1965.

Ryan, Frances B. *Early Days in Escondido.* Escondido, California: Frances and Lewis Ryan, 1970.

---. *Yes, Escondido, There was a Felicita.* N.p.: The Ryans, 1980.

---. *Yesterdays in Escondido.* Escondido, California: F. & L. Ryan, 1973.

Ryan, Frances B. and Ryan, Lewis C. *Escondido As It Was 1900-1950.* N.p.: n.d.

San Diego and the Navy; Unofficial Directory and Guide. Lubbock, Texas: C. F. Boone, n.d.

San Diego-California Club. *San Diego and the Exposition.* San Diego, California: The Club, 1935?

San Diego High School; Centennial History, 1882-1982. N.p.: n.d.

San Diego Magazine. *San Diego, Portrait of a Spectacular City,* by Syd Love and the editors of San Diego Magazine. San Diego: San Diego Magazine Publishing Company, 1969.

San Diego Stadium Story. San Diego, California: Hall & Ojena, 1967?

San Diego Trust & Savings Bank. *San Diego, a Brief History, 1542 to 1888*, compiled by Ed Davidson and Eddy Orcutt. San Diego: Arts & Crafts Press, 1929.

San Dieguito Citizen. *Solana Beach, 40th Anniversary Edition, 1922 to 1962*. Solana Beach, California: n.p., 1962.

Save Our Heritage Organization. *Guide Book for Historic Tours-San Diego*. San Diego, California: The Organization, 197?

Schad, Jerry. *Afoot and Afield in San Diego County*. Berkeley: Wilderness Press, 1986.

---. *Backcountry Roads and Trails, San Diego County*. Beaverton, Oregon: Touchstone Press, 1977.

Schad, Jerry and Krupp, Don. *Cycling San Diego*. San Diego, California: Centra Publications, 1986.

Schaelchlin, Patricia A. *The Little Clubhouse on Steamship Wharf: San Diego Rowing Club 1888-1983*. Leucadia, California: Rand Editions, 1984.

Schwartz, Henry. *Kit Carson's Long Walk and Other True Tales of Old San Diego*. La Mesa, California: Associated Creative Writers, 1980.

Scott, Edward R. *San Diego County Soldier-pioneers, 1846-1866*. San Diego, California: County of San Diego, Board of Supervisors, 1976.

Scripps, Edward Wyllis. *Damned Old Crank: A Self-portrait of E. W. Scripps Drawn from his Unpublished Writings*, ed. by Charles R. McCabe. New York: Harper, 1951.

Shannon, Don. *Mission to Metropolis: A History of San Diego*. National City, California: Bayport Press, 1981.

Smythe, William Ellsworth. *History of San Diego, 1541-1908*. San Diego, California: The History Company, 1907.

Stanford, Leland G. *Footprints of Justice...in San Diego: And Profiles of Senior Members of the Bar and Bench*. San Diego: San Diego County Law Library, 1960.

---. *San Diego Lawyers You Should Have Known*. San Diego: Law Library Justice Foundation, 1971.

---. *San Diego's Legal Lore, and the Bar: History of Law and Justice in San Diego County*. San Diego: Law Library Justice Foundation, 1968.

Stanford, Rolland. *Seeing San Diego: County and City; What to See and Do; Where to go in Southernmost California*. San Diego, California: The Author, 1945.

Starr, Raymond G. *San Diego, a Pictorial History*. Norfolk, Virginia: The Donning Company, 1986.

Stein, Lou. *San Diego County Place-names: Yesterday's People, Today's Geography*. 2nd ed. San Diego, California: Tofua Press, 1978.

Sterling, Robert M. and Looy, Mark. *Athletes Tell Their Unforgettable Moments in Sport*. Champaign, Illinois: Leisure Press, 1986.

Stewart, Donald M. *Frontier Port; A Chapter in San Diego's History*. Los Angeles: Ward Ritchie Press, 1965.

Stories of Old San Diego: Over Two Centuries. San Diego: Committee for the Annual Trek to the Serra Cross, 1966.

Strudwick, June A. *The Thomas Whaley House*. San Diego, California: Historical Shrine Foundation of San Diego County, 1960.

Stuart, Gordon. *San Diego Back Country, 1901*. Pacific Palisades, California: Gordon Stuart, 1966.

Sugg, M. M. *An Armchair Tour of Old San Diego*. San Diego, California: The San Diego County Historical Days Association, 1966.

Swartz, Jack and Campion, George. *Complete Guide to the Nude Beaches of California*. Santa Barbara, California: Pantec Publishing Company, 1978.

Topps Baseball Cards: The Complete Picture Collection, a 35 Year History, 1951-1985. New York, New York: Warner Books, 1985.

Tucker, Joan C. *San Diego and the Southland - Just the Facts: A Guide to Sightseeing*. Leucadia, California: Rand Editions, 1984.

Union-Tribune's Annual Review of San Diego Business. San Diego, California: Union-Tribune Publishing Company, 1987.

Wagner, Ray. *The Story of the PBY Catalina*. San Diego, California: Flight Classics, 1972.

Wagner, William. *Ryan, the Aviator: Being the Adventures and Ventures of Pioneer Airman and Businessman T. Claude Ryan*. New York: McGraw Hill, 1971.

Waldron, Patricia. *Trees of San Diego: A Pictorial Guide*. San Diego, California: San Diego Science Foundation, 1966.

Wegeforth, Harry Milton and Morgan, Neil. *It Began with a Roar: The Story of San Diego's World-famed Zoo*. San Diego, California: Pioneer Printers, 1953.

Wheelock, Walt. *Ferries of the South*. N.p.: La Siesta Press, 1964.

Whitaker, Eileen Monaghan. *Eileen Monaghan Whitaker Paints San Diego*. Text by Don Dedera. La Jolla, California: Copley Books, 1986.

Whitaker, Thomas W. *Torrey Pines State Reserve: A Scientific Reserve of the Department of Parks and Recreation Division of Beaches and Parks, State of California*. La Jolla, California: Torrey Pines Association, 1964.

White, Bob and Halloran, Art. *North County People and Places*. Fallbrook, California: Aero Publishers, 1976.

Wild in the City; the Best of Zoonooz. San Diego: Zoological Society of San Diego, 1985.

Winslow, Carleton Monroe. *The Architecture and the Gardens of the San Diego Exposition; a Pictorial Survey of the Aesthetic Features of the Panama California International Exposition*. San Francisco: Elder, 1916.

Wolin, Rita Larkin. *La Mesa, a Brief History: A Bicentennial Salute, 1976*. La Mesa, California: La Mesa Historical Society, 1976.

Wood, Catherine M. *Palomar from Tepee to Telescope*. San Diego: Frye & Smith, 1937.

Woodward, Arthur. *Lances at San Pascual*. San Francisco: California Historical Society, 1948.

The World Almanac and Book of Facts 1989. New York: World Almanac, 1989.

NEWSPAPERS AND MAGAZINES

Anza-Borrego Desert State Park

Art and Archaeology

Centre City News

Downtown

(Evening) Tribune

Journal of San Diego History

Mountain Empire Monthly

The Neighborhood Reporter

Oceanside Blade-Tribune

Orange County Register

Ramona Sentinal

Reader

San Diego Business Journal

San Diego Economic Bulletin

San Diego Historical Society News

San Diego Historical Society Quarterly

San Diego Home and Garden

San Diego Magazine

San Diego Plus

San Diego Union

Southern California Quarterly

Theatre Tonight!

The Wrangler

Zoonooz

INDEX

378

Dean, Dr. Michael, 168, 173-74
DeBello, John, 192
Deep Sea Drilling Project, 305-6
Deer, 325-26
DeHavilland, Olivia, 166
Del Cerro, 344
Del Coronado Petit Galop, 260
Del Mar, California, 87-88, 138, 190, 284, 304, 332
Del Mar (ferry), 68
Del Mar Fair, 189-90
Del Mar Racetrack, 113-14, 125-6, 131-32, 151-52
Dempsey, Jack, 136
Denver Broncos, 138
Derby, Lt. George H., 216
Derby-Pendleton House, 231
Descanso Library, 254
Desert View Tower, 228
Detroit Tigers, 112
Devil Dogs of the Air, 182
Devine, Andy, 210
Dictionary Hill, 274
Diegueño Indians, 6, 286 see also Indians
Dinosaur Land, 85-86
Dirks, Karen Moe, 150
Discovery, 6
Dive Bomber, 205-6
Diving, 142
Division Street, 290
Dr. Kildare, 204
Dr. Seuss see Seuss, Dr.
Dodge Charger, 88
A Dog Called Bum, 316
Dogs, 315-16
$, 210
Domingo, Placido, 158
Dominicans, 4
Don Diego, 189-90
Down in San Diego, 190
Downs, Johnny, 186, 197-98, 210

D'Oyly Carte Opera Company, 179-80
Duchess of Windsor see Warfield, Wallis
Duchin, Eddie, 210
Dudley Duplex, 311-12
Dudley's Bakery, 352
Dulbecco, Dr. Renato, 96
Dumke, Glenn S., 86
Dunne, Aubrey, 174
Dupee, Walter, 106
Durante, Jimmy, 88
Dutch Flats, 284
Dwan, Allan, 182, 200

Earhart, Amelia, 64
Earp, Wyatt, 26
East County Performing Arts Center, 160
East San Diego, 46, 55, 344
Easy Street, 269
Echeandía, José María, 9, 10
Ecke, Paul, 312, 318
Ecuador, 68
Ederle, Gertrude, 112
Edinburgh, Scotland, 332
Educational Community Complex, 98
Edward VIII of England, 54
Edwards, Phil, 116
Egan, Richard, 194
Eggs, 104, 322
Egyptian Theatre, 202
Eisenhower, Dwight, 104
El Cajon, California, 25-26, 79, 81, 127, 128, 141, 259, 262, 272, 332, 334, 352
El Cajon Boulevard, 80, 198, 254
El Cajon Western Little League, 128
El Camino Real, 272
El Capitan Reservoir, 304

Home Federal Savings and Loan
Association, 102, 236
Honey, 24
Hoover High School, 109, 114,
134, 146, 153, 212
Hopper, Dennis, 192
Hord, Donal, 260, 265-66
Horse rings, 353-54
Horton, Alonzo, 24, 170, 228, 262,
280, 340, 342, 351-52
Horton, Edward Everett, 183-84
Horton, Jamie, 153
Horton Grand Hotel, 34, 178, 227-
28
Horton Hotel, 44, 228
Horton House, 342
Horton Plaza, 32, 69-70, 207, 261-
62
Horton Plaza shopping center, 64,
208, 325-26, 333, 334
Horton's Hall, 170
Hostages, 99-100
Hot Curl, 122
Hot Springs Peak, 300
Hotel Circle, 239-40
Hotel del Coronado, 32, 38, 40, 44,
53, 94, 95-96, 147, 189-90, 209-
10, 219-20, 230, 232, 243-44,
248, 252, 259-60, 289, 320, 350
Hotel Manor, 254
Hotel Robinson, 248
Hotel San Diego, 40, 148, 184
Houghtelin, Abraham, 230
House, Herschel A., 182
House of Hospitality, 266
Houston Astros, 124
Howard, Willing "Wing," 336
Huckleberry Finn see *The Adven-
tures of Huckleberry Finn*
and *Big River: The Adventures
of Huckleberry Finn*
Hughes, Linda Lu, 188

Hugo Award, 223-24
Hunter family, 316
Huntington, Anna Hyatt, 260
Hurricanes, 303-4
Hydrofoils, 340
Hydroplanes, 115-16
Hyer, Martha, 212

I Cover the Waterfront, 216
I.W.W., 44
Ice staking, 242, 248
Iceland Ice Skating Rink, 248
Illusion Theatre, 197
Imig, Larry, 254
Imig Manor, 254
Imperial (ferry), 54
Imperial Beach, 54, 72, 88, 274,
304
Imperial County, 18, 52, 300, 302,
306
Imperial Valley, 218, 228, 273-74,
306
The Indian, 268
Indian Village, 250, 266
Indians, 4, 5-6, 8, 12, 14, 17-18,
170, 215-16, 218, 250 see also
Cahuilla Indians, Cupeño In-
dians, Diegueño Indians, and
Luiseño Indians
"Information Anderson," 70
Institute of Geophysics and
Planetary Physics, 266
Invader, 194
Invaders from Mars, 208
Inyo County, 18
Iran, 99
Irones, Rutheford, 182
Isham, Alfred Huntington, 40
Isham's California Waters of Life,
40
Island of the Blue Dolphins, 217-
18

Israel, Robert D., 36
The Isthmus, 50
Isthmus of Panama, 50, 218 see also Panama Canal
Italians, 30

Jack In The Box, 79-80
Jackass Mail Line, 20
Jackson, Everett Gee and Eileen, 264
Jackson, Helen Hunt, 28, 216, 242, 270
Jacumba, California, 228
Jamacha, 40
Jamul, California, 286
Janssen, David, 186
Janssen, Werner, 152
Japan, 78, 237 see also Yokohama, Japan
Japanese, 30, 78, 83
Japanese tea house and garden, 38, 42, 78
Javelin throw, 146
Jayme, Father Luis, 4
Jennings, Charly, 102
Jeonju, Korea, 332
Jessop, Joseph, 64, 83-84, 351
Jessop Clock, 64, 333-34
Jesuits, 4
"The Jewel of the Hills," 287-88
Jewish resident, first, 19-20
Joan Embery's Collection of Amazing Animal Facts, 94
Johnny Belinda, 204
Johnson, Cheryl and Jerry, 350
Johnson, Capt. Henry James, 32
Johnson, Martin and Osa, 322
Johnson, Nancy, 170
Johnson, William Templeton, 228, 264
Johnston, Abraham, 15-16
Johnston, Bob, 178

Joiner, Jim, 320
Jones, Burton, 190
Jones, Christopher, 193
Jones, David "Deacon," 112
Jones, Randy, 118
Jory, Victor, 186
Josh, 328
Josie's Castle, 204
Jourdan, Louis, 166
Juanita, 68, 348
Juárez, Benito, 18
Judges, 77-78, 288
Julian, California, 26, 135, 256, 316, 334
Julian Drug Store, 334
Julian Hotel, 248

KFMB, 184, 202, 212 see also Channel 8
KGB, 90, 98, 191-92
KGB Chicken, 90, 122
KOGO, 198
Kahle Saddlery, 228
Kahn, Louis, 237-38
Kansas City Barbeque, 182
Kathleen (hurricane), 304
Kearny, Stephen Watts, 13, 14
Kearny High School, 176
Kearny Mesa, 84, 168, 275
Keaton, Buster, 183
Keel, Howard, 168
Keen, Harold, 72
Kellerman, Sally, 210
Kelp, 320
Ken Cinema, 184
Kennedy, John Fitzgerald, 86
Kensington, 344
Khayyám Road, 291
Kicks for Critters, 135-36
Kidd, Admiral Isaac C., 72
Kimball, Frank, 24, 28, 30, 232
Kimball brothers, 24

389

Presidio Hills Golf Course, 230
Presidio Park, 47, 59-60, 267-68, 325-26
Preston, Robert, 171
Price, Vincent, 166
Pulitzer Prize, 155-56, 217-18, 219-20
The Pump House Gang, 127-28, 219-20
Punta Guijarros, 276
"Puppet Lady of San Diego," 177-78
Puppet Theater, 178
Purlie, 176
"Purple Mother," 41-42
Puterbaugh, George, 288
Putnam, Arthur, 267

Quail, 324
Quail Botanic Gardens, 318
Quartermass-Wilde House, 270
Queen Theatre, 197-98
"Quiet Hills Farm," 218
Quin, Ah, 35-36
Quinn, Anthony, 200
Los Quiotes Rancho, 183-84
Quito, Ecuador, 68

Racquetball, 109-10
Raft, George, 210
Railroad stations, 194, 233-34, 251-52
Railroads, 29-30, 99-100 see also Pacific Southwest Railway Museum; San Diego and Arizona RR; San Diego Electric Railway; San Diego, Pacific Beach, and La Jolla RR; and Santa Fe Railroad Company
Railsback, Steve, 210
Rainbow, California, 32

Rainbow, J. P. M., 32
Rainfall, 303-4 see also Flood of 1916
"The Rainmaker," 47-48
Raitt, John, 168
Ramona, California, 58, 117, 270, 287, 300, 322
Ramona (book), 27-28, 216, 270
Ramona (ferry), 68
Ramona Pageant, 190
Ramona Theatre, 188
Ramona's Marriage Place, 242
Rancho Bernardo, 157-58
Rancho de la Misión San Diego de Alcalá, 289
Rancho de la Nación, 24, 289 see also National City
Rancho Drive-in, 206
Rancho Santa Fe, 106, 156-57, 215, 289-90, 318
Rancho Zorro, 290
Rand, Sally, 166
Randall, Tony, 188
Rands, Bernard, 156
Rattlesnake Canyon, 284
Raye, Martha, 168
Reagan, Ronald, 199-200, 350
Ream, Major William Roy, 72
Ream Field, 72
Red Apple Inn, 82
Red-light district see Stingaree
Red Mountain Ranch, 183-84
"Red Rest," 226
"Red Roost," 226
Redbook Magazine, 85
Reef Lounge, 94
Reeve, Christopher, 220
Republican National Convention, 96, 97, 223-24
Republicans, 23-24
Requa, Richard, 48, 52, 272

Restaurants, 61-62, 75-76, 83-84, 93-94, 95-96, 182, 186, 209-10, 229-30, 233-34, 241-42, 244, 248, 249-50, 353-54
Resurrection, 154
Return of the Killer Tomatoes, 192
Reuben, David, 222
Reuben H. Fleet Space Theater, 62, 64, 332
Revolving door, 245-46
Reynolds, Nick, 161-62
Rhinoceros, 327-28
Ribera, 264
Ricco, Lorenzo del, 126
Rickey, George, 262
Riggs, Bobby, 118
Rillispore, 337-38
Rio Theatre, 192
Ripley's "Believe it or Not," 64
Riverside County, 18, 32, 300, 302
Roberts, Elizabeth Judson, 170
Roberts, Randolph, 210
Robertson, Cliff, 188
Robinson, Albert and Margaret, 248
Robinson, Alfred D., 316
Robinson, Arnie, 114, 120
Robinson, "Yankee" Jim, 22
Rockwell, Lewis, 288
Rockwell Field, 288
Rogers, Carl, 98
Rohr, Fred H., 70
Roller coaster, 48, 50, 65-66, 86, 274
Romania, 179-80
Romeo and Juliet, 179-89
Romero, Gustavo, 158
Roosevelt, Eleanor, 72
Roosevelt, Franklin D., 68
Roosevelt, James, 68
Roosevelt, Theodore, 296, 324
Rose, Johnny, 84

Rose, Louis, 20
Rose Canyon, 20
Rose Toyota, 84
Rosecroft Begonia Gardens, 316
Rosenthal, Bernard, 202, 262
Roseville, 20, 30, 54
Roseville (ferry), 54
Rosicrucian Fellowship, 341-42
Rosie and the Originals, 148
Ross, Marion, 206
Rough Water Swim, 117-18, 342
Rowan, Stephen C., 12
Rowing, 110, 120, 130
Roxy West, 254
Royal Palms Hotel, 186
Rozsnyai, Zoltan, 152
Rubenstein, Artur, 236
Ruiz, Francisco María, 230
The Russ, 264, 266
Russ, Joseph, 238
Russ Auditorium, 238
Russ High School see San Diego High School
Russia, 4
Russian Spring, 22
Ruth, "Babe," 111-12
Ryan, Irene, 183
Ryan, Robert, 166
Ryan, T. Claude, 54, 64, 284
Ryan Aeronautical Company, 80
Ryan Airlines, 54, 56, 69

S Mountain see Cowles Mountain
SOHO, 236
Sailing, 107-8, 117-18, 123-24, 125-26, 131-32
St. Augustine High School, 140, 172
St. Didacus, 2
St. Francis Chapel, 256
St. Francis of Assisi, 4
St. Louis, Missouri, 19

398

San Diego Museum of Art, 70, 227, 259, 262, 263-64
San Diego Nissan, 84
San Diego Normal School, 288, 334 see also San Diego State College
San Diego Opera Company, 151-52, 155-56, 157-58, 161-62, 238
San Diego, Pacific Beach, and La Jolla Railway, 34
San Diego Padres, 107-8, 110, 111-12, 115-16, 117-18, 121-22, 123-24, 125-26, 129-30, 131-32, 133-34, 139-40, 141-42, 143-44
San Diego Philharmonic Orchestra, 152
San Diego Police Department, 97-98, 178
San Diego Public Library, 83, 97-98, 178, 227, 266
San Diego Repertory Theatre, 167-68, 210
San Diego River, 8, 216, 300, 304
San Diego Rockets, 110, 134
San Diego Rowing Club (hockey), 144
San Diego Rowing Club (rowing), 130, 243-44
San Diego Sails, 110
San Diego Skyhawks, 144
San Diego Sockers, 133-34
San Diego Stadium, see San Diego Jack Murphy Stadium
San Diego State College (or University), 78, 85-86, 98, 107-8, 114, 119-20, 121-22, 134, 136, 140, 144, 150, 166, 170, 172, 176, 192, 198, 205-6, 222, 224, 236, 245-46, 264, 266, 333-34, 341-42, 346
San Diego State Teachers' College, 334 see also San Diego State College
San Diego State University see San Diego State College
San Diego Sun, 42
San Diego Symphony, 147-48, 149-50, 151-52, 157-58, 159-60, 217-18
San Diego Toros, 139-40
San Diego Trust and Savings Bank, 227, 240, 246, 254
San Diego Unified Port District, 87-88
San Diego Union, 40, 42, 44, 46, 122, 132, 150, 156, 204, 219-20, 231, 266
San Diego Wild Animal Park, 219-20, 305-06, 312, 314, 318, 327-28, 349-50
San Diego Yacht Club, 118, 124, 126
San Diego Zoo, 49-50, 56, 65-66, 72, 93-94, 135-36, 166, 168, 184, 188, 201-2, 306, 307-8, 311-12, 313-14, 319-20, 321-22, 325-26, 328
San Felipe Valley, 20
San Francisco, California, 6, 16, 19, 31, 40, 46, 92, 162, 170, 280, 290
San Francisco Opera Company, 161-62
San Luis Rey River, 8, 304, 318
San Luis Rey Valley, 342
San Marcos, California, 332
San Miguel, 2
San Nicholas Island, 218
San Pasqual, 14, 229, 352 see also Battle of San Pasqual
San Pasqual School, 71-72
San Salvador, 2
San Ysidro, 41, 346
San Ysidro Mountains, 300

401

Trapp Family Singers, 236
TraveLodge, 261-62
Tree streets, 273-74
Trenchard, Sir Hugh "Boom," 96
Tribune see *Evening Tribune*
"Triple-S Commission," 43
Tritons, 336
Trometter, Robert "Bull," 136
Truman, Harry, 322
Tuna boats and tuna fishing, 73-74, 193-94
Tunney, Gene, 136
Turkeys, 321-22
Turner, Lana, 254
Twain, Mark, 216
Twelfth Night, 172, 174
Twin Inns, 250
Two Years Before the Mast, 216

U.S. Army, 21-22, 50, 51-52, 72, 287-88
US Grant Hotel, 44, 96, 200, 262, 342
U.S. House of Representatives, 333-34
U.S. Marines, 135, 181, 182 see also Marine Corps Recruit Depot
U.S. Navy, 72, 73-74, 75-76, 80, 92, 104, 113-14, 151-52, 181, 190, 200, 206, 256, 300 see also Naval Air Station, North Island; Naval Amphibious Base, Coronado; Naval Hospital; and Naval Training Center
USS *Bennington*, 38
USS *Constellation*, 89, 350
USS *Cyane*, 12
USS *Kearsarge*, 152
USS *Kittyhawk*, 350
USS *Neversail*, 336
USS *Ranger*, 350

USS *Recruit*, 76, 335
Ubach, Father Antonio, 28, 248
Unconventional City, 95-96
Uncle Tom's Cabin, 216
Unitas, John, 112
United States International University, 82, 210
University Christian Church, 160
University Heights, 279-80, 294
University of California at San Diego, 89-90, 95-96, 154, 155-56, 204, 263-4, 266, 302, 335-36
University of San Diego, 62
University Towne Centre, 104
Urey, Dr. Harold, 96

Valhalla High School, 128, 142
Vallecito, 20
Valley Center, 280
Vancouver, George, 6
Vaughn, Bert L., 227
Vecchio, Frank, 324
Velásquez, 264
Velodrome, 109-10
Venetia, 50
Veterans' War Memorial, 249
Viejas Days, 91-92
Villa Montezuma, 27-28
Villa Orizaba, 32
The Virginian, 286
Virginian Lane, 285
Vista, 314, 330
Vizcaíno, Sebastián, 2, 276, 282
Voight, Jon, 180
Volleyball, 134, 146, 228

W.P.A., 68, 232
Waddy, Rev. Lawrence, 218
Wagner, Harr, 30, 285
Wales, 274-75
Walker, Robert, 204

World War I, 49-50, 51-52, 74, 136, 250
World War II, 49, 66, 69-70, 71-72, 73-74, 76, 78, 122, 196, 199-200, 228, 242, 252, 256, 300, 301-2, 320, 348
Wrestling, 144
Wright, Frank Lloyd, 225
Wright, Brigadier General George, 22
Wright, Harold Bell, 218
Wright, John Lloyd, 225-26
Wright, Mickey, 140
Wright brothers, 28
Wyatt, Patricia Stose, 110
Wynola, 256

YP, 74
Yankee Stadium, 105
Yantai, People's Republic of China, 332

Yawkey family, 52
Yellow Brick Road, 279
Yellowtail Derby, 138
"Yippee Boats," 74
Yogananda, Paramahansa, 272
Yokohama, Japan, 86, 90, 332
Yours For the Asking, 210
Ysaye, Eugène, 154
Yucatán, Mexico, 228
Yuma, Arizona, 12, 134, 188

ZLAC Rowing Club, 110
Zerbe, Anthony, 180
Zip codes, 345-46
Zoorama, 202, 308
Zoro Gardens, 62
Zoroaster, 62
Zorro, 185-86 see also Rancho Zorro
Zurbarán, 264
Zymo-Xyl, 154

406